Other publications:

Shah, N. A. (2006) *Women, the Koran and international human rights law: The experience of Pakistan.* Leiden: Martinus Nijhoff Publishers.

Self-defense in Islamic and International Law

Assessing Al-Qaeda and the Invasion of Iraq

Niaz A. Shah

palgrave
macmillan

SELF-DEFENSE IN ISLAMIC AND INTERNATIONAL LAW

First published in 2008 by
PALGRAVE MACMILLAN™
175 Fifth Avenue, New York, N.Y. 10010 and
Houndmills, Basingstoke, Hampshire, England RG21 6XS.
Companies and representatives throughout the world.

PALGRAVE MACMILLAN is the global academic imprint of the Palgrave Macmillan division of St. Martin's Press, LLC and of Palgrave Macmillan Ltd. Macmillan® is a registered trademark in the United States, United Kingdom and other countries. Palgrave is a registered trademark in the European Union and other countries.

ISBN-13: 978-0-230-60618-0
ISBN-10: 0-230-60618-0

Library of Congress Cataloging-in-Publication Data

Shah, Niaz A.
Self-defense in Islamic and international law : assessing Al-Qaeda and the invasion of Iraq / by Niaz A. Shah.
p. cm.
Includes bibliographical references and index.
ISBN 0-230-60618-0
1. Self-defense (International law) 2. Self-defense (Islamic law) 3. Qaeda (Organization) 4. Iraq War, 2003- 5. Terrorism. I. Title.

KZ4043.S45 2008
341.6—dc22 2007039539

A catalogue record of the book is available from the British Library.

Design by Scribe Inc.

First edition: March 2008

10 9 8 7 6 5 4 3 2 1

Printed in the United States of America.

Dedicated to the memory of the victims
of "terrorism" and the "war on terror."

Contents

Preface

There are many works focusing on terrorism and, after September 11, 2001, Islamic terrorism. Writers tend to address the issue of terrorism from the perspective of their personal background. In many instances, it is easily discernable whether a work is written from a Western or a Muslim perspective. In two respects, however, this book combines both perspectives. First, I am looking at it from both Islamic and international legal perspectives. Second, I write as someone who was born into and brought up in the Islamic tradition and, since 2001, has earned a living in the West.

I have had the opportunity to talk to people from both worlds. On the issue of terrorism, when I am among Muslims, some will talk as if the entire population in the West is against Muslims and supports the "war on terror," the killing of Muslims, and the destruction of their countries, such as Iraq and Palestine. The assumption is wrong. The most severe critics of the war on terror, for instance, are from the West. If we look at the literature on the legality of the Iraq invasion in 2003, almost every contributor is from the West. Even those who initially supported the war on terror are against the current legal treatment of terror suspects, such as indefinite detention.

It is also the case that many in the West try to paint the picture as if everyone in the Muslim world supports terrorism. Again, this is wrong. The majority of Muslims do not support terrorism. In fact, many are ashamed of the stigma terrorism has brought to Islam. Terrorism has also made the Muslim communities in Europe and elsewhere appear as suspects, causing embarrassment at airports, train stations, random police stops and searches, and so on.

Despite the presence of critics of terrorism and of the war on terror, both in Islamic and Western circles, we often hear only a single point of view. I am looking at the issue of terrorism under Islamic law to show that neither Islamic law nor Muslims support terrorism. I am looking at the war on terror from an international legal perspective (which many Muslims align with the West) to show that many Westerners regard sending of armies in Muslim countries, such as Iraq against international law.

This comparative analysis is intended to contribute to the breaking down of the culture of the single narrative and to a better understanding among people.

NAS
July 19, 2007

Acknowledgments

I want to acknowledge the help and support, academic and otherwise, of many colleagues and friends during the course of writing this book. The list begins with one of the eminent scholars of humanitarian law, Maj-Gen. (retired) APV Rogers, Senior Fellow, Lauterpacht Research Centre for International Law, University of Cambridge. I met him in February 2006 in the library of the Centre by chance when we were searching the same shelf. It never occurred to me then that he would play such a significant part in the development and improvement of the project I had just undertaken. From the very beginning, he had commented on the entire draft honestly and unflatteringly. Rogers looked at every point with military precision. I am enormously grateful to him for his comments as the book would not have been the same without them.

I am also grateful to Tony Ward, University of Hull, for his comments on the draft and general support as a mentor. I am also grateful to Owen Mceldowney, whom I constantly bothered to read different draft chapters. I am also grateful to Brice Dickson, Tom Hadden, Khurshid Iqbal, Tim Sellers, Melvin Dubnick, and Noelle Quenivet for their comments on some draft chapters. The director of Law School at Hull University, Mike Feintuck, kindly allowed me the time I needed for completing the draft. I appreciate it very much.

My batch of Visiting Fellows (January–December 2006) at the Lauterpacht Centre, where I did most of the research, needs special mentioning. I am particularly grateful to Judith Welling (JJ), Emily Crawford, Sara Joseph, Amaka Okany, Elies Van Sliedregt, Melissa Perry, Martin Schaub, Thomas Schultz, David Berry, Ralph Giles, and Gil Limon for their comments and warm company. I am also grateful to Tom Grant, John Barker, M. Shujaullah, and Kevin Boyle for their kind support. I thank Sir Elihu Lauterpacht who is a great source of encouragement. My special thanks are due to Shafqat Shah for her strong support at the last stages of the project. Working with Anthony Wahl, Senior Editor, Palgrave Macmillan, New York, is a genuine pleasure.

About the Author

Niaz A Shah received his PhD from The Queen's University Belfast (2005), took a short course in International Human Rights Law from The University of Nottingham (2001), and received an MA (English) and LLB (1999) from The University of Peshawar, Pakistan. Shah has written widely on human rights issues, such as freedom of religion, honor killing, women's rights, public international law, and Islamic law. He is currently a Lecturer in Law at The University of Hull, United Kingdom.

CHAPTER 1

Introduction

The issue of terrorism is not a new one (Countering Terrorism Strategy, UK, 2006) but the attacks of September 11, 2001, on the United States and the responses of states have changed the notion from terrorism to super-terrorism (Claridge, 2000) and mega-terrorism (Nabati, 2005). The balance between concern for democracy, civil liberties, and rule of law and security is tipping toward concern for security (Haubrich, 2003; Blair, 2005; Amnesty International, 2006). There is one overarching goal: Get the terrorists wherever they are and no matter what it takes (Bush, September 24, 2001). It may involve stretching international law beyond its elasticity (see 4.4); marginalizing the Security Council (see 5.3); breaching human rights standards (see 3.2); forging alliances with dictators (Pakistan) and dynastic rulers (Saudi Arabia); introducing Anglo-American democracy by adopting a short-cut approach[1] and undemocratic means (Afghanistan, Iraq, Palestine). "The rules of the game are changing" (Blair, August 5, 2005, see Mary Robinson cited in Lord Steyn, 2006). Terrorism is not only a challenge to international peace and security (Security Council Res. 1368, 2001; General Assembly, resolution 51/210, 1994) but is also "disrupting some crucial categories of international law" (Cassese, 2001).

When we hear the phrase "war on terror," two main parties enter our minds: Osama Bin Laden's Al-Qaeda, the alleged perpetrator, and the U.S.-led coalition as the victims/defenders. The United States and the United Kingdom claim that terrorism is a serious threat to their security and, therefore, the war on terror is the use of force in self-defense—protecting their national security. President George W. Bush (March 12, 2004) and former Prime Minister Tony Blair (July 6, 2006) argued that Al-Qaeda is a terrorist organization that advocated the killing of Jews and Christians and hates Western values, such as freedom and democracy. This is a grave misrepresentation of what Al-Qaeda claimed in its main document: the 1996 *fatwa* (religious edict) titled "Declaration of War against the Americans Occupying the Land of the Two Holy Places" (hereinafter, Al-Qaeda's Manifesto). This manifesto together with the declaration of Jihad by the World Islamic Front[2] "Jihad against Jews and Crusaders" (1998) provides insight into why Al-Qaeda is using violence against the United States and its allies. In fact, Al-Qaeda justifies its actions under the Islamic legal concept of defensive Jihad (self-defense) to push out of the Arab Peninsula the U.S. forces occupying Muslim's holy places (Bin Laden, 1996). The United States is relying on the right of self-defense grounded in international law (National Security Strategy, 2002) to defend itself against the threat posed by the new wave of terrorism and regimes supporting terrorists, such as Saddam Hussein and the Taliban. This may be called the Security Manifesto of the United States. The United Kingdom also devised its strategy—Countering International Terrorism: the United Kingdom's Strategy in 2006.

1.1 Aim of the Book

The war on terror has caused, and is causing, enormous tension between the Muslim and non-Muslim worlds. Terrorism has also caused, and is continuously causing, greater tension between the Muslim community and others in Europe, the United States, and the rest of the world. The aim of this book is to arrest the growth of this currently enlarging gap by analyzing Islamic and international legal rules on the use of force in self-defense. This book establishes that the rules on the use of force in self-defense in Islamic and international law are compatible. By showing this legal compatibility, the trust of Muslims and non-Muslims worlds may be restored on both systems. It is argued that the Islamic concept of defensive Jihad must not be hijacked to be used as a tool of terror and violence, and the right of self-defense under international law must not be stretched to a breaking point where the defender becomes an aggressor. It is stressed that terrorism must be defeated but only within the boundaries of law, both nationally and internationally.

1.2 Self-defense in Islamic and International Law

This book makes a comparative analysis of the right to self-defense in Islamic and international law in order to find out whether both are compatible, whether Al-Qaeda's declaration of Jihad is Islamic, and whether the U.S.-led invasion of Iraq in 2003 meets the test of international law. To understand the right to self-defense in Islamic law, the concept of Jihad and its two main theories—defensive and offensive Jihad—are explained and applied to the case of Al-Qaeda, testing its justification for declaring Jihad against Anglo-American forces in the Arab Peninsula and elsewhere. In order to understand the right of self-defense in international law, the right of self-defense contained as an exception in article 51 to the general prohibition on the use of force under article 2(4) of the Charter of the United Nations is analyzed and applied to the claim of self-defense of the U.S.-led invasion of Iraq in 2003. Legally speaking, the U.S.-led coalition relied on the Security Council's resolutions 678 (1990), 687 (1991), and 1441 (2002) for invading Iraq; however, self-defense remains the overall unstated ground through out the war on terror (see 5.4).

The main arguments are that both the Koran—the primary source of Islamic law—and international law recognize the right to use force in self-defense as an exception. The Koran (2:190; 22:40) allows a Muslim ruler (Caliph) to use necessary and proportionate force when a Muslim state is attacked or a group of Muslims is persecuted for their belief in Islam but is unable to defend itself. Similarly, international law allows necessary and proportionate use of force in self-defense when there is an armed attack against a state or such attack is imminent. The rules of these legal systems are the expression of the same international legal order. However, both can be misinterpreted and misapplied. The invasion of Iraq and the declaration of Jihad by Al-Qaeda are cases in point (it is argued that the invasion of Iraq in 2003 and the declarations of Al-Qaeda in 1996 and World Islamic Front in 1998 are both illegal).

The second argument is the warning regarding the fast changing nature of conflicts in Afghanistan and Iraq. These conflicts are constantly deteriorating and many Muslims who were initially against Al-Qaeda might think differently now. Muslims are disenchanted with the Anglo-American foreign policy and have started disliking their presence in Muslim lands. The governments of Afghanistan and Iraq neither wield power nor represent the will of their nations. The lives of these new democracies depend on the presence of Anglo-American forces in Iraq and Afghanistan. The governments in Iraq and Afghanistan are considered Anglo-American puppets. The damage in terms of Muslim lives and property is enormous and is immensely worrying the Muslim world (see 3.3). Human rights breaches has become a pattern, and there is no end in sight for these conflicts. The reconstruction is either slow or does not happen at all. The future holds no hope. All these elements taken together are making the conflicts of Afghanistan and Iraq strong candidates for the declaration of the Koranic (legitimate) Jihad as these circumstances might compel mainstream Muslim leaders (not necessarily pro

Anglo-American governments or Al-Qaeda) to declare Jihad by consensus. This kind of consensus declaration of Jihad would be Islamic and compatible with international law (see 2.2.4).

1.3 Significance of Comparative Approach

This book looks at the current issue of terrorism from both Islamic and international law perspectives. The significance of the Islamic approach is that Al-Qaeda relies mainly on the Koran to warrant its call for defensive Jihad, so it is appropriate to employ the same source to test its claim. It is more convincing, as many Muslims tend to prefer Islamic law to international law, to argue that Al-Qaeda's declaration is against both the Koran and international law. It would have greater impact to talk to Muslims in the language of the Koran: The law of Allah (God) does not permit unnecessary violence (see 3.4.1.2). In addition, it would appeal to the international community by explaining that it is a misrepresentation of the Koran to think that it supports terrorism. In fact, terrorism is a severely punishable act under Islamic law (Vogel, 2002). Analyzing the invasion of Iraq in 2003, according to international law, demonstrates that it was illegal and the invaders and the occupiers should be held accountable.

Looking at the right of self-defense from Islamic and international law perspectives makes perfect sense as both legal systems allow the use of force in self-defense as an exception. In Islamic tradition, it is the right of states to declare war in self-defense (Jihad). A non-state actor such as Al-Qaeda has no authority to do so unless a ruler is on the side of invaders (see 2.2.4). According to the strict reading of article 51 of the Charter, the use of force in self-defense is allowed when there is an armed attack against a state or such an attack is imminent and until the Security Council comes into action. Self-defense under the Charter is the right of states only. It is this use of self-defense by and against non-state actors from two different legal systems, which ties in the study together. In the Muslim world, we hear voices predominantly against the West; in the non-Muslim world, we see greater skepticism against Islam. The comparative study, as well as presenting both versions of terrorism and the war on terror, strikes at the heart of the culture of single narrative in the Muslim and non-Muslim world.

1.4 Contextual Interpretation of the Koran

To understand the Koranic concept of Jihad as self-defense and its position on terrorism and the right of self-defense under international law, this book adopts the approach of contextual interpretation. The contextual interpretation of the Koran has three dimensions. First is the social context: Arab tribal society. Second is the historic context: seventh-century Arabia with tribal wars. Third is the Koranic context: when and why a particular verse permitting the use force was revealed, and what is the overall approach of the Koran toward the use of force? Special attention is given to those verses of the Koran which, when taken out of their context, often give distorted meanings. For instance: "But when the forbidden months are past, then fight and slay the Pagans wherever ye find them, and seize them, beleaguer them, and lie in wait for them in every stratagem (of war); but if they repent, and establish regular prayers and practise regular charity, then open the way for them: for Allah is Oft-forgiving, Most Merciful" (Koran, 9:5). However, when verses such as these are studied according to the suggested contextual interpretation of the Koran, the real meanings surface.

To understand the real spirit and purpose of the right to self-defense in international law, its prohibition on the use of force except in self-defense is analyzed in its historical context to find out how and when it can be applied, particularly to non-state actors, such as Al-Qaeda. In both cases of Islamic and international law, the formative contexts of rules on self-defense are analyzed to discover its real meaning and spirit and how it applies to the problem of terrorism and the war on terror.

1.5 Why the Koranic Approach?

There are four major sources of Islamic law: the Koran, the *Sunnah* (model behaviour of the Prophet Muhammad), *ijma* (consensus of opinion), and *qiyas* (analogical deductions) (Kamali, 2000; Hallaq, 2005; Esposito and DeLong-Bas, 2001). This study uses the primary source of Islamic law—the Koran—to explain its rules on the use of force in self-defense. The use of the phrase "Islamic law" instead of "the Koran" in the title is intentional. There are two main reasons for relying on the Koranic approach (see Shah, 2006). First, it is a principle of Islamic law that the Koran is the first source to start in order to find an answer to any Islamic issue. If the jurists do not find an answer in the Koran, they will seek it in the second and third sources of Islamic law (Rahim, 1911). Hence, it is natural to start with the Koran. Second, the Koran provides sufficient evidence on the subject of self-defense so we do not need to go outside the Koran. If the Koranic evidence were lacking, naturally we would turn to the *Sunnah* followed by third and fourth sources of Islamic law. The strength of the Koranic approach is that it relies on the undisputed source of Islamic law. The Koranic approach would be acceptable to both Shias and

Sunnis, thus it would be applicable to the entire Islamic world. It is in contrast to those studies, which focus on classical jurists of the four Sunni schools. Studies of this nature represent the view of Sunni Islam only. The proposed Koranic approach is not sectarian, it is holistic.

1.6 Is there Islamic International Law?

This section will answer two questions: Is there an Islamic international law, and is it appropriate to compare the perceived Islamic religious law with the assumed secular international law? The answer to the first question is both no and yes. The negative answer signifies that there was no codified Islamic international law for centuries as we had in Europe, such as the Convention for the Protection of Human Rights and Fundamental Freedoms (1950) or the European Community Act (1972). This might have led to the belief, specifically in the non-Muslim world, that there is no Islamic international law. It is clear from what follows that this view is erroneous. The positive answer has two aspects: (a) Islamic international law always existed in its uncodified form, that is, in the form of its sources, such as the Koran; and (b) the codified and binding corpus of Islamic international law is fast growing. The two prominent illustrations of codified law are the Convention of the Organisation of the Islamic Conference on Combating International Terrorism (1999) and the Arab Charter on Human Rights (2004) of the League of Arab States. There is a host of other bilateral and multilateral treaties binding different Muslim states. All these treaties are professedly based on Islamic legal tenets.

Answer to question whether it is appropriate to compare Islamic law with international law is yes. Islamic law is and is not religious. Islamic law is religious in the sense that it is based and derived from the Muslims' divine text, the Koran and the *Sunnah*. The subject matter, however, of Islamic law covers spiritual, moral, the hereafter, and secular affairs. In simple terms, Islamic law covers the relation of man to God and man to man. Islamic international law falls in the secular domain of worldly affairs: how Muslims states shall conduct their relations among themselves and with the international community. In this sense, Islamic law is not religious as the subject matter is not religious. The comparison of Islamic international law is not much different from comparing European public law with international law.

1.7 Scope of the Book

The scope of this book is to look at the right of self-defense from the perspectives of Islamic law and international law and testing the declaration of

Al-Qaeda's Jihad in self-defense and the Iraq invasion of 2003. As some scholars of Islam argue, Islam is a religion meant for humanity and should be spread to the rest of the world peacefully. However, if there are political and material obstructions placed in the way to do so, then it should be done forcefully (see 2.3). It is beyond the remit of this book to address the conception of Jihad as a mechanism of spreading the religion of Islam. The focus is not on Islam as a faith either. The focus rather is on the grounds for the use of force in self-defense in the Koran. It is also beyond the scope of this study to look at the history of Jihad and how it was interpreted over fourteen hundreds years. The focus is the Koranic concept of Jihad and how it can be related to the conflicts of our age. This book addresses the invasion of Iraq from the perspective of international law and whether the U.S.-led invasion of Iraq stands the test of international law. It is also beyond the remit of this book to look at the Iraq invasion from a "just war" perspective.

1.8 Structure of the Book

This book consists of seven chapters divided into three parts. Part I consists of two chapters. Chapter 2 covers the Koranic concept of Jihad and the theories of Jihad as understood in its historic and Koranic contexts. Chapter 3 tests the Koranic foundation of the declaration of Jihad by Al-Qaeda. Part II consists of Chapters 4 and 5. Chapter 4 discusses the right of self-defense in international law. Special attention is paid to preemptive self-defense. Chapter 5 looks at the evidence of weapons of mass destruction before the invasion of Iraq in 2003. It also tests the validity of the "revival theory" of the United States: The Security Council's authorization of "the coalition of the willing" to use force in 1990 against Iraq is revived to use force against Iraq in 2003. Chapters 6 and 7 form Part III. Chapter 6 makes a comparison of the right to self-defense under the two legal systems—Islamic and international law—and concludes that both are compatible and can coexist. The conclusion shows Muslims' disenchantment with international legal order, Western domination of international institutions, and Westerners' hypocritical approach toward democracy and human rights in the Muslim world. Al-Qaeda's declaration of Jihad is un-Koranic (illegitimate), but many Muslims might see logic in it and sympathise with it if Muslim lands remain under what Muslims consider an Anglo-American occupation (see generally Honderich, 2002; Fanon, 1965).

The translation of the Koran by Abdullah Yusuf Ali (1989) is used throughout this book unless indicated otherwise. The reason for using Ali's translation is that it is considered authoritative in the Muslim world. The superior courts in the Indian sub-continent cite it as an authority. For instance, the Supreme Court of India has relied on it in the case of *Shah Bano* (AIR 1985 Supreme Court 945), the Federal Shariat Court of Pakistan in the case of *Hazoor Bakhash* (PLD 1981 FSC 145), and the Dhaka High Court, Bangladesh in the case of *Hefzur Rahman* (47 [1995] Dhaka Law Reports 54). The choice of spelling the Qur'an as "Koran" is mine. In the Koranic citation, chapter (*sura*) comes first followed by verse number, such as 9:5. The use of the phrase "Muslim lands" is intentional in order to cover those Muslim-populated areas that are not governed by Muslims. The phrase, however, does cover modern Muslim nation-states. From time to time, Islamic law and the Koran are used interchangeably. The phrase "Muslim ruler" refers to a Caliph but also includes the head of a modern Muslim nation-state.

References

Ali, Y. (1989) *The meaning of the holy Qur'an*. Maryland: Amana Corporation.

Amnesty International (2006) Report on the UK Anti-terror measures. AI Index: EUR 45/004/2006.

Blair, T. (2006) Blair Speech in Los Angles. July 6. Available at: http://www.pm.gov.uk/output/Page9948.asp.

———. (2005) Full text of Blair statement on extremism. *Times Online*. August 5. Available at: http://www.timesonline.co.uk/article/0,,22989-1722621,00.html.

Bush, G. (2004) Remarks by the President and Mrs. Bush in Interview by Television of Spain. 12 March. Available at: http://www.whitehouse.gov/news/releases/2004/03/20040312-7.html.

———. (2001) President Freezes Terrorists' Assets. September 24. Available at: http://www.whitehouse.gov/news/releases/2001/09/20010924-4.html.

Cassese, A. (2001) Terrorism is also disrupting some crucial categories of international law. *European Journal of International Law*, 21(5), pp.993–1001.

Claridge, D. (2000) Exploding the myths of superterrorism. In Taylor, M. and Horgan, J. (eds.). *The Future of Terrorism*. London: Frank Cass. pp.69–78.

Esposito, J. and DeLong-Bas, N. J. (2001) *Women in Muslim family law*. 2nd ed. Syracuse: Syracuse University Press.

Fanon, F. (2005) *The wretched of the earth*. Grove Press.

General Assembly, (1994) Measures to eliminate terrorism. Available at: http://www.un.org/documents/ga/res/49/a49r060.htm.

Hallaq, W. (2005) *The origins and evolution of Islamic law*. Cambridge: Cambridge University Press.

Hazoor Bakhash (1981) *Federal Shariat Court* (All Pakistan Legal Decisions), 145.

Haubrick, D. (2003) September 11, Anti-Terror Law and Civil Liberties: Britain, Germany and France Compared. *Government and Opposition*, 38(1), pp.3–28.

Hefzur Rahman (1995) *47 Dhaka Law Reports*, 54.

Honderich, T. (2002) *After the terror*. Edinburgh University Press.
Kamali, M. H. (2000) Law and society, the interplay of revelation and Reason in the Shariah. *In* Esposito, J. (eds.) *Oxford history of Islam*. Oxford University Press.
Laden, B. (1996) Declaration of war against the Americans occupying the land of the two holy places. Available at: http://www.pbs.org/newshour/terrorism/international/fatwa_1996.html.
Nabati, M. (2003) International law at a crossroads: Self-defense, global terrorism, and pre-emption (a call to rethink the self-defense normative framework). *Transnational Law and Contemporary Problem*, 13, pp.771–802.
Rahim, A. (1911) *Muhammadan jurisprudence*. Lahore: PLD Publishers.
Shah, N. A. (2006) *Women, the Koran and international human rights law: The experience of Pakistan*. Lieden: Martinus Nijhoff.
Security Council (2002) S/RES/1441. November 8. Available at: http://daccessdds.un.org/doc/UNDOC/GEN/N02/682/26/PDF/N0268226.pdf?OpenElement.
——— (2001) UN Security Council resolution 1368 (2001). Available at: http://www.unhchr.ch/Huridocda/Huridoca.nsf/(Symbol)/S.RES.1368+(2001).En?Opendocument.
——— (1991) S/RES/687. April 3. Available at: http://daccessdds.un.org/doc/RESOLUTION/GEN/NR0/596/23/IMG/NR059623.pdf?OpenElement.
———, (1990) S/RES/678. November 29. Available at: http://daccessdds.un.org/doc/RESOLUTION/GEN/NR0/575/28/IMG/NR057528.pdf?OpenElement.
Shah Bano (1985) *All India Reports*, Supreme Court, 945.
Steyn, Lord (2006) Democracy, the rule of law and the role of judges. *European Human Rights Law Review*, 3, pp.243–53.
United Kingdom (2006) Countering International Terrorism: the United Kingdom's Strategy, 2006.
United Nations (1945) The Charter of the United Nations.
United States (2006) The national security strategy of the United States of America. Available at: http://www.whitehouse.gov/nsc/nss/2006/nss2006.pdf.
——— (2002) The national security strategy of the United States of America. Available at: http://www.whitehouse.gov/nsc/nss.html.
Vogel, F. (2002) The trial of terrorists under classical Islamic law. *Harvard International Law Journal*, 43, pp.53.
World Islamic Front (1998) Jihad against Jews and Crusaders. Available at: http://www.fas.org/irp/world/para/docs/980223-fatwa.htm.

PART I

CHAPTER 2

Self-defense in Islamic Law[1]

Jihad has become a common tool in the hands of Muslim organizations, particularly those engaged in conflicts, such as in Kashmir, Chechnya, Palestine, Iraq, and Afghanistan. At the same time, the word "Jihad" portrays negative connotations in much of the non-Muslim world, more specifically so in the West. In many non-Muslim gatherings, the word Jihad raises serious eyebrows and very few are able to draw a distinction between Jihad and terrorism. In the non-Muslim world, different denominations are used for the phenomenon of Jihad: extremism, radicalism, fundamentalism, and (after the emergence of Al-Qaeda) terrorism and even mega-terrorism. These Muslim organizations, however, regard themselves as struggling for self-determination (e.g., in Kashmir and Chechnya) or engaged in self-defense, such as Al-Qaeda claims. There seems to be a great deal of misunderstanding among Muslims and non-Muslims about the meaning and spirit of Koranic Jihad. The scholarship on Jihad reflects that it is not only laypersons that are confused or misinformed. Scholars of Islam, both in Western and Islamic worlds, also do not agree on a single interpretation of Jihad. Therefore, there are different and distorted meanings of Jihad.

The recent proliferation of writing on Islamic Jihad as a form of extremism and terrorism has become a growing industry. A common weakness of much of those writings—a good deal of it by self-proclaimed "authorities" with only superficial experience in the Islamic world—is that they are based on secondary sources and, in many cases, hearsay. These accounts, therefore, are twice removed from reality. In most cases, publicists have no clear grasp of the Islamic legal system, culture, and language. This becomes acute in the case of Koranic justification and conduct of Jihad. It has led to such a great misunderstanding that one would hope to reintroduce Jihad to the non-Muslim world—and to some Muslims—on new and objective terms.

Focusing on the primary source of Islamic law, the Koran, this chapter examines the concept of Jihad, theories of Jihad, and who—state or non-state actors—may declare Jihad. This approach is in contrast to those writers who have written at length on the subject with little or no reference to the original source, such as John Kelsay (1993) and Sohail Hashmi (1996). In many such instances, the authors engage in the historic development of Jihad through secondary sources rather than following the Islamic legal rule of Koranic primacy in the hierarchy of legal sources. The Koran articulates clear rules for the justification and conduct of Jihad, peace processes, resumption of hostilities, and rewards for taking part in and punishments for not participating in Jihad. This chapter is focused on the Koranic justification of Jihad although some verses that are not directly relevant to the subject are reproduced in order to clarify the context and throw further light on the meanings of those under discussion. As will be evident, all the Koranic verses are mutually complementary and can be misunderstood unless considered as parts of one integral whole.

2.1 The Concept and Kinds of Jihad

Jihad is derived from the Arabic word *Juhd*, literally meaning to "exert," "strive," and "struggle" (Koran, 6:108; 22:77). Jihad is of two main kinds: greater or major Jihad and lesser or minor Jihad. Greater Jihad is a process of self-purification. The lesser or minor Jihad signifies fighting in self-defense or defending other Muslims. In my opinion, Jihad is a search. On a personal level, it is a search for self-satisfaction by winning the pleasure and blessing of God. This internal search could be regarded as major Jihad. On the external level, Jihad is a search for self-protection in several ways, including self-defense, self-determination, and the search for how to remove obstructions hindering self-protection. The search for self-protection does not mean necessarily through violent means. The resolution of an international issue by intense diplomatic negotiations is a perfect example of Jihad. Jihad by sword is the last resort.

2.2 Defensive and Offensive Theories of Jihad

The Koran allows necessary and proportionate use of force in self-defense. This is known as the "defensive" theory of Jihad. However, there are scholars of Islam who argue that Islam is a religion for humankind and that Muslims are under an obligation to spread the faith of Islam peacefully and, if there are obstructions to achieving this end, then by force. This is known as the "offensive" theory of Jihad.

2.2.1 Defensive Jihad: Use of Force in Self-defense

The study of the Koranic verses reproduced in this chapter shows that the use of force in self-defense is an exception to its general prohibition. As the name suggests, "defensive" Jihad means to use force in self-defense. Self-defense may be individual or collective. The Koran covers both kinds. The defensive theory of Jihad is discussed under three sub-sections: the grounds for the use of force, when self-defense ends, and limitations on the use of force.

2.2.1.1 Grounds for the Use of Force

The Koran mentions two clear grounds for engaging in defensive Jihad: when a Muslim land is attacked or when such an attack is imminent; or when Muslims are persecuted for believing in Islam but are unable to defend themselves. The latter shows that the Koran allows intervention on humanitarian grounds.

Regarding self-defense, the Koran says, "to those against whom war is made, permission is given (to fight), because they are wronged" (22:39). This was the first time, immediately after the Prophet Muhammad migrated to Madina (Ali, 1989:832), that the Koran gave permission to use force in self-defense after Muslims were persecuted for thirteen years in Mecca (Daryabadi, 2002:603). The verse is in the passive "against whom war is made" (Ali, 1989:832) and therefore, indicates that the permission given is when Muslims are "wronged," that is, attacked. The permission to use force hinges on "wronging" Muslims. The phrase "who fight you" shows that Muslims cannot be aggressors (Daryabadi, 2002:68; see Hamidullah, 1956; Mohammad, 1985). This verse prohibits aggression. The Koran (2:190) further says: "fight in the cause of Allah those who fight you, but do not transgress limits." This verse was revealed one year after the Prophet Muhammad migrated from Mecca to Madina (Asad, 1997:512), which he did to avoid further persecution. In this verse, the Koran specifies to fight those who are at war with you, which can be anyone such as Jews, Christians, Pagans, and so on, and only combatants, excluding noncombatants.

Regarding collective self-defense, the Koran (4:75) says: "And why should ye not fight in the cause of Allah and of those who, being weak, are ill-treated (and oppressed)?—Men, women, and children, whose cry is: 'Our Lord! Rescue us from this town, whose people are oppressors; and raise for us from thee one who will protect; and raise for us from thee one who will help!'"

Verse 22:39 is different than verse 4:75. Verse 22:39 allows the use of force in self-defense whereas the latter permits the use of force in the defense of those who are persecuted for believing in Islam but are unable to defend themselves. In other words, verse 4:75 allows the use of force in collective self-defense and for humanitarian purposes. The Koran (22:40) further specifies the nature of persecution: "(They are) those who have been expelled from their homes in defiance of right—(for no cause) except that they say, 'our Lord is Allah.'" The threshold for using force in collective self-defense is that the level of persecution must be so severe as to compel Muslims to leave their home such as some cases of Palestinians expulsion by Israel, not otherwise. The Koran (3:113–14) recognizes that Jews and Christians are upright and righteous people and believe in God, therefore, Muslims may join in their collective defense:

> Not all of them are alike: Of the People of the Book are a portion that stands (For the right): They rehearse the Signs of Allah all night long, and they prostrate themselves in adoration. (3–113)
>
> They believe in Allah and the Last Day; they enjoin what is right, and forbid what is wrong; and they hasten (in emulation) in (all) good works: They are in the ranks of the righteous. (3–114)

However, it must be kept in mind that these verses address the specific situation of Muslims in the seventh-century Arab society, but in general they may cover all those who believe in God. Muslims may also join in the collective self-defense of non-Muslims if they have entered into an alliance of a military nature (see 1.3.2). The Koran does not prohibit such an alliance.

2.2.1.2 When Self-defense Ends

The Koran does not provide carte blanche permission to use force in self-defense. It clearly stipulates when the use of force shall end: "And fight them on until there is no more Tumult or oppression, and there prevail justice and faith in Allah. But if they cease, let there be no hostility except to those who practise oppression" (Koran, 2:193). Yusuf Ali (1989:78) argues that "If the opposite party ceases, to persecute you, your hostility ends with them as a party, but it does not mean that you become friends to oppression. Your fight is against wrong, there should be no rancour against [them]." Verse 2:193 mentions two objectives to be achieved to bring the use of force in self-defense to an end: the end of oppression or the achievement of peace. There is, however, an exception to this rule: Hostility continues with those elements who "practice oppression." In an analogous way, the Koran (8:39) says: "and fight them on *until* there is no more tumult or oppression, and there prevail justice and faith in Allah altogether and everywhere; but if they cease, verily Allah doth see all that they do." This verse clearly reiterates what verse 2:193 purports: "If they cease from fighting and from the persecution of truth . . . they should [not] be harassed with further hostility" (Ali, 1989:423). However, verse 8:39 has an additional phrase, "altogether and everywhere," suggesting that the norm applies to all Muslims' conflicts compared to verse 2:193, which addresses a specific event.

2.2.1.3 Limitations on the Use of Force in Self-defense

War in Islam is basically defensive. Defense is by nature a limited venture; that is why Allah said soon after this permission, *and do not exceed the limit* (Tabatabai, 1892–1981).[2] The Koran lays down express limits on the use of force in self-defense: necessity and proportionality. The Koran does not allow the use of force unless it becomes necessary, that is, when Muslims are attacked or persecuted individually and collectively. The use of force is allowed until either the persecution ends by defeating the perpetrators, or the opposite party ceases fighting because of a peace treaty. The clear message of verses 2:190 and 2:192 is that the use of force is permissible "only in self-defense" and the Koran does not allow "aggression" (Asad, 1997:41). "War is permissible . . . under well-defined limits. When undertaken, it must be pushed with vigour (but not relentlessly), but only to restore peace and freedom for the worship of [God]" (Ali, 1989:76). Therefore, the use of force is limited to restoring freedom and peace for Muslims.

The second limitation is the principle of proportionality. The Koran (42:40) says: "The recompense for an injury is an injury equal thereto (in degree): but if a person forgives and makes reconciliation, his reward is due from Allah." Verse 40:40 clearly sets out the limits and extent regarding the use of force but *rewards* forgiveness and reconciliation. Nevertheless, it does not mean that the Koran disapproves a proportionate response: "If any do help and defend themselves after a wrong (done) to them, against such there is no cause of blame" (42:41). "And if ye do catch them out, catch them out no worse than they catch you out: But if ye show patience, that is indeed the best (course) for those who are patient" (16:126). The main courses shown are forgiveness and no more than what is proportional. The Koran does not allow transgression of these limits: "but do not transgress limits" (2:190). Exceeding these limits is punishable.

The greater emphasis of the Koran on accepting the offer of peace may fall under the category of proportionality, but it can also be treated as a separate limitation on the use of force. The Koran (8:61) says: "But if the enemy incline towards peace, do thou (also) incline towards peace, and trust in Allah." The implication of this verse is that even if they offer peace only with a view to deceive, this offer of peace must be accepted, as all judgment of their intention is based on outward evidence (Razi, cited in Asad, 1997:249). In other words, mere suspicion is not an excuse for rejecting an offer of peace (Asad, 1997:249). "While we must always be ready for a good fight lest it be forced on us, even in the midst of the fight we must always be ready for peace if there is any inclination towards peace on the other side. There is no merit merely in fighting by itself" (Ali, 1989:429). Yusuf Ali (1989:76) contends that peace cannot be withheld when the enemy comes to terms. I agree with Ali on the point that Muslims cannot refuse the offer of peace because the Koran (2:192) says: "But if they cease, Allah is Oft-forgiving, Most Merciful." As the war is in the cause of Allah—defending Muslims and their land—and Allah is merciful and forgiving, so shall be the adherents of Allah's religion. The reiteration of accepting peace is the reason that Islam is regarded as the religion of peace. Self-defense ends at the offer of peace and beginning of peace negotiations. The reason is that the grounds triggering the use of force—tumult and oppression—disappear and so does self-defense. The Koran (4:90) states: "If they withdraw from you but fight you not, and (instead) send you (Guarantees of) peace, then Allah Hath opened no way for you (to war against them)." Verse 4:90 does not allow the continuation of the use of force when there is an offer of peace.

The Koran makes a clear distinction between those who keep their covenants and those who do not. It says that there can be no treaty with those who breaks their covenants when they get an upper hand: "How (can there be such a league), seeing that if they get an advantage over you, they respect not in you the ties either of kinship or of covenant" (Koran, 9:8), but with "those with whom ye made a treaty near the sacred Mosque? As long as [they] stand true to you, stand ye true to them" (Koran, 9:7). In another context, the Koran (2:194) lays down the same rule: "The prohibited month for the prohibited month—and so for all things prohibited—there is the law of equality. If then any one transgresses the prohibition against you, transgress ye likewise against him. But fear Allah, and know that Allah is with those who restrain themselves." Those who exceed these limits and kill are as guilty as if they have killed the entire humankind: "If any one slew a person—unless it be for murder or for spreading mischief in the land—it would be as if he slew the whole people: and if any one saved a life, it would be as if he saved the life of the whole people" (Koran, 5:32). The sum total of the grounds for resorting to force and its limitations reflect the true Koranic concept of Jihad: necessary and proportionate use of force in individual and collective self-defense. Allama Tabatabai (1892–1981) neatly sums up the law and its limitations:

> These five verses together promulgate a single law covering all its limits and details. *And fight in the way of Allah is* the basic law; *and do not exceed the limit* puts disciplinary restriction on it; *And kill them wherever you find them* defines the limits of pressure; *and do not fight with them at the Sacred Mosque until they fight with you therein* puts a restriction according to the place; *and fight with them until there is no more mischief* (disbelief) shows its duration; *The sacred month for the sacred month, and reprisal* (is lawful) *in all sacred things* explains that this legislation is based on the principle of retaliation in fighting and killing, it is paying them in their own coin (emphasis in original).

Verse 9:29 reiterates these limitations but goes one step further: "Fight those who believe not in Allah nor the Last Day, nor hold that forbidden which hath been forbidden by Allah and His Messenger, nor acknowledge the religion of Truth, (even if they are) of the People of the Book, until they pay the Jizya (poll tax) with willing submission, and feel themselves subdued." Some scholars interpret this verse as if it had scrapped all the Koranic limitations on the use of force. Ibn al-Qayyim (cited in Qutb, 2003:5) interprets this verse as if the Prophet Muhammad is ordered to fight his enemies from among the earlier faiths until they submit to his authority or pay *Jizia* or embrace Islam. According to Maududi (1994:202), the purpose of fighting is to put an end to the sovereignty and supremacy of the unbelievers. The authority to rule should only be vested in those who follow the true faith, that is, Islam. Unbelievers should live in subordination.

Verse 9:29 gives a different meaning when interpreted in its Koranic context. Let us deal with the question of *Jizia* first. The root meaning of *Jizia* is "compensation" (Ali, 1989:445) and "satisfaction" (Asad, 1997:262). The derived or technical meaning is a poll tax levied from those who were not Muslims but were willing to live under the protection of the Islamic state (Ali, 1989:445). There is no fixed amount but it may be as paltry a sum as five pence in the United Kingdom. Women, children, poor, slaves, monks, and hermits are exempted from paying a poll tax. Being a tax on able-bodied men, it is in a sense a commutation for military service. However, the word *Yadin* (literally meaning, hand), occurring in verse 9:29, has different interpretations. Hand is usually considered as a symbol of power and authority. Ali interprets it as "token of willing submission" and Asad as "with a willing hand." Rashid Rida (cited in Asad, 1997:262) takes the word *Yad* (singular of *Yadin*) in a metaphorical sense and relates the phrase to the financial ability of the person liable to pay *Jizia*. The *Jizia* is thus partly symbolic and partly commutation for military service. As the amount is insignificant and exemptions are many, the symbolic nature predominates (Ali, 1989:445). All non-Muslims citizens who volunteer for military service are exempt from the payment of *Jizia*. As in Islam Jihad or participation in war is religiously sanctioned but at the same time Islam does not force non-Muslims to follow its tenets, it is understandable to levy symbolic poll tax instead. This is how the religious freedom of non-Muslims is respected and protected. Non-Muslims were also exempt from paying *Zakat* (poor tax), which the Muslims were obligated to pay. Exemption from Jihad and *Zakat* together worked to the advantage of non-Muslims (Mohammad, 1985:390). *Jizia* was not a specific Islamic invention but was the norm of the time. "Several of the early caliphs made peace treaties with the Byzantine Empire some of which even required them to pay tribute [*Jizia*] to the Byzantines" (Streusand, 1997).

Verse 9:29 must be read in the context of a clear-cut Koranic rule: The use of force is allowed in self-defense only. The rule of verse 9:29 to fight is relevant only in the event of aggression committed against the Muslim community or state. The phrase "nor hold that forbidden which hath been forbidden by Allah and His Messenger" probably points toward the prohibition of aggression by all apostles of God. This forbidden thing, in the context of permitting fighting, might mean aggression (Asad, 1997:261). This interpretation is more plausible as the verse occurs in the chapter dealing with the subject of war, particularly conduct of war and resumption of hostilities.

The historical context of 9:29 is that it was revealed in Madina. Chapter 9 of the Koran deals with three themes: Muslims' first expedition to pilgrimage in Mecca (Dhu al-Qadah 9 AH./631 CE); the preparation for the battle of Tabuk (Rajab 9 AH /631 CE); and strongly censuring those Muslims who stayed behind during the battle of Tabuk (Maududi, 1994:176). The Madinan period is the time when the Muslims were struggling to consolidate their nascent community, which was surrounded by hostile tribes and political alliances. In this state of uncertainty, Muslims had two options: peace treaties with other tribes or war until hostile tribes were subdued. For Muslims, it is irrelevant whether these hostile groups were Christians, Jews, or Pagans. The Prophet Muhammad fought his own tribe, Quraish, as it threatened and attempted, during the battle of Badr, to conquer Madina where Prophet Muhammad had migrated. Keeping in view the Koranic and historic contexts, the most probable interpretation is that verse 9:29 addresses those unbelievers who either were aggressors or there was a well-founded fear that they would attack Muslims. The meaning seems specific to those historical events and may not be characterized as a general norm of Islamic law applicable in all times and all situations.

2.2.2 Anticipatory Jihad

The Koran also allows necessary preparation and the use of force when an attack on Muslim land is imminent. It was a practice among the warring Arab tribes to conclude peace treaties, but in many instances the terms of these treaties were never honored. The following Koranic(8:56) verse reflects this tendency: "They are those with whom thou didst make a covenant, but they break their covenant every time, and they have not the fear (of Allah)." The breaking of covenants has two implications. First, entering into covenants with non-Muslims is not only permissible but also desirable. Second, the Muslims may resort to war only if and when the other party is openly hostile to them (Asad, 1997:248–49). In such circumstances, the Koran (8:58) gives conditional permission: "If thou fearest treachery from any group, throw back (their covenant) to them, (so as to be) on equal terms." The "reason to fear treachery" must not, of course, be based on mere surmise but on clear, objective evidence (Asad, 1997:249). "For Allah loveth not the treacherous" is a clear warning to the Muslims that before breaking the covenant and declaring war, there should be clear evidence of treachery regarding the other side (Tabari, cited in Asad, 1997:249). "It is obligatory on the part of the Muslim head of government to apprise the enemy beforehand of the non-existence of pacts and treaties. Fighting without this previous notice is unlawful" (Daryabadi, 2002:346). Once treachery is established, in the same chapter the Koran (8:60) says: "Against them make ready your strength to the utmost of your power, including steeds of war, to strike terror into (the hearts of) the enemies."

The prime example of anticipatory self-defense is the Battle of Badr (624 CE), which is the subject matter of chapter 8, "Al-Anfal" ("Spoils of War"), of the Koran. After thirteen years of persecution, the Prophet Muhammad migrated from Mecca to Madina where he consolidated the Muslim community in a short span of time. He had concluded alliances and peace treaties with neighboring tribes and his influence was growing. This alarmed the powerful tribes of Mecca, particularly the Quraish, because Muslims could get control of the main trading route between Mecca and Syria passing near Madina. The Quraish apprehended that the growing power of Muslims in Madina might jeopardize their trade with Syria. They sent an expedition toward Madina to crush the Muslim power. When the Prophet Muhammad received this news, he led a small force out of Madina to thwart an imminent attack on Madina (Maududi, 1994:119–34).[3]

2.2.3 Who May Declare Defensive Jihad?

According to the Koran, it was the Prophet Muhammad, and after his death a Caliph (Muslim ruler), who has the authority to declare defensive Jihad. "In its classical interpretation it was left to the Imam or Caliph who was the head of Muslim polity to declare Jihad" (Mohammad, 1985:390). The Koran (8:65) says: "O Messenger, rouse the Believers to the fight" and "consult them in affairs (of moment). Then, when thou hast Taken a decision put thy trust in Allah" (Koran, 3:159). After a decision is taken by "mutual consultation" the citizens of a Muslim state are required to follow the decision of those who are in authority: "O ye who believe! Obey Allah, and obey the Messenger, and those charged with authority among you" (Koran, 4:59). The Koran does provide a procedure for the resolution of differences among Muslims, for example the ruler and the ruled: "If ye differ *in* anything among yourselves, refer it to Allah and His Messenger, if ye do believe in Allah and the Last Day: That is best, and most suitable for final determination" (Koran, 4:59). It means if Muslims "differ in anything" among themselves, the matter shall be decided according to the Koran (the words of God) and the *Sunnah*: the model behavior of the Prophet Muhammad. Verse 4:59 gives priority to the words of God both in obedience and for dispute resolution, hence it is imperative to turn to the Koran and what it says on the point in issue.

The declaration of war (defensive Jihad) is an issue of public safety. The Koran (4:83) states that any matter related to public safety should be referred to the Prophet Muhammad or to those charged with authority among the Muslims: "When there comes to them some matter touching (Public) safety or fear, they divulge it. If they had only referred it to the Messenger, or to those charged with authority among them, the proper investigators would have tested it from them (direct)." This verse shows that all matters related to public safety shall be referred to the Prophet Muhammad and, after his death, to those who are in authority. Individuals shall not divulge it or spread panic about it (Ali, 1989:211). As the Prophet Muhammad had passed away, the other option is to refer the matter to those who are "charged with authority." Some organizations or individuals may differ with the given government on the issue of public safety. In such a situation, it may be derived from the previous three verses that the test is the public support because God had only "charged" the Prophet Muhammad with authority. After his departure, it is up to Muslims to charge someone else with authority to rule according to the Koran and the *Sunnah*. If the public trusts and believes that the government is Islamic, then it is up to the government to decide on the issue of public safety. In this case, the opposing individual view or group of individual views has no authority. However, if the given government loses public support and trust because it is considered un-Islamic, then those who have the support and trust of the public can take decisions on public safety after being put in a position of authority according to Islamic law.

2.2.4 Declaration of Jihad by Non-state Actors

This signifies that there could be a situation where individuals (or leaders not in government), by consensus, may be able to declare Jihad. Individuals or group of individuals may declare Jihad if the following conditions are met: (a) a Muslim land is attacked, (b) the ruler is on the side of the invader, and (c) a well-founded fear exists that the ruler will not protect the lives and properties of Muslims. In such a case, if there is consensus among Muslim leaders, they may declare Jihad in defense of Muslims. The classic case is the Russian invasion of Afghanistan in 1979. The Afghan leaders declared Jihad against the invaders as well as the pro-communist ruler of Afghanistan. Muslims around the world joined the Afghan Jihad. This kind of Jihad would be considered a war in self-defense or defensive Jihad, although it would not be declared by a Muslim ruler. This kind of self-defense is compatible with article 51 of the Charter of the United Nations, the right to self-determination under the Charter (articles 1(2); 55), and article 1 of the International Covenant of Civil and Political Rights, 1966 (see generally, Fanon, 1965; Honderich, 2002). The right of self-defense under article 51 is available to states only, but in a case where the head of a state does not represent the will of his population or work against the interests of his country, the consensus declaration of war by other Muslim leaders should be taken as a legitimate substitute.

In sum, the Koran provides clear rules for defensive Jihad: necessary and proportionate use of force in individual and collective self-defense. The two Koranic grounds for the use of force are when a Muslim land is attacked or such an attack is imminent, or when a group of Muslims are persecuted for believing in Islam but are unable to defend themselves. The permission to use force is not unlimited. The Koran imposes three limitations on the use of force. Force is not allowed (a) if the opposite party ceases fighting Muslims, (b) when there is an offer of peace, or (c) when oppression and persecution of Muslims ends. The treaties made with non-Muslims must be respected. Hostilities shall only be resumed if the ground for triggering the use of force in self-defense is revived. Only the ruler of a Muslim state, not non-state actors, may declare Jihad. However, if the ruler is on the side of the invaders, then Muslim leaders, by consensus, may declare Jihad.

2.3 Offensive Jihad

The offensive theory of Jihad is founded on two premises: the universality of Islamic faith and the obligations of its followers to spread it to the rest of the world. However, if the proselytizing process is obstructed, those obstructions shall be removed by force if Muslims are capable to do so. Therefore, it is called offensive theory of Jihad. The two supporters of the offensive theory of Jihad, who have immensely influenced the debate on Jihad in the twentieth century, are Maududi and Qutb.

Sayyid Abul A'la Maududi (1996:86) argues that Muslims are supposed to serve the entire humanity and the best way to serve it is to invite people to goodness and prevent them from doing evil, that is, the good and evil based on his understanding of true Islamic teachings. Maududi (1996:53–82) does believe in defensive Jihad in order to preserve Muslims and their power from elimination. However, he (1996:85–149) argues that once Muslims have gained sufficient power, they should strive to remove mischief from the earth and establish the rule of God. It may be done peacefully or by force, if necessary, hence the justification for offensive Jihad. According to him, the Koran allows Muslims to use the sword for two purposes: to preserve Muslims and their power from being eliminated and to use the accumulated power to remove mischief from the entire world establishing the rule of Allah.

Sayyid Qutb (2003:18–20), influenced by Maududi, argues that to say that Jihad is merely defensive war is to "underrate the Islamic way of life, places its importance below that of the homeland." He (2003:20–21) believes that "justification for Jihad is inherent in the nature of this faith . . . defending the homeland of Islam is the means to establish God's authority within it, and to use it as the base from which to address all mankind. Islam is a message to all humanity, and the whole earth is its sphere of action." According to Qutb (2003:28), Jihad includes "efforts to change people through verbal advocacy. It also includes the possible armed struggle to end an oppressive system and establish [Islamic] justice." "Islam is not a party of preachers and missionaries but rather of divine enforcers. Its mission is to blot out, by force if necessary, oppression, moral anarchy, social disorder and exploitation . . . and replace evil with good" (Qutb, 2003:34). Any efforts to spread Islam might face obstacles. Islam aims to remove these obstacles so that it can address people freely and appeal to their minds and consciences in order to have genuine freedom of choice (Qutb, 2003:21). The ultimate aim of Jihad is "universal revolution" to "replace the dominance of non-Islamic systems" (Qutb, 2003:36). Jurists such as Ibn Taymiyyah took a more activist position: A ruler who fails to enforce Sharia rigorously in all its aspects, including Jihad, forfeits his right to rule (cited in Streusand, 1997). Similarly, Muhammad Mutahhari (1986:89) deems Jihad defensive but that includes defense against oppression. He considers an attack on a polytheist country legitimate, not to impose the religion of Islam but to eliminate the evils of polytheism. Both Maududi and Qutb rely on the following verses to support their theory of offensive Jihad:

> Ye are the best of peoples, evolved for mankind, enjoining what is right, forbidding what is wrong, and believing in Allah. (3:110)

> Let there arise out of you a band of people inviting to all that is good, enjoining what is right, and forbidding what is wrong. (3:104)

> (They are) those who [Muslims], if We establish them in the land, establish regular prayer and give regular charity, enjoin the right and forbid wrong. (22:41)

The theory of offensive Jihad does not stand up to the Koranic scrutiny. There is no doubt that the Koran declares Islam to be a religion for humankind. There is also no doubt that the Koran enjoins its adherents to spread the message of Islam to the rest of the world. Nevertheless, I do not agree with Maududi and Qutb's offensive theory of Jihad for three major reasons. First, a contextual interpretation of the verses they rely on brings a different meaning to them. The verses do not support the offensive theory of Jihad. Second, the Koran provides elaborate rules for propagating Islam, which do not include the use of force. Third, their interpretation is against the Koranic code of armed conflict based on the principle of neutrality.

Let us start with the contextual interpretation of the verses used in support of offensive Jihad. Verses 3:104 and 3:110 were revealed in the context of making a comparison of Muslims with those People of the Book (the followers of divine scripture) who had given up their faith and were engaged in strife and dissention. These verses, in fact, allude to an ideal Muslim community: happy, untroubled by conflicts or doubts, sure of itself, united, and prosperous because it invites people to goodness and forbids wrong (Ali, 1989:154). To make the context clear, verse 3:110 is reproduced in full:

> Ye are the best of peoples, evolved for mankind, enjoining what is right, forbidding what is wrong, and believing in Allah. If only the People of the Book [followers of scriptures such as Jews, Christians etc.] had faith, it were best for them: among them are some who have faith, but most of them are perverted transgressors. (3:110)

The following two verses throw further light on the real meaning and context of verse 3:110, particularly the concept of "enjoining good and forbidding evil."

> The Believers, men and women, are protectors one of another: they enjoin what is just, and forbid what is evil: they observe regular prayers, practise regular charity, and obey Allah and His Messenger. (9:71)

> Those that turn (to Allah, in repentance; that serve Him, and praise Him; that wander in devotion to the cause of Allah; that bow down and prostrate themselves in prayer; that enjoin good and forbid evil; and observe the limit set by Allah.—(These do rejoice). So proclaim the glad tidings to the Believers. (9:112)

Verse 3:110 is related to how a Muslim community should be and how it may achieve happiness and felicity. It should establish prayer, pay *Zakat* (poor tax), promote good, and forbid evil (Yusuf, 1989:310). They should practice charity and participate in Jihad. Only those who have sufficient knowledge of Islam may invite people to good and forbid evil, because only the knowledgeable may know the difference (Usmani, 1993:81). Jihad is one of the features of an ideal Muslim community. It is not a means of forbidding an evil the way Maududi and Qutb describe. In addition, one of the requirements of "enjoining good and forbidding evil" is to possess sufficient knowledge of Islam, whereas Jihad becomes compulsory on every ordinary Muslim if a Muslim land is under attack. In some cases, Jihad is optional for able-bodied men. The order of "enjoining good and forbidding evil" is for Muslims regarding other Muslims in order to avoid the situation of the People of the Book mentioned in verse 3:110. For instance, regarding the People of the Book, the Koran (5:79) says that they failed to invite good and forbid evil, hence there is dissention and strife among them. To argue, as Maududi and Qutb do, that this rule applies to non-Muslims as well means nothing but subjecting non-Muslims to the Islamic code of good and evil. Conversely, it is a germane norm of Islamic law that Islamic law applies only to Muslims. For instance, the 1979 Hudood Ordinance of Pakistan prohibits Muslims from drinking alcohol but places no such restrictions on non-Muslims. This brings us to the second argument that the offensive theory of Jihad contradicts the Koranic concept of freedom of religion.

The Koran believes in the right to freedom of religion and explains the rules for propagating Islam and the different stages involved in the process. First, the Koran sets out the general rule of absence of compulsion in religion: "Let there be no compulsion in religion" (2:256). This verse has two implications. First, it makes clear that no one is compelled to adopt Islam as his or her religion. Second, once someone embraces Islam, he or she should not be forced to follow what others believe. The Koran (16:125) goes one step further and lays down the guidelines for preaching Islam: "Invite all to the way of God with wisdom and beautiful preaching, and argue with them in ways that are best and most gracious." After imparting the message of

Allah in "ways that are best and most gracious," the Koran (18:29) states: "Say, '[t]he truth is from your Lord': Let him who will believe, and let him who will reject (it)." The Koran thus elaborates the stages for preaching religion: (a) there is no compulsion in religion, (b) invite all to the way of God graciously, and after invitation (c) people should be left free to choose to believe or not to believe (Shah, 2005).

It is interesting to note that both Maududi and Qutb have a similar view of freedom of religion. Relying on verse 2:256, Maududi (1996:17) says that the best way for us is to present our religion and its teaching to the world together with our reasoning for it. We should leave it to the people to accept or reject it. To get to the contextual meaning of this verse, he goes further and explains the occasion and context of its revelation. It was the tradition of Arabs in Madina, before the migration of Prophet Muhammad from Mecca to Madina, for a woman whose children died in infancy to say that she would raise a particular child as a Jew if it remained alive. This was in fact to please the gods so her child might live longer. In this way many children became Jews. With the arrival of Prophet Muhammad to Madina, the local people tried to convert their Jewish children to Islam, because they reckoned Islam as a better religion. On this occasion verse 2:256 was revealed, prohibiting forceful conversion of Jewish children to Islam.

The point of departure comes when Maududi (1996:164–65) says that the rule regarding freedom of religion remains the same and so does the rule regarding "enjoining good," that is, by persuasion and peaceful means. However, the rule regarding "forbidding evil" changes if there is "mischief and evil" on the earth, and Muslims have sufficient power to remove it by force. He fails to cite any Koranic evidence to back up his argument. Moreover, I have never come across a verse where the Koran conditions the use of force in order to forbid evil on the military capabilities of Muslims. Both Maududi and Qutb cite verse 2:251: "And did not Allah Check one set of people by means of another, the earth would indeed be full of mischief." However, verse 2:251 is not relevant to the point Maududi and Qutb are making. First, it shows the procedure of how one group was checked by another group but does not provide a ground for the use of force. Second, the word "check" does not necessarily or usually include the use of force. If Maududi and Qutb's concept of "evil and mischief" means attacking and persecuting Muslims, then force may be used. But this is not what they mean by "evil and mischief." For Maududi it means immorality (1996:105–9) and an un-Islamic way of life (1996:170–75). For Qutb (2003:36), it means the removal of "un-Islamic systems." This, in my opinion, amounts to an imposition of Islam by force, which the Koran clearly prohibits.

Third, the offensive theory of Jihad is against the Koranic code of armed conflict with non-Muslims and the inherent principles of neutrality, that is, fight only those who fight you. The Koran provides express rules on living in peace with non-Muslims as well as making peace treaties with them if they are inclined toward peace. Islam obligates Muslims to honor their covenants with non-Muslims. If the covenant with the Pagans is not dissolved and they are not engaged in aiding someone else against Muslims, then Muslims are required to complete their pledge with them. The Koran (9:4) says:

> (But the treaties are) not dissolved with those Pagans with whom ye have entered into alliance and who have not subsequently failed you in aught, nor aided any one against you. So fulfil your engagements with them to the end of their term: for Allah loveth the righteous.

Verse 9:4 spells out two conditions for not fulfilling treaties with Pagans: if Pagans break the terms of the treaty or aid someone with whom Muslims are in conflict. Absent these conditions, Muslims are required to observe the treaties until the end if time-specific. After the end of treaties, the general Koranic rule applies: Necessary and proportionate use of force may be used in self-defense only. It does not mean the declaration of war. The Koran encourages just and kind dealing with everyone: Jews, Christians, Pagans, and so on:

> Allah forbids you not, with regard to those who fight you not for (your) Faith nor drive you out of your homes, from dealing kindly and justly with them: for Allah loveth those who are just. (60:8)

The critics of Islam say that the Koran tolerates Jews and Christians but not unbelievers. The Jews and Christians may live in subordination in a Muslim state and the rest should be converted to Islam or killed (Khadduri, 1955). The Koranic evidence provides a different view. Verse 9:4 is Pagan-specific and does not mention that after ending treaties with them, convert or kill them. Rather the Koran (9:5) says: "If one amongst the Pagans asks thee for asylum, grant it to him, so that he may hear the word of Allah. And then escort him to where he can be secure." Verse 60:8 applies to everyone, including Pagans, and the Koran encourages just dealings with everyone. The Koranic (60:9) rules of friendship do not exclude non-Muslims:

> Allah only forbids you, with regard to those who fight you for (your) Faith, and drive you out of your homes, and support (others) in driving you out,

> from turning to them (for friendship and protection). It is such as turn to them (in these circumstances), that do wrong.

Many Muslims cite the following two verses to justify alienation from non-Muslims:

> Let not the believers take for friends or helpers Unbelievers rather than believers: if any do that, in nothing will there be help from Allah except by way of precaution, that ye may Guard yourselves from them. But Allah cautions you (To remember) Himself; for the final goal is to Allah. (3:28)
>
> The Unbelievers are protectors, one of another: Unless ye do this, (protect each other), there would be tumult and oppression on earth, and great mischief. (8:73)

These are wartime verses stating not to trust those Pagans, Christians, and Jews with whom Muslims are at war. They may not apply in a state of peace or neutrality. The Koran (8:72) also absolves Muslims of the protection of those Muslims who do not join them in the war:

> Those who believed, and adopted exile, and fought for the Faith, with their property and their persons, in the cause of Allah, as well as those who gave (them) asylum and aid—these are (all) friends and protectors, one of another. As to those who believed but came not into exile, ye owe no duty of protection to them until they come into exile; but if they seek your aid in religion, it is your duty to help them, except against a people with whom ye have a treaty of mutual alliance. And (remember) Allah seeth all that ye do.

Verses 9:4, 60:8, and 60:9 have one dominant theme: Fighting is permitted only with those who fight or drive Muslims out of their homes. Absent these conditions, the Koran (3:108) stands for just dealings: "And Allah means no injustice to any of his creatures."

The critics of Islam also developed a theory that Islam was spread by sword. Maududi (cited in Qutb, 2003:25) describes it as follows:

> For a considerable time now unfriendly interpreters have been adding spin to it as if it were nothing but pure zealotry—giving an image of a horde of religious fanatics surging forward, swords in hand, beards tucked under their lips, and chanting *Allahu Akbar* (God is great). To intensify this imagery, their eyes are shown as filled with blood. Wherever they see an infidel (non-Muslim) they lay their hands on him and force him to declare that there is no deity except God or face execution. The spin masters have thus painted us masterly with their tag: "This nation's history smells of blood."

This theory, however, does not pass the test of history. Muslims ruled Spain for eight centuries and it was a perfect opportunity for Muslims to convert, for instance, all Christians and Jews to Islam. However, historical evidence presents a different picture: Thousands of Christians lived side by side with Muslims under Muslim rule. For Jews, it was a golden age. The Indian subcontinent is another illustration. The Muslims invaded India in 712 CE and ruled almost all of it until the British arrival in the eighteenth century. Millions of Hindus and members of other religious minorities lived under Muslim rule. At the time of partition in 1947, Hindus outnumbered Muslims (Prasad, 1959). The Ottoman Empire is another instance. The presence of thousands of non-Muslims in modern Muslim nation-states reflects the current Muslim states practice of negating this theory. History testifies in favor of the Koranic norm by showing that there is no compulsion in Islam. To say that Islam was spread by the sword is ignorance of history. It would be more convincing to argue that Islamic rule was expanded by conquests, which is completely different from converting non-Muslims to Islam forcefully. Islamic empire building is not different from other instances of empire building, such as British or French. No British colony, such as India, invited the British to colonize India.

The views of Maududi and Qutb regarding Jihad as self-defense and freedom of religion conform to the Koran. Their views of the universality of Islamic faith are understandable. However, their arguments for the use of force for subjecting non-Muslims to the rule of Allah do not conform to the Koranic messages of peace and freedom of religion. The most problematic is their concept of "evil and mischief" and their removal by force. It seems that they regard all moral, political, and social systems that are not Islamic as "evil and mischief." For them the panacea for all "evil and mischief" is its replacement with "good," which means the rule of Allah. The Koran (2:191; 2:217) does mention that "tumult and oppression are worse than slaughter," which Maududi (1996:104) and Qutb (2003:18) cite to build their arguments. However, these two verses give the opposite meanings when read in full; it means Muslims shall not be oppressed and prevented from believing in Islam:

> And slay them wherever ye catch them, and turn them out from where they have Turned you out; for tumult and oppression are worse than slaughter; but fight them not at the Sacred Mosque, unless they (first) fight you there; but if they fight you, slay them. (2:191)

> They ask thee concerning fighting in the Prohibited Month. Say: "Fighting therein is a grave (offence); but graver is it in the sight of Allah to prevent access to the path of Allah, to deny Him, to prevent access to the Sacred

> Mosque, and drive out its members." Tumult and oppression are worse than slaughter. Nor will they cease fighting you until they turn you back from your faith if they can. (2:217)

In these verses "tumult and oppression" means turning Muslims out of their home and preventing them from access to the path of Allah. The Koran allows the use of force in these cases. This take us back to the grounds for defensive Jihad, which is when Muslims are attacked (turned out of their homes) and persecuted for believing in Islam (prevented from the path of Allah). This is a reiteration of the grounds for self-defense rather than the introduction of new ground for the use of force. The repetition strengthens the theory of defensive Jihad and the fact that these are the *only* Koranic grounds for the use of force.

The offensive theory of Jihad seems in conflict with the major themes of the Koran, such as peace, freedom of religion, and justice for all of God's creatures. The contextual interpretation of the verses cited in support of the offensive theory supports these Koranic themes rather than the offensive theory of Jihad. However, it might be helpful to understand Maududi and Qutb's arguments if they are studied within the political context and landscape they lived in. Maududi wrote his book on Jihad (in Urdu language) in 1926 when the Indian subcontinent was under British rule and political heat was gathering fast to overthrow the foreign yoke. He founded his own religious political party called Jamat Islami in 1936. "Jihad for [Maududi] was akin to war of liberation" (Streusand, 1997). Based on Maududi and Hassan Al-Bana's view, the Egyptian Islamic Brotherhood came into existence in 1928. Sayyid Qutb, himself an Egyptian, was its key member. The Brotherhood focused on the removal of the then government, as they considered it un-Islamic: "For them, as for Ibn Taymiya, [J]ihad includes the overthrow of governments that fail to enforce Shari'a" (Streusand, 1997). To get popular support, both Maududi and Qutb tried to anchor their arguments firmly in the Koran. The political climate of the time may partly explain their offensive view of Jihad: overthrow of foreign and un-Islamic political regimes. Similarly, Ibn Taymiyyah's war against Tatars furnishes a clue for why he adopted an extreme view of Jihad. The Tatars threatened the borders of Islam by attempting to cut a swath across Central Asia and Asia Minor. "Ibn Taymiyyah's call for *[J]ihad* was, at its root, a call for defense against invasion" (Silverman, 2002:81; Mohammad, 1985:393). Ibn Taymiyyah (cited in Munir, 2003:403) says that if Jihad was meant for preaching religion and was one of such means, then there would be no exception not to kill women and children. Their exception is strong evidence that the fight is against those who fight against us to push back their wickedness (see generally, Kruse, 1956).

2.4 Dar Al-Islam (Abode of Islam) and Dar Al-Harb (un-Islamic Abode)

Some publicists tend to divide the world into Dar al-Islam and Dar al-harb. They consider Dar al-Islam to be always at war with Dar al-harb until it is conquered. "Islam expresses . . . division between friend and foe . . . by dividing the world into the D*ar al-harb*—the domain of war—and the *Dar al-Islam*—the domain of Islam, where war is forbidden" (Westbrook, 1992–93:819). Majid Khadduri is the prominent follower of this theory. He (956:358) argues that Islam, emerging in the seventh century of the Christian era as a conquering power with world domination as its ultimate objective, refused to recognize legal systems other than its own. Islam was willing to enter into temporary peaceful relations with other states pending consummation of its world mission. On the assumption that the aim of Islam was the whole of mankind, the world was sharply divided under the law of Islam between the Dar al-Islam and the Dar al-harb. The Muslims were under legal obligation to reduce the latter to Muslim rule in order to achieve Islam's ultimate objective, namely the enforcement of God's law over the entire world. The instrument by which the Islamic state was to carry out that objective was called the Jihad, which was always just if waged against the infidels and the enemies of the faith. Thus, Jihad was the Islamic *bellum justum* (Khadduri, 1956:359). For Khadduri (1955:59), Jihad is "a sanction against polytheism and must be suffered by all non-Muslims who reject Islam . . . [it] is the litigation between Islam and polytheism; it is also a form of punishment to be inflicted upon Islam's enemies and the renegade from the faith" Abdullahi An-Na'im (1988:328) suggests that there is progression in the Koranic sanction from the use of force in self-defense to the use of force in the propagation of Islam lending support to Khadduri's view. Some publicists follow the theory of Islam versus the rest of the world without putting it to the Koranic test. Ali and Rehman (2005) and Mushkat (1986–87) are two examples.

2.4.1 Contextual Interpretation of the Koran

I do not agree with Khadduri as the Koran does not divide the world into Dar-al-hard and Dar al-Islam. It is the invention of latter writers (Engineer, 2006). An-Na'im's argument is not convincing as he fails to provide supporting

Koranic evidence. Let us deal with Khadduri's argument first. To make his point, Khadduri relies on selective verses and plucks them out of their proper context. He does not attempt to connect one verse to another to reach a proper understanding. All the relevant verses are analyzed below in their historic and Koranic context.

2.4.1.1 Historic Context

The seventh-century Arab society was divided into tribes. Tribal wars were common features of Arab political existence. There was no unified legal system. Individuals owed their allegiance to the tribal head and the interests of the tribe were supreme (Smith, 1903). The tribe as a group was responsible for the survival of its members and interests (Rahim, 1911). By necessity, tribes were forced to enter into alliances with other tribes either by means of intertribal marriages or political covenants (Watt, 1966). Might was right and a small incident could spark a violent tribal conflict (Hitti, 1961). Fred Donner (1991) argues that the Muslim valuation and articulation of Jihad is just as much, if not more, a product of history as it is of religion. "In this society, war . . . was in one sense a normal way of life; that is, a 'state of war' was assumed to exist between one's tribe and all others, unless a particular treaty or agreement had been reached with another tribe establishing amicable relations. In a sense, one might say that Arabia only survived as an entity by virtue of a primitive version of the Cold War 'balance of terror'" (Donner, 1991). Islam emerged and had to survive in these circumstances and "fighting, sometimes preemptively, sometimes defensively, was understood to be the only way to do so" (Jackson, 2002).

2.4.1.2 Koranic Context

The verses of the Koran may be divided into the particular and the general. The particular verses of the Koran in terms of this discussion are those dealing with wars of Muslims with non-Muslims in the early days of Islam. The general verses of the Koran related to this discussion are those dealing with non-Muslims, such as Christians and Jews, during peacetime and how to propagate Islam. The particular verses of the Koran dealing with Jihad may be divided into the following categories: (a) justification of Jihad, (b) exhorting Muslims to Jihad, (c) conduct of Jihad, and (d) reward for participating, and punishment for not participating, in Jihad. This chapter is concerned with verses dealing with the justification of Jihad as previously indicated. Verses such as: "Will ye not fight people who violated their oaths, plotted to expel the Messenger, and took the aggressive by being the first (to assault) you?" (9:13); "O Messenger, rouse the Believers to the fight" (8:65); and "Go ye forth, (whether equipped) lightly or heavily, and strive and struggle, with your goods and your persons, in the cause of Allah" (9:4) fall under exhorting Muslims to Jihad. The following verses are related to the conduct of Jihad:

> When ye meet the Unbelievers (in fight), smite at their necks; At length, when ye have thoroughly subdued them, bind a bond firmly (on them): thereafter (is the time for) either generosity or ransom: Until the war lays down its burdens. (47:4)
>
> But when the forbidden months are past, then fight and slay the Pagans wherever ye find them, and seize them, beleaguer them, and lie in wait for them in every stratagem (of war); but if they repent, and establish regular prayers and practise regular charity, then open the way for them: for Allah is Oft-forgiving, Most Merciful. (9:5)
>
> The reward of those who "strive and fight with their wealth and their persons: for them are (all) good things: and it is they who will prosper." (9:88)
>
> But those who are slain in the Way of Allah—He will never let their deeds be lost. (47:4)

Khadduri (1955) builds his arguments based on verses related to the conduct rather than the justification of Jihad. This leads him to the conclusion that the Koran allows the use of force for converting non-Muslims to Islam or that the standing order is to kill them where Muslims find them. This implies that the Koran justifies the genocide of non-Muslims. This conclusion is wrong and unfounded for two main reasons. First, these verses are clearly related to the conduct and not the justification of Jihad. Hence, the application of these verses is confined to the state of war. They do not formulate a general rule. Second, the Koran (2:190) says to fight "those who fight you," meaning that women, children, and the elderly shall not be killed during the war. If the Koranic command were a general order to eliminate Jews, Christians, and Pagans, it would not have specified its order to only kill able-bodied Jews, Christians, Pagans, and so on. The Koran would have said: Kill all Jews, Christians, and others irrespective of age and gender. Again, the Koran 9:6 states: "If one amongst the Pagans ask thee for asylum, grant it to him, so that he may hear the word of Allah. And then escort him to where he can be secure" (see Maududi, 1990:191). The Koran does not say "seize and kill him" instead of "escort him to where he can be secure."

Moreover, the Koran believes that Jews and Christians are rightly guided people and the Koran confirms the truth of Gospel and Jewish Scripture.

> They [People of the Book] believe in Allah and the Last Day; they enjoin what is right, and forbid what is wrong; and they hasten (in emulation) in (all) good works: They are in the ranks of the righteous. (3:114)

> Let the people of the Gospel judge by what Allah hath revealed therein. (5:47)

> It was We who revealed the law (to Moses): therein was guidance and light. By its standard have been judged the Jews, by the prophets who bowed (as in Islam) to Allah's will, by the rabbis and the doctors of law. (5:440)

> To thee We sent the Scripture in truth, confirming the scripture that came before it, and guarding it in safety: so judge between them by what Allah hath revealed, and follow not their vain desires, diverging from the Truth that hath come to thee. To each among you have we prescribed a law and an open way. (5:48)

The Koran allows both Jews and Christians to be judged according to what was revealed to them (5:47): It did not say either to kill them all or judge them by the Koranic standard. In general, the social code of the Koran encourages mixing and good relations with Jews and Christians when not at war. For instance, the Koran (5:5) states:

> The food of the People of the Book is lawful unto you and yours is lawful unto them. (Lawful unto you in marriage) are (not only) chaste women who are believers, but chaste women among the People of the Book, revealed before your time.

The Koran believes in peaceful coexistence with the rest of the world. Like all other religions, Islam encourages self-propagation. The Koran therefore, provides a set of rules on how to propagate Islam. The Koran does not support the theory of the division of world into two hostile camps: Dar al-Islam and Dar al-harb. As the subsequent pages further clarify, the Koran never divides the world on these lines.

2.4.2 The Theory of Abrogation: Nasakh

Those scholars who argue that the Koran allows the use of force in self-defense and the propagation of Islam rely on the theory of abrogation (*nasakh*). The word *nasakh* literally means "to copy a book" (Kathir, 2000:325). In the discussion of the Koran, it means to "remove" or "annul" one verse of the Koran by another subsequent verse. Abrogation, however, does not entail obliteration of a verse, turning it into a nonbeing. Its only effect is the cancellation of the order that the verse had promulgated

(Tabatabai 1892–1981). "The Nasakh only occurs with commandments, prohibition, permissions, and so forth. . . . The meaning of Nasakh in the case of commandments is removing the commandment and replacing it by another" (Kathir, 2000:325). An-Na'im (1988:324–29) argues that the Koran allows the use of force for two purposes: self-defense and propagation of Islam. However, latter verses of chapter 9, which dissolved all treaties with non-Muslims, abrogated the earlier verses permitting the use of force in self-defense. The verses revealed afterward are in force, which, by his interpretation, allows the use of force for propagating Islam. "The verses of this chapter [9], such as 5, 12, 13, 29, 36, 73, and 123, contain the clearest sanction for the use of force against non-Muslims, and are generally considered to have repealed or superseded all previous verses which prohibit or restrict the use of force. In particular verse 5 . . . is said to have repealed . . . over one hundred preceding verses of the Qur'an which instruct Muslims to use peaceful means and arguments to convince unbelievers to embrace Islam" (An-Na'im, 1988:327). Chapter 9 of the Koran have repealed "all previously revealed inconsistent verses of the Qur'an" (An-Na'im, 1988:328). He argues that this shows progression from the use of force in self-defense toward the use of force in the propagation of Islam. However, he (1988:328) does say that "it should be possible for modern Muslim jurists to reverse this process of abrogation in order to re-instate the principles of peaceful co-existence with non-Muslims."

I have two main objections to An-Na'im's argument: (a) the set of verses he relies on is not related to the propagation of Islam at all, and (b) he does not produce any evidence from the Koran to support his argument of abrogation. An-Na'im relies on verse 9:5 and 9:29 to derive a rule that claims the Koran allows the use of force for propagating Islam. To make the context and meanings clear and provide readers an opportunity, let us reproduce all the relevant verses:

> A (declaration) of immunity from Allah and His Messenger, to those of the Pagans with whom ye have contracted mutual alliances. (9:1)
>
> Go ye, then, for four months, backwards and forwards, (as ye will), throughout the land, but know ye that ye cannot frustrate Allah (by your falsehood) but that Allah will cover with shame those who reject Him. (9:2)
>
> And an announcement from Allah and His Messenger, to the people (assembled) on the day of the Great Pilgrimage—that Allah and His Messenger dissolve (treaty) obligations with the Pagans. If then, ye repent, it were best for you; but if ye turn away, know ye that ye cannot frustrate Allah. And proclaim a grievous penalty to those who reject Faith. (9:3)

> (But the treaties are) not dissolved with those Pagans with whom ye have entered into alliance and who have not subsequently failed you in aught, nor aided any one against you. So fulfil your engagements with them to the end of their term: for Allah loveth the righteous. (9:4)
>
> But when the forbidden months are past, then fight and slay the Pagans wherever ye find them, and seize them, beleaguer them, and lie in wait for them in every stratagem (of war); but if they repent, and establish regular prayers and practise regular charity, then open the way for them: for Allah is Oft-forgiving, Most Merciful. (9:5)
>
> If one amongst the Pagans asks thee for asylum, grant it to him, so that he may hear the word of Allah. And then escort him to where he can be secure. That is because they are men without knowledge. (9:6)
>
> But if they violate their oaths after their covenant, and taunt you for your Faith—fight ye the chiefs of Unfaith: for their oaths are nothing to them: that thus they may be restrained. (9:12)
>
> Will ye not fight people who violated their oaths, plotted to expel the Messenger, and took the aggressive by being the first (to assault) you? Do ye fear them? Nay, it is Allah Whom ye should more justly fear, if ye believe! (9:13)
>
> Fight those who believe not in Allah nor the Last Day, nor hold that forbidden which hath been forbidden by Allah and His Messenger, nor acknowledge the religion of Truth, (even if they are) of the People of the Book, until they pay the Jizya with willing submission, and feel themselves subdued. (9:29)
>
> The number of months in the sight of Allah is twelve (in a year)—so ordained by Him the day He created the heavens and the earth; of them four are sacred: that is the straight usage. So wrong not yourselves therein, and fight the Pagans all together as they fight you all together. But know that Allah is with those who restrain themselves. (9:36)
>
> O Prophet! strive hard against the unbelievers and the Hypocrites, and be firm against them. (9:73)
>
> O ye who believe! fight the unbelievers who gird you about, and let them find firmness in you: and know that Allah is with those who fear Him. (9:123)

It is important for the proper understanding of these verses to know the historic context, that is, the period of history they were revealed in. Muslims had different mutual alliances and peace treaties with several non-Muslim tribes. "The contents of chapter nine are related to the events arising from the *Treaty of Hudaybiyah* (6 A. H. / 628 C.E.)" (Maududi, 1990:176) between the

Prophet Muhammad and Quraish. By the terms of this treaty, Banu Khazagh became the Muslims' ally whereas Banu Bakr became the Quraish's ally. Banu Bakr, aided by the Quraish, attacked Banu Khazagh thus breaching terms of the treaty (Usmani, 1993:249). Quraish, apprehensive at the growing power of Muslims, prepared for decisive war. However, Prophet Muhammad made a sudden attack on Mecca in 8 A H/629 CE, conquering it with little difficulty. At that moment, Muslims still had time-specific and open-ended treaties with other tribes. It was a period of violent tribal and communal wars and Muslims were engaged in the wars of survival and self-consolidation. In the heat of military and political struggles, verses 1–37 were revealed in 9 AH/631 CE. The specific occasion of revelation is when the Prophet Muhammad sent Abu Bakr as a leader of the Pilgrims to Mecca. These verses were revealed in the absence of Abu Bakr. Therefore, the Prophet Muhammad sent his cousin Ali to Mecca to recite these verses publicly (Maududi, 1990:187). The reason is that the Koran (8:58) does not allow attacking those who have a treaty with Muslim unless the treaty is terminated openly.

Now as the historic context and purpose is clear, the simple interpretation seems to be that the Koran declared immunity for those Pagans with whom Muslims had mutual alliances. The treaties with the rest of the Pagans are dissolved except, the Koran reiterates, with those Pagans who are neither fighting with nor aiding someone against Muslims. All warmongers and mischief-makers were given a four-month grace period with the option to either repent from what they were doing (i.e., hostile activities against Muslims) or embrace Islam. If none of these options were availed of after four months, the state of war begins. Once the war begins all the tactics of war will apply, such as killing, ambushing, and beleaguering. However, there is one exception where these tactics cease to apply: If a Pagan asks for asylum, it shall be granted so that he may hear the word of God. After that, Muslims are required to send him to a place where he will be safe, namely an area of his own choosing. Muslims are also exhorted to be firm in war (Koran, 9:73). The subject matter of these verses is the conduct of Jihad and the armistice code of the Koran.

By this interpretation, these verses do not introduce new grounds for the use of force. They also do not require Muslims how to propagate Islam. They rather address the status of treaties in force among Muslims and different tribes as well as why and when hostilities shall resume. It is greatly surprising that An-Na'im contends that these verses introduce a new rule: propagating Islam by force by abrogating the previous verses and permitting the use of force in self-defense. There is nothing in the Koran that directly or indirectly hints toward An-Na'im's conclusion. These verses address a particular issue at a particular time and their interpretation is tied to that moment and event in history. They do not create a new universal rule obligating all Muslims to kill all Pagans at all places and at all times.

An-Na'im's argument of abrogation is seriously flawed. I do not agree with him for two reasons. First, he makes a general statement that over one hundred verses are abrogated without pinpointing the abrogating and abrogated verses. I gather from his assertion that certain verses of chapter 9 abrogate verses related to freedom of religion, self-defense, and anticipatory self-defense. An-Na'im (1987:325) accuses others of failing "to take account of verses of the *Qur'an* that suggest aggressive Jihad." However, he never specifies a verse abrogating the use of force in self-defense only. His argument is not convincing because those who produce evidence from "the book of God will be acceptable" (Ibn Taymiyyah, 712 AH). The Koran does abrogate verses of the previous religions as well as Koranic verses: "None of Our revelations do we abrogate or cause to be forgotten, but We substitute something better or similar" (2:106). Whenever the Koran intends to repeal a rule, it is made clear (16:89). For instance, for Muslims, Jerusalem was the Qibla, that is, a point of focus that Muslims face during prayer. Prophet Muhammad turned his face from old Qibla, Jerusalem, toward new Qibla, Kaba, after he received revelation during prayer (Koran, 2:142). Since then, Kaba is the new Qibla for Muslims. In other instances, the Koran indicates how to deal with a particular issue in future. For example, the Koran (4:15) forbids lewdness but hints toward a different punishment in the future. Verse 24:2, revealed after 4:15, provides the indicated punishment. There is no such indication in the Koran regarding the abrogation or revelation of a different rule for self-defense. Relying on Tabari, Asad (1997:41) writes that "this early, fundamental principle of self-defense as the only possible justification of war has been maintained through out the Qur'an is evident from 60:8 as well as the concluding sentence of 4:9, both of which belong to a latter period than the above verse." Ibn Kathir (2000:527) argues that the interpretation that verse 9:5 has abrogated the verses permitting the use of force in self-defense is not plausible. Shah Wali Ullah (2005:39–50) does not list as abrogated those verses that An-Na'im regards as abrogated.

The second reason I do not agree with An-Na'im is that he suggests that Muslims jurists may revoke the process of abrogation, meaning that the use of force for the propagation of Islam may be reversed with the use of force in self-defense. This is a fundamental change in Islamic law and clearly against the Koran. Abrogation is the right of God, and the only human agent through whom God revealed the Koran was the Prophet Muhammad. The mission of Islam was completed shortly before the Prophet Muhammad passed away: "This day have I perfected your religion for you, completed my favour upon you, and have chosen for you Islam as your religion" (Koran, 5:3). This is the last verse chronologically marking the end of Muhammad's ministry (Ali, 1989:245). The process of revelation and abrogation stops here. This leaves no room for An-Na'im's argument. In my opinion, Muslim jurists may interpret verses differently, but they cannot abrogate or reinstate abrogated verses. For instance, can Muslim jurists change the Qibla? The answer is no.

It is significantly important to note that both Maududi and Qutb do not cite the verses that An-Na'im cites to support their offensive theory of Jihad. They rely on a different set of verses. Commenting on verse 9:5, Qutb (2003:69 Vol. 8) writes that the declaration of war "was not meant as a campaign of vengeance or extermination, but rather as warning which provided a motive for them to accept Islam." Citing verse 9:6, Qutb (2003:69 Vol. 8) further says: "Islam . . . does not seek to exterminate all idolaters. . . . On the contrary . . . individual idolaters who are not a part of hostile and belligerent are guaranteed safety in the land of Islam. God instructs His Messenger to give them asylum so that they may listen to God's word and become aware of the nature of the Islamic message before they are given safe conduct to their own domiciles [lands]."

The argument of progression, the changing of rule of peaceful propagation of Islam to propagation by force, is erroneous. Qutb (2003:20–21) summarizes Ibn Qayyim's argument of progression—which An-Na'im seems to follow—in the following words:

> The first revelation given to the Prophet by his Lord . . . was His order to him, "*Read in the name of your Lord who created man out of a germ-cell.*" (96:1–2). This was the start of the Prophethood. The instruction . . . was read within himself. He subsequently revealed to him: "*You are enfolded, arise and warn*" (74:1–2). This means that God made him a prophet by telling him to read and He gave him his mission . . . God then ordered him to warn his immediate clan. Subsequently, he gave the same warning to his own people, then to the surrounding Arabian tribes, then to all Arabs, then to the mankind generally. For more than a decade . . . Muhammad . . . continued to advocate the faith without resorting to fighting. . . . Throughout this period he was ordered to stay his hand, forbear patiently and overlook all opposition. Latter, God gave him permission to migrate [from Macca to Madina] and permitted him to fight. He then instructed him to fight those who wage war against him and to maintain peace with those who refrain from fighting him. At a latter stage, God ordered him to fight the idolaters until all submission is made to God alone.

This is a very concise summary of the way Islamic religion evolved from one person, Prophet Muhammad over the period of approximately twenty-three years, to an Islamic state. Gradualism and pragmatism are the marks of the Koranic revelation process (Shah, 2006). The Koran, in more than one place, says how and why verses were revealed gradually:

> By degrees shall We teach thee to declare (the Message), so thou shalt not forget. (87:6)

> Those who reject Faith say: "Why is not the Qur'an revealed to him all at once?" Thus (is it revealed), that We may strengthen thy heart thereby, and We have rehearsed it to thee in slow, well-arranged stages, gradually. (25:32)

> (It is) a Qur'an which We have divided (into parts from time to time), in order that thou mightest recite it to men at intervals: We have revealed it by stages. (17:106)

These verses reflect how and why the Koran was revealed in a gradual way. The gradualism and progression of the Koran is easy to comprehend. The change from the beginning of Muhammad's prophethood to the establishment of Islamic polity in Madina required different rules. The progression of rules from dealing with individuals to communities is natural and reflects the Koranic realism. In this process of gradual revelation of the Koran, some verses were abrogated. As previously indicated, the Koran (2:106) says that "none of Our revelations do. We abrogate or cause to be forgotten, but We substitute something better or similar" There does not seem to be such clear rules changing the principles of the use of force in self-defense to the use of force for the propagation of Islam.

According to An-Na'im, one of the central themes of the Koran is upholding good and forbidding evil, but the Koran does not "explicitly specify the ways in which this obligation is to be discharged" (1988:332). Therefore, he relies on the second source of Islamic law,[4] which encourages direct action against evil. Contrary to An-Na'im's view, the Koran does provide guidance how to respond to evil:

> Those who patiently persevere, seeking the countenance of their Lord; Establish regular prayers; spend, out of (the gifts) We have bestowed for their sustenance, secretly and openly; and turn off Evil with good: for such there is the final attainment of the (eternal) home. (13:22)

> Repel evil with that which is best: We are well acquainted with the things they say. (23:96)

> Nor can goodness and Evil be equal. Repel (Evil) with what is better: Then will he between whom and thee was hatred become as it were thy friend and intimate! (41:34)

2.4.3 Is the Koran Self-contradictory?

Closely related to the theory of abrogation is an argument that the Koran suffers from serious contradictions (Tibi, 1996; An-Na'im, 1988). To reconcile different parts of the Koran with each other, the theory of abrogation is employed. For many scholars, this is the only way to do so. In general, I do believe on theory of abrogation: Some verses were repealed by others, but I do not accept the argument that the Koran is self-contradictory. Let us interpret the Koran by the Koran itself (Tabatabai, 1892–1981), that is, what the Koran says on the Koranic consistency. "Do they not consider the Qur'an (with care)? Had it been from other Than Allah, they would surely have found therein much discrepancy" (Koran, 4:82). In another place, the Koran (39:23) says: "Allah has revealed (from time to time) the most beautiful Message in the form of a Book, consistent with itself, (yet) repeating (its teaching in various aspects)." Bassam Tibi and others asserting contradiction in the Koran never produced and juxtaposed two or more verses to prove their claim or disprove the Koranic claim. I never come across any verse relevant to the topic under discussion that contradicts another relevant verse. When read with care, the Koran identifies different stages of Jihad: (a) justification, (b) exhorting and raising the morale of Muslims, (c) conduct of Jihad, (d) booty of war, and (e) reward for those who take part and punishment for those who do not take part in Jihad. The Koran is consistent in covering all stages of warfare, although the relevant verses are scattered in the Koran and revealed at different periods. This is understandable because the Koranic revelation is piecemeal and issue-oriented. Some rules are repeated for emphasis. The best example is the repetition of grounds for the use of force in self-defense.

It is very hard to accept the views of Khadduri and An-Na'im after reading the Koranic verses related to the conduct of Jihad and relations with Jews and Christians outside wartime. These verses are consistent with each other and make perfect sense if understood in their proper internal and external context. For instance, the verse stating to smite the necks of Jews, Christians, and Pagans is understandable because this is what happens in any battlefield. This is what happened in World War I and II. The worst instance is the use of an atomic bomb by the United States. Many people are being killed in the current conflicts in Afghanistan and Iraq (see 3.2). These verses were revealed in the age of tribal wars when it was common to use steeds and swords to subdue and kill opponents. Since the Muslims were fighting with Jews, Christians, and Pagans, there are many references to them. If Muslims were at war with Communists, Hindus, and Buddhists in seventh-century Arab society, we would have found Koranic references to killing or making treaties with them. For instance, the history of the Indian subcontinent from the eighth to the eighteenth century furnishes examples of Muslims wars with Hindus and others (Qureshi, 1962). The Koranic order of killing Jews and Christians is particular and limited to the able-bodied and those engaged in warfare with Muslims. The general injunctions of the Koran regarding them are that they are the rightly guided people and do not prevent Muslims "from dealing kindly and justly with them" (60:8).

2.5 Conclusion

It is established that the Koran allows necessary and proportionate use of force in self-defense, that is, defensive Jihad. The ruler of a Muslim state is allowed to declare Jihad, and non-state actors have no such authority unless the Muslim ruler is on the side of the invaders or working against the interests of Muslims. The offensive theory of Jihad is unfounded and conflicts with fundamental principles of the Koran, such as freedom of religion and its code of armed conflict (i.e., neutrality). The division of the world into Dar al-Islam and Dar al-harb is not Koranic. The Koran is absolutely consistent and spells out consistent rules for three different situations: state of neutrality, state of peace, and state of war.

References

Ali, Y.(1989) *The meaning of the holy Qur'an.* Maryland: Amana Corporation.

Ali, S. and Rehman, J. (2005) The concept of Jihad in Islamic international law. *Journal of Conflict and Security Law*, 10, pp.321–45.

An-Na'im, A.(1988) Islamic ambivalence to political violence: Islamic law and international terrorism. *German Yearbook of International Law*, 31, pp.307–36.

———. (1987) Islamic law, international relations, and human rights challenge: Challenge and response. *Cornell International Law Journal*, 20, pp.317–36.

Asad, M. (1997) *The message of the Koran*. Gibraltar: Dar Al-Andalus.

Daryabadi, A.M. (2001) *The glorious Quran: Text, translation & commentary.* Leicester: The Islamic Foundation.

Donner, F. (1991) The sources of Islamic conception of Jihad. I*n* Kelsey, J. and Johnson, J. (eds.) *War and Jihad: Historical and theoretical perspectives on war and peace in Western and Islamic traditions.* New York: Greenwood Press.

Engineer, A. (2006) On Kufr, Jihad, cow slaughter and Dar Al-Harb. Newsletter of Institute of Islamic Studies, Mumbai. Available at: http://www.csss-isla.com.

Fanon, F. (1965) *The wretched of the earth*. New York: Grove Press.

Hamidullah, M. (1956) *The Muslim conduct of state*. Lahore, Pakistan: Ashraf Publishers.

Hitti, P.(1961) *History of the Arabs*. London: McMillan.

Honderich, T. (2002) *After the terror*. Edinburgh: Edinburgh University Press.

Jackson, S.(2002) Jihad and the modern world. *Journal of Islamic Law and Culture*, Spring/Summer, pp.1–26.

Kathir, Ibn. (1301–73) *Tafsir Ibn Kathir* (Al-Mubarakpuri, S. trans. 2000) Vols I and IV Riyadh: Darussalam.

Kelsay, J. (1993) *Islam and war: A study in comparative study*. Kentucky: John Knox Press.

Khadduri, M. (1956) Islam and the modern law of nations. *American Journal of International Law*, 50, pp.358–71.

———. (1955) *War and peace in the law of Islam*. Baltimore: John Hopkins University Press.

Kruse, H. (1956) *The foundation of Islamic international law*. Karachi: Pakistan Historical Society.

Maududi, S. A. (1996) *Al-Jihad Fil-Islam* (Urdu). Lahore, Pakistan.

———. (1990) *Towards understanding the Quran* (Z. Ansari, trans). Vol. III. Delhi: Markazi Maktaba Islami. (Original work published 1942–73).

Mohammad, N. (1985) The Doctrine of Jihad: An introduction. *Journal of Law and Religion*, 3, pp.381–98.

Mushkat, R. (1986–87) Is war ever justifiable? A comparative survey. *Loyola Of Los Angles International and Comparative Law Journal*, 9(2), pp.227–318.

Mutahhari, M. (1986) Jihad in the Qur'an: First lecture. *In* Mehdi Abedi and Gary Legenhausen (eds.), *Jihad and Shahadat: Struggle and martyrdom in Islam: Essays and addresses by Ayatollah Mahmud Taleqani, Ayatullah Murtada Muttahari and Dr. Ali Shari'ati*. Houston: Institute for Research and Islamic Studies.

Prasad, I.(1959) *A short history of Muslim rule in India*. The Indian Press Ltd. Allabad.

Qureshi, I. (1962) *The Muslim community in the Indo-Pakistan sub-continent*. Gravenage.

Qutb, S.(2003) *In the shade of the Quran*, Vol. 8 and 9, (Salahi, M. A. trans). Leicester: The Islamic Foundation. (Original work published 1950–1960s).

Rahim, A. (1911) *Muhammadan jurisprudence*. Lahore: PLD Publishers.

Shah, N.A. (2006) *Women, the Koran and international human rights law: The experience of Pakistan*. Lieden: Martinus Nijhoff Publishers.

———. (2005) Freedom of religion: Koranic and human rights perspectives. *Asia-Pacific Journal on Human Rights and the Law*, 6(1–2), pp.69–88.

Silverman, A. (2002) Just war, Jihad, and terrorism: A comparison of Western and Islamic norms for the use of political violence. *Journal of Church and State*, 44, pp.73–92.

Smith, W. (1903) *Kinship and marriage in early Arabia*. Cook (eds.) Adam And Charles Black London.

Streusand, D. (1997) What does Jihad means? *Middle East Quarterly*, September. Available at: http://www.meforum.org/article/357.

Tabatabai, A. (1892–1981) *Al-Mizan* [Koranic commentary]. Available at: http://www.almizan.org/.

Taymiyyah, Ibn (2005) *Risala Usul Tafseer* (Ansari Urdu, trans). Lahore, Pakistan: Al-Faisal Nashran. (Original work published 712).

Tibi, B.(1996) War and peace in Islam. In Nardin, T. (ed.) *The ethics of war and peace: Religious and secular perspectives*. New Jersey: Princeton University Press. pp.128–45.

Usmani, S.A. (1993) *Al-Koran: Translation and commentary* (Urdu). Madina, Saudi Arabia: Shah Fahad Koran Complex.

Wali, Ullah.S. (2005) *Al-Fozul Al-Kabir* (Abdullah Urdu, trans.). Lahore, Pakistan: Al-Faisal Nashran.

Watt, W. M. (1969) *Muhammad at Medina*. Karachi: Oxford University Press.

Westbrook, D. (1992–93) Islamic International Law and Public International Law: Separate Expression of World Order. *Virginia Journal of International Law*, 33, pp.819–97.

Yusuf, S.D. (1991) *Koran, translation and commentary*. Junaghari (Urdu, trans). Madina, Saudi Arabia: Shah Fahad Koran Complex.

CHAPTER 3

Al-Qaeda, the Koran, and Politics of Terrorism

It is widely believed that the violent activities of Al-Qaeda emanate from the teachings of Islam. The reason is simple: Al-Qaeda claims to be a Muslim organization and makes frequent references to the Koran and other sources of Islamic law to justify its declarations of Jihad against the Anglo-Americans and their allies. This has led to thinking that the Koran is the main source of inspiration for Al-Qaeda's type of Jihad. Chapter 1 in this book has established that the Koran does not support offensive Jihad. The Koran allows necessary and proportionate use of force for individual and collective self-defense only. It is important to note that, as we shall see later, Al-Qaeda claims that its Jihad is in self-defense, that is, relying on defensive theory of Jihad. This implies that Al-Qaeda is following the defensive rather than extreme interpretation of Jihad. It is a case of misapplication rather than extreme interpretation. This chapter has three main objectives. First, to challenge the Koranic foundation of Al-Qaeda's 1996 "Declaration of War against the Americans Occupying the Land of the Two Holy Places" and the World Islamic Front's 1998 declaration of "Jihad against Jews and Crusaders." This chapter argues that Al-Qaeda's declaration of Jihad is un-Koranic (illegitimate) for two main reasons: As a non-state actor, it does not have the authority to declare Jihad, and the circumstances in 1996 and 1998 did not warrant individual declaration of Jihad. In addition, targeting civilians by Al-Qaeda exceeds the Koranic limits on the use of force in self-defense. Second, this chapter gives clear warning that if the Anglo-American forces do not leave Muslim lands, Muslims leaders (which may not necessarily include Al-Qaeda or the pro-Western Muslims rulers) may, by consensus, declare Koranic (legitimate) Jihad. It is also probable that more and more Muslims leaders may start, overtly or covertly, supporting Al-Qaeda. If such a support passes the threshold of "sufficient Muslim leaders' consensus," it will provide Islamic legitimacy to an otherwise un-Islamic Jihad. Jihad of this kind will be legal according to international legal standards: the use of force in self-defense, self-determination, and law of occupation (see 2.2.4). The point made is not to support Al-Qaeda or the pro-Anglo-American governments in the region but to make a case for the legitimate rights of common people. Third, it analyzes the Islamic and non-Islamic causes of terrorism and concludes that to look for an explanation for Al-Qaeda's violence in Islam in isolation from non-religious causes is misleading. The theory of "reactive terror" provides the most plausible explanation for terrorism. Some Muslims strongly believe that their land and religion is under attack and react to the situation with violence. Religion is used as a tool to support the militancy of organizations, such as Al-Qaeda. This chapter concludes by stressing to refocus attention on the non-Islamic causes of terrorism if we seriously want to reign in the rising tide of so-called Islamic terrorism.

3.1 Manifesto of Al-Qaeda

Al-Qaeda, over the years, has issued several statements in press interviews, videos, and on the Internet. They deal with different aspects of the plight of Muslims, justification of Al-Qaeda's activities, and sometimes take solace from harm inflicted on its perceived enemy. This chapter looks at the declarations of 1996 and 1998, since these contain the core of Al-Qaeda's justification of Jihad, specifically the 1996 declaration. This is why I call it the Manifesto of Al-Qaeda. Sometimes, it is described as a "Ladenese Epistle" (Lawrence, 2005:23). The Manifesto is a well crafted and candid expression of what Al-Qaeda considers "oppression" of and "aggression" against Muslims across the world: in the Middle East, Central Asia, Southeast Asia, the Horn of Africa, the Caucasus, and the Balkans. The Manifesto furnishes many illustrations showing the "plight" of Muslims, "plunder" of Islamic wealth of oil in the Middle East and Anglo-American backed "corrupt" and "dictatorial" Muslim polities. The Manifesto attempts to arouse Muslim men, youth, and women to their duty of Jihad to defend Muslims against "aggression" and end their "oppression." Bin Laden argues that the Koran supports his call for Jihad. The Manifesto is discussed under the following subheads.

3.1.1 Aggression against Muslims

The Manifesto is a "magnificent piece of eloquent, at times even poetic Arabic prose" (Lewis, 1998)[1] full of citation from the Koran. It sets the stage before calling on Muslims to wage Jihad. It describes the plight of Muslims all over the world in the following words:

> It should not be hidden from you that the people of Islam had suffered from aggression, iniquity and injustice imposed on them by the Zionist-Crusaders alliance and their collaborators; to the extent that the Muslims blood became the cheapest and their wealth as loot in the hands of the enemies. Their blood was spilled in Palestine and Iraq. The horrifying pictures of the massacre of Qana, in Lebanon are still fresh in our memory. Massacres in Tajakestan, Burma, [Kashmir], Assam, Philippine, Fatani, Ogadin, Somalia, Erithria, Chechnya and in Bosnia-Herzegovina took place, massacres that send shivers in the body and shake the conscience. All of this [happened] and the world watch[ed] . . . and not only didn't respond to these atrocities, but also with a clear conspiracy between the USA and its' allies and under the cover of the iniquitous United Nations, the dispossessed people were even prevented from obtaining arms to defend themselves. The people of Islam awakened and realised that they are the main target [of] aggression. . . . All false claims and propaganda about human rights were hammered down and exposed by the massacres that took place against the Muslims in every part of the world. . . . The latest and the greatest of these aggressions . . . is the occupation of the land of the two Holy Places . . . by the armies of the American Crusaders and their allies.

The Manifesto shows real conflicts involving Muslims all over the world, human rights breaches on massive scale, and the way these conflicts were (and are) handled by the Western powers, the United Nations, and other regional organizations, such as NATO. Al-Qaeda, as we shall see later, considers the Saudi government to be corrupt and an agent of the United States. Therefore, it regards the presence of U.S. forces in the Arab peninsula, despite the fact that Saudi government invited them, as an occupation.

3.1.2 Objectives of Al-Qaeda

The Manifesto clearly spells out the objectives: "We wish to study the means that we could follow to return the situation to . . . normal. . . . And to return to the people their own rights." The overarching aim is to restore the situation to normal in the Muslim lands: returning Muslims their rights, which they had lost after the arrival of Western powers in the Muslim lands. "In order to re-establish the greatness of this Ummah [all Muslims are collectively called Ummah] and to liberate its occupied sanctities." We should "expel the occupying enemy from the country of the two Holy places." The

Manifesto does not state that Al-Qaeda wants to Islamize the West or turn the United States, the United Kingdom, or any other Western state into Islamic states. The only stated objective is to stop Western (mainly Anglo-American) aggression against Muslims and return to Muslims control of their lands and resources.

3.1.3 Means to Achieve Objectives

Alluding and praising the bombings in Al-Khobar (1995) and Riyadh (1996) in Saudi Arabia, the Manifesto states that "due to the imbalance of power between [Al-Qaeda's] armed forces and the enemy forces, a suitable means of fighting must be adopted, i.e. using fast moving light forces that work under complete secrecy. In other words, to initiate guerrilla warfare, where the sons of the nation . . . take part in it. . . . Our youths knew that the humiliation suffered by the Muslims as a result of the occupation of their sanctities can not be kicked and removed except by explosions and Jihad." In other words, Al-Qaeda justifies its conduct of Jihad on the basis of an imbalance of military power between the Anglo-Americans and Al-Qaeda. This includes suicide bombings and targeting civilians (see 3.4.1.4; 3.4.2).

3.1.4 Saudi Regime: Agent of the United States

Al-Qaeda considers the Saudi regime as the agent of the United States. The regime invited the U.S. troops in the 1990s to protect its oil fields from Iraq, but the United States never left. Al-Qaeda considers their presence as an occupation of the land of the two Holy Mosques. Al-Qaeda accuses the United States of shedding the blood of innocent Iraqi men, women, and children. According to Al-Qaeda, the American aim in attacking Iraq is to provide strategic advantage to Israel, to get control of the region, and to loot the Islamic wealth of oil. "The presence of the USA Crusader military forces on land, sea and air of the states of the Islamic Gulf is the greatest danger threatening the largest oil reserve in the world." "Therefore [Al-Qaeda] agreed that the situation cannot be rectified (the shadow cannot be straightened when its' source, the rod, is not straight either) unless the root of the problem is tackled. Hence, it is essential to hit the main enemy who divided the (Ummah) into small and little countries and pushed it, for the last few decades, into a state of confusion(Al-Qaeda, 1996)." "The [Saudi] regime is fully responsible for what had been incurred by the country and the nation; however the occupying American enemy is the principal and the main cause of the situation.

Therefore efforts should be concentrated on destroying; fighting and killing the enemy until . . . it is completely defeated" (Al-Qaeda, 1996). As an agent of the United States, the Saudi regime has no legitimacy for Al-Qaeda. Hence, the United States and the regime are both legitimate targets.

After describing the relation between the United States and the Saudi regime, the Manifesto turns to the relation between the Saudi regime and the citizens of Saudi Arabia. The charge sheet of the Saudi regime constitutes a good part of the Manifesto:

> Injustice had affected the people of the industry and agriculture. . . . The situation at the land of the two Holy places became like a huge volcano at the verge of eruption that would destroy the Kufr [infidelity]. . . . The explosions at Riyadh [1995] and Al-Khobar [1996] is a warning of this volcanic eruption emerging as a result of the severe oppression, suffering, excessive iniquity, humiliation and poverty. . . . Everybody talks about the deterioration of the economy, inflation, ever increasing debts and jails full of prisoners. . . . [The regime is] ignoring . . . Shari'ah law; depriving people of their legitimate rights; allowing the American to occupy the land of the two Holy Places [and had] imprison[ed] . . . sincere scholars. Through [this] course of action, the regime has [lost] its legitimacy. The inability of the regime to protect the country, and allowing the enemy of the Ummah . . . to occupy the land for the longest of years . . . heavy spending on these forces . . . [oil] prices are fixed to suit the American economy ignoring the economy of the country; expensive deals were imposed on the country to purchase arms; [all this compels] people [to] ask what is the justification for the very existence of the [Saudi] regime then?

The main allegations against the Saudi regime is the invitation of U.S. troops who now occupy the Holy places; heavy spending on these forces; expensive arms deals with the United States and others; the deterioration of economy; misapplication of Sharia and other human rights violations, such as the repression of scholars and of the Saudi citizens. The charge sheet covers political, military, economic, and social aspects of Saudi Arabia affecting Saudi citizens.

3.1.5 Exhaustion of Peaceful Means

To counter the belief that Al-Qaeda has an inclination for unnecessary violence, the Manifesto claims that first efforts were made to rectify the situation by peaceful means. Force is used after the exhaustion of peaceful means. Individuals and groups "wrote [to the Saudi regime] with . . . passion, diplomacy and wisdom asking for corrective measures and repentance from the "great wrong doings and corruption" that had engulfed even the basic principles of the religion and the legitimate rights of the people." The Saudi regime, however, refused to listen. Therefore, "it is no longer possible to be quiet. It is not acceptable to give a blind eye to this matter."

3.1.6 Reach of Al-Qaeda's Call

The reach of Al-Qaeda is global: It calls on Muslims all over the world to wage Jihad against the United States and her allies. Once the charge sheet against the United Sates and the Saudi regime is complete, the Manifesto cleverly invokes the Koran, sayings of the Prophet Muhammad, Muslim jurists, Arab ancestral bravery, and poetry in order to frame its appeal within Islamic legal sources and Arab code of bravery. The Manifesto appeals to the Saudi army, youths, women, and scholars in an effort to win their hearts for its call. Thereafter, the appeal naturally shifts to the Muslim world, stressing upon them that the urgency "to liberate their sanctities is the greatest of issues concerning all Muslims. It is the duty of every Muslims in this world."

3.1.7 World Islamic Front's Declaration, 1998

In 1998, Al-Qaeda issued another declaration of Jihad together with other organizations. Its tone and style is not much different from the declaration of 1996. The declaration begins with citations from the Koran. Its message is couched in poetic Arabic prose. The reasons for the declaration of Jihad are the same as given in the 1996 declaration. It appeals to Muslims all over the world. The declaration explains the motive of U.S. presence in the Arab Peninsula. "Americans' aims behind . . . wars [in the Muslim world] are religious and economic [and] to serve the Jews' petty state." The declaration stresses upon Muslims that Islamic scholars had "throughout Islamic history unanimously agreed that [J]ihad is an individual duty if the enemy destroys the Muslim countries." "The ruling to kill the Americans and their allies—civilians and military—is an individual duty for every Muslim who can do it in any country . . . in order to liberate the Al-Aqsa Mosque and the holy mosque [in Mecca] from their grip, and in order for their armies to move out of all the lands of Islam, defeated and unable to threaten any Muslim." The politically significant difference is that the leaders of Jihad groups from Egypt, Pakistan, and Bangladesh signed the declaration. It is an attempt to broaden the scope of their appeal, draw a greater number of recruits, and increase support for their call.

These two documents show Muslims as oppressed and their lands as under non-Muslim foreign occupation. Those Muslims rulers who have invited or side with foreign troops are called the agents of the West. They are considered as neither true Muslims nor true leaders. Therefore, these governments have no legitimacy and are legitimate targets for Al-Qaeda. Al-Qaeda sees the war as an economic and political "war of values." It is described as a "Crusade" against Islam by "Judo-Christian Alliance" and their protégés in the Muslim world. The invaders are interested in the Islamic wealth of oil. Their Muslim agents in the Muslim world support the invaders in their designs. Al-Qaeda's warning to Muslims is stark: Islam is under threat. In contrast to the Western puppet Muslims regimes, Al-Qaeda regards itself as the faithful defender of Islam. It urges Muslims to embrace its call for Jihad to protect Muslim lands from the enemy and their Muslim agents. The ultimate aim is to throw the invaders out, remove their agent regimes from the Muslim lands, and restore power to and rights of Muslims. The language of both declarations is defensive through and through. There is no indication of aggression against anyone unless it is in perceived self-defense (cf "Counter Terrorism Strategy," UK, 2006).

3.2 The Koranic Foundation of Al-Qaeda's Jihad

Al-Qaeda Manifesto is a powerful expression of the serious issues concerning the Muslim world in the 1990s. These issues range from the presence of U.S. troops (in fact their control of the region); civilians maiming and deaths on massive scale (United Nations Iraq Mission, 2006; United Nations Iraq Mission, 2007); persistent Israeli incursions into Palestinian territory; assassinating all those whom Israel thinks have to be killed; the inability of the international community and organizations to protect Muslims lands; failing to solve the conflict of Palestine to the persistent violations of human rights by the Saudi regime. Most of these issues are well-founded and supported by independent evidence from the 1990s (Human Rights Watch, 1991).[2] The evidence, detailed in this chapter, shows that the situation has worsened after 2001.

The killing of civilians is of great concern from the beginning of the Iraq invasion in 2003. "More than a year after the occupation of Iraq, civilians are still being killed unlawfully every day by Coalition Forces, armed groups and individuals" (Amnesty International, May 11, 2004). "In a number of cases UK soldiers have opened fire and killed Iraqi civilians in circumstances where there was apparently no imminent threat of death or serious injury to themselves or others'. . . . Soldiers resorted to lethal force even though the use of such force did not appear to be strictly necessary in order to protect life" (Amnesty International, May 11, 2004). The United States Pentagon (May 4, 2007) report says: "Approximately 10% of soldiers and marines report mistreating non-combatants (damaged/destroyed Iraqi property when not necessary or hit/kicked a non-combatant when not necessary)."[3] This percentage is despite the fact that 40 percent of soldiers would not report abuse by fellow soldiers (Pentagon, May 4, 2007). The United Kingdom's Intelligence and Security Committee (2005:29 paragraph 110) investigation indicates that "there were fewer than 15 occasions when UK intelligence personnel reported actual or potential breaches of UK policy or the international Conventions." The killing of twenty-four civilians in Haditha (Iraq) in late 2005 shocked the world.[4] In 2006, President Karzai wept in his televised speech saying that we cannot prevent terrorists from Pakistan. We cannot prevent NATO from bombing terrorists. And our children are dying (UK Foreign and Commonwealth Office, April 18, 2007:33). President Karzai (*BBC*, May 3, 2007) also warned: "Afghan patience was wearing thin over the killing of civilians by Western forces hunting Taliban fighters" In June 2007, "more than 200 were killed by coalition troops in Afghanistan" (*Guardian*, July 1, 2007). The Afghanistan Independent Human Rights Commission (AIHRC) (April 13, 2007) concluded its inquiry into the deaths of twelve civilians in March 2007 by the U.S. Marines that the force used was "certainly excessive and disproportionate to any threat faced."[5] "Their actions thus constitute a serious violation of international humanitarian law standards" (AIHRC, 2007b).[6] Millions of people have lost their homes and are displaced in Iraq. The United Nations High Commissioner for Refugees reported that "by April 2007, there were believed to be well over 4 million displaced Iraqis around the world, including some 1.9 million who were still inside Iraq, over 2 million in neighbouring Middle Eastern countries, and around 200,000 further afield." Some displaced women have started to work as prostitutes in neighboring countries, such as Syria (*New York Times*, May 19, 2007).

Human rights breaches across the Muslim world by the Anglo-American forces and the Muslim governments they support are another area of concern. For example, on the state of human rights conditions in Saudi Arabia, the U.S. Department of State said (2001): "The Government's human rights record remained poor. Citizens have neither the right nor the legal means to change their government. Security forces continued to abuse detainees and prisoners, arbitrarily arrest and detain persons, and hold them in incommunicado detention." In addition, there were allegations that security forces committed torture. Amnesty International (2006) criticized the election of

Saudi Arabia to the United Nations Human Rights Council because of its poor human rights record. The abuse and torture of detainees in Abu Ghraib shocked the world (United Nations, E/CN.4/2006/120; Amnesty International, Open Letter to President George W. Bush, May 7, 2004). The annual human rights report of the British Foreign and Commonwealth Office reported "grave deterioration" in human rights conditions in Iraq since February 2006 (April, 18, 2007:33). The United Nations Iraq Mission (March 2007) also expressed concern over human rights violations. The United States National Intelligence Estimate (January 2007) says that "the term 'civil war' accurately describes key elements of the Iraqi conflict." Israel aggression against Palestinian civilians in summer 2006 is described as a 'collective punishment' (Hilsum, July 7, 2006). The Palestinians cannot move freely on their own lands. The World Bank report (May 9, 2007) says: "Freedom of movement and access for Palestinians within the West Bank is an exception rather than a norm," which is affecting the revival of economy. During the 2006 Israel-Lebanon (Hezbollah) war, "Israeli forces had committed indiscriminate and disproportionate attacks, pursuing a strategy which appeared intended to punish the people of Lebanon and their government for not turning against Hezbollah, as well as harming Hezbollah's military capability" (Amnesty International, 2006). The United Nations Human Rights Council passed a resolution (A/HRC/S-2/2, August 11, 2006) strongly condemning the "massive violations of human rights" in Lebnon by Israel. The United Nations High Commissioner for Human Rights, Louise Arbour, (*BBC*, July 20, 2006) showed concern that crimes against humanity might have been committed in Lebanon and called for an international inquiry.

Several suspected terrorists were kept in secret prisons in Europe run by the American CIA from September 11, 2001 to 2005 after concluding agreements with NATO and some European states. The Council of Europe (Marty's) report (June 8, 2007) concluded:

> What was previously just a set of allegations is now proven: large numbers of people have been abducted from various locations across the world and transferred to countries where they have been persecuted and where it is known that torture is common practice. There is now enough evidence to state that secret detention facilities run by the CIA [existed] in Europe from 2003 to 2005, in particular in Poland and Romania with the permission of the highest state official.

General Taguba's report (March 2004) of the United States into the Abu Ghraib abuses concluded:

> Several US Army Soldiers have committed egregious acts and grave breaches of international law at Abu Ghraib/BCCF and Camp Bucca, Iraq.

> Furthermore, key senior leaders in both the 800th MP Brigade and the 205th MI Brigade failed to comply with established regulations, policies, and command directives in preventing detainee abuses at Abu Ghraib (BCCF) and at Camp Bucca during the period August 2003 to February 2004.

The Human Rights Watch (2004:1) reported:

> Since late April 2004, when the first photographs appeared of U.S. military personnel humiliating, torturing, and otherwise mistreating detainees at Abu Ghraib prison in Iraq, the United States government has repeatedly sought to portray the abuse as an isolated incident, the work of a few "bad apples" acting without orders. . . . This pattern of abuse did not result from the acts of individual soldiers who broke the rules. It resulted from decisions made by the Bush administration to bend, ignore, or cast rules aside.

Human Rights Watch (2004:1) also reported: "Detainees in U.S. custody in Afghanistan have testified that they experienced treatment similar to what happened in Abu Ghraib—from beatings to prolonged sleep and sensory deprivation to being held naked—as early as 2002." The International Committee of Red Cross (2004) reported "brutality against protected persons upon capture . . . sometimes causing death or serious injury" in Iraq between March and November 2003. When the abuses committed by the British troops in Iraq were challenged in the highest court of the United Kingdom, House of Lords, the British government strongly argued that the Human Rights Act, 1998 (UK) does not apply to British troops outside the United Kingdom (*Al-Skeini & Others*, [2007] UKHL 26, paragraph 4).

Al-Qaeda's allegations of corruption and expensive arms deals between the Saudis and Anglo-Americans are well-founded. The Serious Fraud Office of the United Kingdom was investigating corruption allegations in £40bn al-Yamamah arms deal between BAE Systems (UK leading arms company) and Saudi Arabia when the British Attorney General suddenly halted the investigation.[7] The Attorney General and former Prime Minster Tony Blair claimed that the investigation was damaging national interests and British foreign policy in the Middle East. They denied that economic concern influenced their decision. (*Guardian*, December 16, 2006). "Arms sales to Saudi Arabia represent the biggest export deals in British history" (*New York Times*, December 15, 2006). The United States recently concluded $5–10 billion arms deals with Saudi Arabia and other states in the region (*New York Times*, April 5, 2007). Some politicians share Al-Qaeda's claim that oil was a factor in the invasion of Iraq in 2003. Tony Benn, a British MP, (March 22, 2006) openly said that the United States went into Iraq for oil. The Australian Defense

Minister, Bredan Nelson, suggested that protecting Iraq's huge oil reserves was a reason for the continuing deployment of foreign troops (*Guardian*, July 5, 2007). The 9/11 Commission Report (2004) of the United States Congress recommended to "build a relationship beyond oil" with the region.

The inconsistent application of international law, double standard on democracy, and human rights and the monopoly of international institutions such as the United Nations Security Council (see 7.1.2), International Monetary Fund, and World Bank by the Western powers is an issue of concern and dismay in countries around the world (Reuter, 2004). For instance, the Security Council cannot pass a resolution that will go against the Anglo-American interests because they will exercise veto. These and all others issues raised in Al-Qaeda's Manifesto of 1996 and beyond are well-founded and are and should be of great concern for the international community. The question, however, is whether Islamic law permits Al-Qaeda to declare Jihad in these circumstances and whether the means used by Al-Qaeda are justified. The answer to this question depends on the answers to two further questions: What constitutes self-defense in Islamic law, and does Islamic law allows nonstate actors to declare war?

3.2.1 Self-defense in Islamic Law

As Chapter 1 of this book shows, the Koran allows necessary and proportionate use of force in self-defense when a Muslim land is attacked or such attack is imminent, or when a group of Muslims are persecuted for believing in Islam but are unable to defend themselves. When Al-Qaeda declared Jihad in 1996 and 1998, no Muslim country was under direct attack. No attack was imminent on a Muslim country either. In some regions, such as Kashmir, Palestine, and Chechnya, Muslims were in conflict with India, Israel, and Russia, respectively. In these conflicts, incidents of Muslim persecution were reported but Muslims, at the same time, were able to inflict harm on their persecutors. Muslim states and citizens also provided overt and covert help to Muslims engaged in militant struggle. For instance, India constantly accuses Pakistan of supporting Kashmir freedom fighters (terrorists for India). Al-Qaeda rightly refers to the killing of Iraqi men, women, and children in the first Gulf War in 1990s and thereafter. These killings, however, were the result of a conflict of different nature. Iraq attacked Kuwait, another Muslim country. With the help of the international community, Kuwait was liberated in 1991.

Al-Qaeda's declaration of Jihad against the Saudi regime does not seem to be justified. The government claims to be applying Sharia law. In fact, many human rights organizations accuse Saudi Arabia of following the strictest interpretation of Islamic law, resulting in human rights violations (Amnesty International, 2001; Human Rights Watch, 2005). The courts and businesses are working not necessarily the way one would like them to operate, but there are no serious internal disturbances or radical opposition groups against the government. People seem to live normal lives, as would be expected in that region. The regime's military ties with the United States, arms deal with Anglo-Americans, and sale of oil and ill governance, breaches of civil liberties, and so on do not give rise to the right of declaration of Jihad by non-state actors. The circumstances in 1996 and 1998 did not warrant Al-Qaeda's declaration of Jihad.

3.2.2 Can Al-Qaeda Declare Jihad?

Al-Qaeda is a non-state actor. The Koran is clear on the question of whom to follow in public affairs: someone who is in authority, namely the ruler of a Muslim state. As declaration of Jihad (war) is an important public decision, the ruler of a Muslim state must make it after careful consideration and consultation with *Shura* (Council or Parliament). After the emergence of nation-states, the ruler of a particular Muslim state may declare Jihad for the Muslim state concerned. It is the right of a ruler to call upon other Muslim states and allies for collective self-defense. Non-state actors cannot declare Jihad unless the ruler is on the side of the invaders and Muslim leaders by consensus declare Jihad (see 4.4.4).

As previously stated, in 1996 and 1998, no Muslim state was under attack from non-Muslim forces. No armed attack on a Muslim state was imminent either. There are fifty-seven Muslim states according to the membership of the Organisation of Islamic Conference (OIC). None of them has either declared Jihad in self-defense or called upon other Muslim rulers and allies for collective self-defense. The declarations of Al-Qaeda in 1996 and 1998 have no Koranic foundation on two counts: No Muslim state was under attack requiring declaration of Jihad in self-defense, and there was no situation where a Muslim land was under attack and the ruler was on the side of the invader, justifying individual declaration of Jihad.

3.3 Changing Nature of Conflicts in Afghanistan and Iraq

After September 11, 2001, new conflicts began in the Muslim world, namely Afghanistan and Iraq. The United States accused Al-Qaeda of carrying out attacks on them. The international community—including Muslims—sympathized with the United States and many Muslims supported the U.S.-led invasion of Afghanistan in October 2001. The aim of attacking Afghanistan was to "bring [America's] enemies to justice" (Bush, September 20, 2001) and to "bring those responsible to account" (Blair, September 14, 2001). The Taliban regime, Al-Qaeda's host, was ousted, which was welcomed both within and outside Afghanistan. Al-Qaeda was not destroyed but its ability was damaged greatly (Bush, 2001). A U.S.-led coalition invaded Iraq in March 2003. The aim was to "disarm" Saddam (Bush, 2001; Blair, 2001) of his supposed weapons of mass destruction (WMD). The invasion of Iraq is controversial (Chapter 5 in this book argues that Iraq's invasion in 2003 is illegal) but there was some international support in the beginning. The expectations were that, after achieving the stated goals in Afghanistan and Iraq, the Anglo-American troops would leave and control would return to Afghans and Iraqis. However, with the passage of time two facts emerged: The liberators/invaders failed to bring stability to Afghanistan and Iraq, and they have not left these countries.[8] Instead, elections were held under the supervision of the Anglo-Americans. Pro Anglo-American governments came to power both in Afghanistan and Iraq. Foreign troops guard these governments in Iraq and Afghanistan. President Bush and former Prime Minister Blair repeatedly claimed that democracy is up and running in Afganistan and Iraq against the ground realities: absolute choas and anarchy.

The tone and rationale has considerably changed over the years regarding why Anglo-American troops went into Afghanistan and Iraq. The focus is now on reforming the value system, at several levels, in these countries rather than catching Bin Laden or destroying WMDs in Iraq. A few citations from President Bush and former Prime Minister Blair's speeches point toward this conclusion:

> Our mission in Iraq is clear. We're hunting down the terrorists. We're helping Iraqis build a free nation that is an ally in the war on terror. We're advancing freedom in the broader Middle East. We are removing a source of violence and instability, and laying the foundation of peace for our children and our grandchildren. (Bush, June 28, 2005)

> America's mission in Iraq is to defeat an enemy and give strength to a friend—a free, representative government that is an ally in the war on terror, and a beacon of hope in a part of the world that is desperate for reform. (Bush, June 28, 2005)

> If we do not defeat the terrorists or extremists in Iraq, they will gain access to vast oil reserves, and use Iraq as a base to overthrow moderate governments

> across the broader Middle East. . . . Our troops are fighting a war that will set the course for this new century. . . . This war is an ideological conflict. (Bush, October 26, 2006)
>
> The war we fight today is more than a military conflict; it is the decisive ideological struggle of the 21st century. (Bush, August 31, 2006)
>
> The point about these interventions, however, military and otherwise, is that they were not just about changing regimes but changing the values systems governing the nations concerned. The banner was not actually "regime change" it was "values change." (Blair, July 6, 2006)
>
> We are fighting a war, but not just against terrorism but about how the world should govern itself in the early 21st century. (Blair, July 6, 2006)
>
> The moment we decided not to change regime but to change the value system, we made both Iraq and Afghanistan into existential battles for Reactionary Islam. We posed a threat not to their activities simply: but to their values, to the roots of their existence. (Blair, July 6, 2006)
>
> It is not wanting Muslim countries to modernise but to retreat into governance by a semi-feudal religious oligarchy. (Blair, July 6, 2006)
>
> Whatever the outward manifestation at any one time—in Lebanon, in Gaza, in Iraq and add to that in Afghanistan, in Kashmir, in a host of other nations including now some in Africa—it is a global fight about global values; it is about modernisation, within Islam and outside of it; it is about whether our value system can be shown to be sufficiently robust, true, principled and appealing that it beats theirs. (Blair, July 6, 2006)
>
> What is happening today out in the Middle East, in Afghanistan and beyond is an elemental struggle about the values that will shape our future. (Blair, July 6, 2006)

Blair continued with his "war of values" at home as well. He said Muslims had a "duty to integrate." "Our tolerance is part of what makes Britain, Britain. Conform to it; or do not come here" (Blair, December 8, 2006).

The Defense Science Board (2004)[9] of the United States reported:

> In stark contrast to the cold war, the United States today is not seeking to contain a threatening state empire, but rather seeking to convert a broad movement within Islamic civilization to accept the value structure of Western Modernity—an agenda hidden within the official rubric of a "War on Terrorism."

The Defense Science Board (2004) hinted at how to proceed:

> If we really want to see the Muslim world as a whole, and the Arabic-speaking world in particular, move more toward our understanding of moderation and

> tolerance, we must reassure Muslims that this does not mean that they must submit to the American way. . . . To succeed, we must understand the United States is engaged in a generational and global struggle about ideas, not a war between the West and Islam.

Bin Laden and many other Jihadi organizations warned Muslims in the 1990s that the West is against Islam and the United States is at the head of this war. Mainstream Muslims did not pay heed to these warnings. However, there is now growing awareness in the Muslim world regarding the Anglo-American strategy: "If ordinary Muslims doubted the designs ascribed to the West by [B]in Laden before the invasion of March 2003, and all that has followed, considerably fewer are likely to do so today" (Lawrence, 2005:xxiii). Muslims have shown "deep resentment [to] American occupation" (Woodward, 2006:372) and many are becoming sympathizers and might be lukewarm supporters.

There is growing opposition from the mainstream Muslims to the Anglo-American presence in the Muslim world. Anglo-American's policies toward Muslims lent support to Al-Qaeda's argument: They are neo-imperialists. "There is a constant evidence that American presence is creating a fearful backlash throughout the Muslim world that empowers the fanatics far more than it frightens them. [President Bush] has failed to offer the country a new, realistic reason for being there" (*New York Times*, September 12, 2006). "The United States has responded to the growing threat of suicide terrorism by embarking on a policy to conquer Muslim countries—not simply rooting out existing havens for terrorists in Afghanistan but going further to *remake* Muslim societies in the Persian Gulf. . . . The close association between foreign military occupation and the growth of suicide terrorists movements in the occupied regions should make us hesitant over any strategy centering on the transformation of Muslim societies by means of heavy military power" (Pape, 2005:6). Sir Richard Dannat, the British Army Chief of Staff, expressed (October 12, 2006) concern, thus, "We are in a Muslim country [Iraq] and Muslims' views of foreigners in their country are quite clear. . . . We should 'get ourselves out sometime soon because our presence exacerbates the security problems.'" The classified, but apparently leaked, National Intelligence Estimate of the United States says: "The Iraq war has made the overall terrorism problem worse" (*New York Times*, September 24, 2006). Within the Middle East, the Anglo-American invasion of Iraq has created a fertile recruitment ground for [B]in Laden's conception of Jihad against the West" (Lawrence, 2005: xv). The National Intelligence Council of the United States reported (January 2005) that Iraq and other conflicts could provide training and recruitment ground for Islamist militants, much as Afghanistan did for the founding generation of Al-Qaeda during the war against the Soviet occupation in the 1980s. The Ministry of Defense for the United Kingdom, reported that the war in Iraq has acted as a recruiting sergeant for extremists across the Muslim world (*Guardian*, September 28, 2006).

The nature of conflicts in Afghanistan and Iraq is fast-changing. Muslims are disenchanted with the Anglo-American foreign policy and have started disliking their presence in the Muslim lands. The July 2007 National Intelligence Estimate of the United States confirmed that extremism is fast-growing among the broader Sunni communities. The governments of Afghanistan and Iraq neither wield power nor represent the will of their nations, as they are seen to have come to power with the help of invaders/victors. For instance, the United States suggested building a wall dividing Shias and Sunnis in Baghdad, Iraq. Prime Minister al-Maliki objected to the erection of wall but the United States went ahead with the construction (*New York Times*, April 22, 2007). Thousands and thousands of Muslims are killed per month (United Nations Iraq Mission, 2007). The damage to Muslim properties is enormous. The natural resources such as oil are contracted to Anglo-American companies. The future holds no hope for this and next generations in these countries. All these elements not only confirm what Bin Laden said in 1996, but are also making the conflicts of Afghanistan and Iraq strong candidates for the declaration of the Koranic (legitimate) Jihad by Muslims leaders. Muslim leaders do not mean Al-Qaeda or the pro-Anglo-American governments. It means the ordinary Muslims. This will be a war for people's rights, not terrorism or extremism.[10] If this kind of declaration of Jihad is made, it would be compatible with the international law of self-defense—the right to self-determination and the law of occupation (see 2.4.4).

3.4 Causes of Terrorism

In Western and many other non-Muslim countries, it is a commonly held view that terrorism emanates from Islam and the "evil ideology" of Al-Qaeda is based on the Koran (see "Counter Terrorism Strategy," UK, 2006). Very often, non-Islamic reasons are not mentioned or very few are inclined to analyze them for Islamic militancy. This gives a partial view of why terrorists are terrorists. To avoid falling into this common trap and in order to do justice to the subject, the causes of terrorism are divided into two broad categories: Islamic and non-Islamic. This is also to take into account the other version of the story: why some Muslims have taken arms against Anglo-Americans and their allies. In July 2007, in the United Kingdom the terror threat level was raised to "critical" after explosives were found in a car in London busy

Haymarket and a blazing Jeep was driven into the terminal of Glasgow airport. There are two important points to note here. First, the British media was showing pictures of the blazing car for three days. On the same day, eighty civilians were killed by NATO forces in Afghanistan. No media outlet commented on it or tried to link the killings of Muslims in Afghanistan to what was attempted by Muslims in the United Kingdom. Second, the perpetrators of the London and Glasgow incidents turn out to be either Muslim foreign doctors or students in the United Kingdom. As the usual and mundane explanation—someone paid a visit to a madrassa in Pakistan and became radical overnight—does not apply here, no one raised the issue of why educated and intelligent Muslims with the prospect of bright futures would engage in such activities. The aim here is not to support the position of terrorists but to provide a full view of the matter and better understanding of what the West (mainly Anglo-Americans) say and what the Muslims say. The aim, as indicated earlier, is to strike at the culture of a single narrative.

3.4.1 Causes Attributed to Islam

There is a belief that Islam is an extreme religion. This is why organizations such as Al-Qaeda rely on the Koran for supporting their violence. The impression created is that the Koran is the fountain of inspiration for Jihadis without any link to non-Islamic external factors. What follow are commonly heard arguments.

3.4.1.1 Establishment of Islamic State

We hear very often that the militants want to establish a worldwide Islamic state. There is also a fear in some Western circles that extremists might capture power, implement harsh Islamic laws, and probably damage Western interests in the Muslim world. The first argument is unfounded and the second has no legal or moral weight. Al-Qaeda never advocated for a world Islamic state. The focus of all its statements, released in various forms, is the expulsion of foreign troops from Islamic lands (see Lawrence, 2005). These statements do refer to the "rule of Islamic law" and "system of Allah," but these essentially signify the establishment of the rule of Allah in the lands of Muslims, which Al-Qaeda considers to be under un-Islamic occupation. If the purpose of Al-Qaeda's struggle was establishing an Islamic state rather than protecting the Islamic system under threat, it might have started at a different point of history and in a completely different set of circumstances. The fact that Al-Qaeda's armed struggle started when Anglo-Americans landed in Muslim lands—whereas Islam is 1,400 years old—points more toward the plausibility of self-defense interpretation rather than the establishment of a world Islamic state. "It is true that suicide organisations often have additional goals such Hamas and Al-Qaeda's aim to build Islamic states in Palestine and the Arab peninsula respectively. The existence of these goals should not distract us from the fact that the proximate, operational goal is to gain control of territory" (Pape, 2005:28), which "the terrorists view as their homeland" (Pape, 2005:23). For instance, after the Soviet withdrawal from Afghanistan, Bin Laden ended his Jihad against the Russians. The Afghan Mujahidin (those who engage in Jihad) did not take Jihad to Moscow. The second argument about the rise of political Islam should not be of concern to anyone. Over one billion Muslims have a right to self-determination like anyone else. The argument has no legal or moral strength.

3.4.1.2 Violence and the Koran

For Bin Laden and his followers, this is a religious war, a war for Islam against infidels, and therefore, inevitably, against the United States, the greatest power in the world of infidels (Lewis, 2004: xv). The U.S. strategy of war presumes that suicide terrorism is mainly a product of an evil ideology called Islamic extremism that will produce terrorists wherever it exists, regardless of U.S. military presence (Pape, 2005:251). This "presumption is wrong and misleading" (Pape, 2005:251). I agree with Pape for two reasons. First, the Koran allows necessary and proportionate use of force in self-defense. Second, if a very small minority of Muslims justify their activities—which are punishable by Islamic law—based on their view of Islam, their view is as misguided as those who say that Islam advocates violence. The extremists and their activities neither represent the worldview of all Muslims nor constitute the Koranic concept of Jihad. For instance, the British National Party, which is generally considered a racist outfit, does not represent the views of mainstream British citizens. Nor does the pornography industry, dominated by Western men and women, represents the general morality of the West.

3.4.1.3 Evil Islamic Ideology

President Bush and former Prime Minister Blair claimed, on a number of occasions, that terrorism, an "evil ideology," comes from Islam. First, it has been previously established, that Islam does not support terrorism. Second, Anglo-Americans demonstrate their inconsistent approach toward Jihad and Bin Laden. In 1979, the former Soviet Union invaded Afghanistan. It outraged the Muslim world and the non-Communist part of the international community. Afghan leaders, not the ruling group, declared Jihad against the Russians. Abdullah Azzam (1985) issued the most important declaration of

Jihad: "Defense of the Muslim Lands: The First Obligation after Iman [Faith]." The aim of Azzam's declaration of Jihad was to expel the Russians out of Afghanistan. "If a piece of Muslim land the size of a hand span is infringed upon, then Jihad becomes [individual obligation] on every Muslim." Azzam is considered the mentor of Bin Laden and his declaration of Jihad against Russians became a model for Bin Laden's declaration of Jihad against the United States (Suellentrop, 2002). This Jihad was funded and supported in every respect by the United States, the United Kingdom, Saudi Arabia, and Pakistan. "The United States and Saudi Arabia together funnelled some $3.5 billion into Afghanistan and Pakistan during the Afghan war" (Stern, 2004:117). CIA, MI6, and Pakistan's Inter Service Intelligence (ISI) were the brains behind the Jihad (Coll, 2005) and "external patrons of the [*M*]*ujahidin*" (Lawrence, 2005: xii). The United States, the United Kingdom, and Pakistan—funded by Saudi Arabia—created Taliban in late 1990s (Rashid, 2002; see 9/11 Commission Report, 2004). The Taliban regime was the unfortunate result of the Anglo-American and Pak-Saudi alliance.

The Mujahidin were supported in 1980s. The Taliban were created and supported in the 1990s. However, Taliban, today's Mujahidin fighting Anglo-Americans, are called terrorists. In the 1980s, Islam was not an extremist religion and Bin Laden and his mentor Azzam were not terrorists. They were the heroes of the Afghan Jihad: a war of liberation from the communists.[11] The religion is the same (Islam), Jihadis are the same (Bin Laden), the landscape is the same (Afghanistan), but this time, for Al-Qaeda, the invaders are different—the capitalists, not the Communists. With the change of invaders, the label shifts from Mujahidin to terrorists.

3.4.1.4 Suicide Bombing

The Western media articulates the view that suicide bombers kill themselves because they are brainwashed by the masters of terror. These people "do tell us something about motivations, they are completely incapable of explaining why these attacks begin at a particular time, and in a particular place, why they spread throughout the world in a very specific patterns; and why some militants organisations have employed them while others haven't" (Reuter, 2004:9). As explained above, Al-Qaeda contends that because of numerical and technological superiority of the enemy, it resorts to suicide bombing. Apparently, believing that Palestinians struggle for self-defense, Al-Qardawi (July 7, 2004) argues that suicide bombing is justified because Palestinians do not have tanks, F-61s, and so on. The only weapon they have is their bodies and they are using it. The desperation drives them to give the most precious thing—life—by doing the maximum damage possible on what they consider invaders.

Similar logic was extended by Royal Air Force (RAF) commander of the United Kingdom in one of the RAF exercises in April 2007. The elite Group One pilots were asked: "Would you think it unreasonable if I ordered you to fly your aircraft into the ground in order to destroy a vehicle carrying a Taliban or al-Qaida commander?" (*The Sun*, April 3, 2007). The British Ministry of Defence (*The Sun*, April 3, 2007) said that Air Vice-Marshal Walker did not say he would order his crews on suicide missions:

> As part of a training exercise he wanted them to think about how they, and their commanders, would react faced with a life and death decision of the most extreme sort—for example, terrorists trying to fly an aircraft into a British city, being followed by an RAF fighter which suffers weapons failure. These are decisions which, however unlikely and dreadful, service people may have to make and it is one of many reasons why the British people hold them in such high esteem.

The logic advanced by the RAF and Al-Qaeda—which Qardawi thinks is justified—is not different. Al-Qaeda reckons that Anglo-Americans have landed in their lands and that their presence is a serious threat to Islam and Islamic wealth. As Al-Qaeda has no organized military, the only effective way to fight and expel them is suicide bombing. The lack of weapons by Al-Qaeda seems to be compatible with RAF's "suffering failure of weapons." Clearly, one is a state and the other is a non-state actor, but the point is to see the logic of their arguments.

Suicide bombing is of invaluable propaganda value. The bombers send a message to their own people: Follow our example—the cause is greater than our (and your) lives. They say to the outside world, we fear humiliation more than we fear death, and, therefore, we have no fear of your well-trained and well-equipped armies, or your high-tech arsenal (Reuter, 2004:3). The political logic of suicide bombing is that it pays off and Al-Qaeda knows it (Pape, 2005). The effective staging of suicide bombings and the dramatic fallout they provoke have encouraged the adoption of the practice by political groups of widely diverse hues (Reuters, 2004:13). The attackers know that their enemy is stronger in a conventional military sense. Yet they also believe that their enemy is weaker in a deeper spiritual sense: They have grown soft, want to live and live well, and are afraid of death. This is the rationale for suicide bombers' irrational abandonment of the natural will to survive embracing death (Reuters, 2004). This shows the power of the powerless and the powerlessness of the powerful.

Although Islamic groups receive the most attention in the Western media, suicide terrorism was not introduced by Islamic organizations (Pape, 2005:16).

Groups professing different or no religion carried out suicide attacks (see Rapport, 1984). Tamil Tigers, a declared terrorist organization in Sri Linka, have killed two heads of states: Rajiv Ghandi of India and Ranasingha Premadasa of Sri Lanka. The Kurdish Workers Party (PKK)—mainly secular—has carried out several suicide attacks against Turkish military targets (Pape, 2005:16). The Japanese Kamikazes were "desperate to stop the advance of the American invasion fleet . . . the Japanese high command organized a variety of 'special attacks' organizations whose pilots—commonly called kamikazes—agreed to crash their aeroplanes, gliders, and even manned torpedoes into US vessels" (Pape, 2005:13, see Bloom, 2005). The Kamikazes may not be considered suicide terrorists as they were carrying out orders of a government, but the purpose was to defeat the enemy that they thought was stronger in military power. The sacrifice of their lives was for the defense of their country. The Kamikazes were neither Christians nor Muslims, but their logic is similar to that of modern suicide terrorists. The Irish Revolutionary Army (IRA) carried out several terrorist attacks against the British military targets, because the IRA wanted them to be out of their land. In this case both sides were Christians or at least from the Christian world. Irish terrorism (Stone, 2006) bears resemblance to the Iraq-Iran war of the early 1980s where both parties were Muslims who invoked the Islamic concept of Jihad and people from both sides wanted to lay down their lives for their countries.

William Shakespeare wrote: "As flies to the wanton boys, are we to gods. They kill us for their sport" (*King Lear*: Act IV Scenes i–ii). The general impression that Muslim suicide bombers probably kill people for no good reasons is misleading. Muslim suicide bombers do not seem to be "wanton boys" killing themselves and others for a "sport." On the contrary, they intensely believe that their land and faith are under attack, and they have a duty to defend Muslim land and their faith. Yusuf Qardawi (cited in Reuter, 2004:122) makes a distinction between suicide and martyrdom. A person who commits suicide kills himself for his own benefit. However, a person who becomes a martyr sacrifices himself for his faith and nation. Whereas a person who kills himself has given up all hope in himself and God, the Mujahid (the warrior), has total faith in God's mercy. He does battle with the enemy with his new weapon, which Providence has put in the hands of the weak so that they are in position to fight the powerful and the arrogant.

3.4.1.5 Martyrs among Virgins in Paradise

There are many references to martyrdom in the statements of militant organizations. For instance, a short poem believed to be written by Bin Laden in

2003 (see Lawrence, 2005) reads:

> So let me be a martyr
> Dwelling in a high mountain pass
> Among a band of knights who,
> United in devotion of God,
> Descend to face armies

This and similar references to martyrdom in Jihadi literature has led to a belief that martyrdom is an ultimate goal of Jihad.

The concept of martyrdom, as contained in the Koran, is not an end in itself. It will help if we look at the circumstances in which the concept was introduced during the early wars of Islam. In the seventh-century Arab society, looting, trading caravans, and invading other tribes and lands in order to capture their riches was a norm. To purge the Arab rules of warfare, the Koran introduced a fundamental rule: Fighting shall be, in the cause of Allah, necessary and proportionate use of force in self-defense. The concept of martyrdom was introduced when some Muslims felt afraid and subdued because of large enemy forces. To raise their morale and strengthen their wills, several Koranic verses were revealed, all of which fall in the exhortation category (see 2.4). The Muslim warriors were told not to show their backs to their enemy, strike terror in enemy's heart, be firm against them, and smite their necks during fighting. Despite brave fighting, if a Muslim is fallen in a battlefield for the cause of Allah, such a warrior is a martyr whom Allah will reward immensely. Those who die in the cause of Allah are not dead: "And say not of those who are slain in the way of Allah. 'They are dead.' Nay, they are living, though ye perceive (it) not" (Koran, 2:154); "They rejoice in the bounty provided by Allah" (Koran, 3:170).

The Koranic aim was not the achievement of martyrdom per se but to encourage brave and valiant fight against the enemy forces. The practice of Prophet Muhammad shows that one's life must be saved so far as possible. For instance, when the persecution of Prophet Muhammad reached its height in Mecca, he migrated to Medina. On the night of migration, the henchmen of his Meccan persecutors chased him. When the prophet and his friend, Abu Bakr, realized that they were being chased, they hid in a cave to save their lives. They escaped a certain death and martyrdom. If martyrdom were the aim of a Muslim's life, the Prophet Muhammad would have never missed this perfect opportunity.

3.4.2 Targeting Civilians

Al-Qaeda is targeting civilians. They are considered legitimate targets. This has created a belief that the Koran supports the killing of non-Muslim civilians. The Koran does not condone such killings. Al-Qaeda's logic is that "they pay taxes to their government, they elect their president, their government manufactures arms and gives them to Israel and Israel uses them to massacre Palestinians. The American Congress endorses all government measures and this proves that the entire America is responsible for the atrocities perpetrated against Muslims" (Bin Laden, 2001; see Lawerence, 2005). Al-Qaeda's argument suffers from two serious flaws. First, all the citizens of the United States and the United Kingdom have certainly not voted for Bush and Blair in general elections. Even if they have done so and pay taxes, it is not certain that they also support the "war on terror." We have seen many anti-war demonstrations both in the United States and the United Kingdom. There is a strong anti-war group called the Anti-War Coalition in the United Kingdom. The second and most important point is that no matter how high the level of civilian support for Anglo-American government is, the Koran (2:190) does not allow the killing of "those who do not fight," which means non-combatants. This is an absolute Koranic prohibition and there is no exception to the rule. Al-Qaeda's targeting of civilians exceeds the Koranic limits. The Koran does not allow killings of those who nurse the wounded in the battlefield, women who cook food for combatants, for example.

3.4.3 The Koran in the Hands of Terrorists

The Koran does not support terrorism, why then do the terrorists rely on it so heavily? There are two possible explanations for this. First, the Koran advocates defensive Jihad, which is the use of force in self-defense. The concept exists and history furnishes instances where force was used for defending Muslim lands. Second, the Koran is an undisputed primary source of Islamic law. Any argument, which is presented in this way, seems to represent the Koranic view and attracts greater number of recruits and sympathizers. It is an Islamic tactic geared toward Muslims and has worked well in many cases. These factors have made the concept vulnerable to misuse. The Koran may be cited to back up a call for Jihad, which may not neatly fit into the Koranic concept of Jihad. As previously indicated, this is a case of a misapplication of the Koranic concept of Jihad.

It is not novel that someone would cite scripture to give authority or strengthen one's case for anything. Shakespeare wrote: "The devil can cite scripture for his purpose" (*The Merchant of Venice*, Act 1, Scene iii). Many Christians are against the Iraq war, but President Bush (September 11, 2001) cites Psalm 23: "Even though I walk through the valley of the shadow of death, I fear no evil, for you are with me." President Bush (September 20, 2001) also seems to believe that God is on his side in his war on terror: "Freedom and fear, justice and cruelty, have always been at war, and we know that God is not neutral between them." Saddam Hussein was seen holding the Koran during his trail and very often referred to God and Islam, but he did not implement Islamic law when he was in power. Even Adolph Hitler cited the Bible (see AbuKhalil, 2002).

3.4.4 Non-Islamic Causes

Apart from Islamic reasons for terrorism, another set of reasons is also wholly or partly considered responsible for terrorism. They are fanaticism, poverty, psychological disorder, and terrorists' hatred toward freedom and democracy. They are discussed one by one in this section.

3.4.4.1 Fanaticism

Since the attacks of September 11, 2001, many "conjured up pictures of demons: suicide bombers were described as fanatics and lunatics" (Reuter, 2004:7). Former Prime Minster Blair said: "[Al-Qaeda] has an ideology, a world-view; it has deep convictions and the determination of the fanatic. It resembles in many ways early revolutionary Communism" (Blair, July 6, 2006). To argue that fanaticism is a reason for terrorism is untenable. Neither the leader, Bin Laden, nor the suicide bombers are fanatics. "Bin Laden is a rational man" (Mann, 2005; cf: "Counter Terrorism Strategy," UK, 2006). The way all operations are planned and carried out reflects sound planning and military acumen. The cogency, relevant reasoning, and timing of all Bin Laden's statements show great strategic and political wisdom and Mann's assessment seems justified. Supporting Reuter's (2004) assessment, Stern (2004) argues that "suicide-killers are not irrational fanatics but cost-effective weapons by rational organisations." To many Westerners, Bin Laden "is the incarnation of villainy. . . . But for millions of Muslims around the world, including many who have no sympathy with terrorism, [B]in Laden is an heroic figure" (Lawrence, 2005: xvii).

3.4.4.2 Poverty

Poverty is sometimes mentioned as a reason for terrorism. Muslim youths may be drawn to terrorism because of destitution and marginalisation in society. The analysis of suicide terrorism does not indicate poverty as a reason for terrorism. For instance, all the nineteen hijackers of September 11, 2001, were educated and came from middle-class families. Many of them went to Western universities (Reuter, 2004). "The attackers weren't poor; they didn't come from the ghetto that is Gaza; they hadn't personally been mistreated by any Western power far less robbed of their freedom. They were neither hermit-like fanatic, nor had they undergone years of brainwashing in isolated camps before being sent out as robots to steer the captured planes to their doom. On the contrary, the three attackers who had lived in Germany for years fell within everyday spectrum of normality. Although they were at times introverted and antisocial, they could also be warm hearted and friendly" (Reuter, 2004:7; see Pape, 2005). Reuter (2004:10) argues that "The presupposition that the attackers consist solely of fanatical, single, uneducated men from the slums is simply wrong: women and secular people are just as likely to blow themselves and . . . the readiness to commit such an act increases with the person's level of education. Neither is the unchanging misery of their living conditions the crucial factor; if it was, half of the Somali population would have already blown itself up" (see also Hoffman, 2003). The July 7, 2005, bombers were bright and intelligent men who had bright and successful futures in the United Kingdom (Taylor, April 25, 2007). Tony Blair (July 6, 2006) argued that it is "rubbish to suggest that [terrorism] is the product of poverty. It is true it will use the cause of poverty." There are many poor people in the world that do not become terrorists. Neither fanaticism nor poverty seems to be a plausible explanation for suicide terrorism (see 9/11 Commission Report, 2004).

3.4.4.3 Psychological Dimension

The language used for describing suicide bombers tends to show that they may be suffering from some sort of psychological problems, for example, they may be harbouring suicidal inclinations or are simply psychopaths. However, the study of the behavior of suicide bombers shows that they are normal people and lived normal lives. For instance, the September 11 hijackers were normal young men. Most of them used to drink alcohol and had normal relations with partners. They were liked in the community they lived in (9/11 Commission Report, 2004). Their peers and teachers found them normal persons (Pape, 2005). This suggests suicide bombers do not suffer from any deadly psychological problems.

Related to this argument is the argument of indoctrination and brainwashing of Muslim youths by the extremists' organizations. The point of indoctrination is often made in a way that gives the impression that indoctrination is an Islamic "pill" or an "injection" that, when applied, transforms its taker instantly: A normal human becomes a terrorist. This is an over simplification of the phenomenon. It seems that those who turn to terrorism have strong feelings of anger against the perpetrators of atrocities committed in the Muslim countries, such as Iraq, Afghanistan, and Palestine. Their trip to Pakistan or Afghanistan is the point where they think to sacrifice their lives for what they strongly believe is in defense of Muslims and Islam. Joining training camps for terrorism does not seem to be the beginning; it is rather the end—time to sacrifice.

3.4.4.4 Hatred for Democracy and Freedom

President Bush and former Prime Minister Blair repeatedly told the world that terrorists are mass murderers. They hate us because of our "freedom" and "democracy." "On September the 11th, enemies of freedom committed an act of war against our country. . . . They hate our freedoms—our freedom of religion, our freedom of speech, our freedom to vote and assemble and disagree with each other . . . [they] follow in the path of fascism, and Nazism, and totalitarianism" (Bush, September 11, 2001). Since September 11, President Bush reiterates the motif of freedom and democracy on the one side and terrorism on the other. "The war we fight today is more than a military conflict; it is the decisive ideological struggle of the 21st century. . . . On one side are those who believe in the values of freedom and moderation—the right of all people to speak, and worship, and live in liberty. And on the other side are those driven by the values of tyranny and extremism—the right of a self-appointed few to impose their fanatical views on all the rest. . . . They're successors to Fascists, to Nazis, to Communists, and other totalitarians of the 20th century" (Bush, 2006).[12] Former Prime Minister Blair uses the same language (see Blair, July 6, 2006).

The careful analysis of the statements of Al-Qaeda, Bush, and Blair show that the mantra "terrorists versus freedom and democracy" is without any foundation. First, Al-Qaeda does not states that it hates American "freedom" or "democracy." On the contrary, Al-Qaeda repeatedly claims that it is fighting for the freedom of Muslim lands. "There is no terrorist in the world who is a terrorist because he hates freedom. By far, the majority of terrorists are fighting for freedom of some group that does not have it. In the case of Iraq, it is freedom from American occupation; with the Irish Republican Army, it was freedom from British rule; with the Palestinians, it is freedom from Israeli occupation; and so forth. It is absurd to suppose that a human being sitting around suddenly stands up and says: 'You know, I hate freedom. I think I'll go blow myself up'" (Reese, 2003). Second, the United States and the United Kingdom are not the only free and democratic countries. Several countries in the West may make a valid claim of being free and democratic (e.g. Norway, Denmark, Sweden, Switzerland). Why does Al-Qaeda not terrorize these countries? This selective hatred of Al-Qaeda toward two free and democratic countries makes us wonder whether this is the actual reason. Bin Laden was funded and participated—with overt British and U.S. backing—in the Afghan Jihad against Russia. Was he against freedom and democracy then, too? It does not seem without logic that Al-Qaeda's wrath against the United States and the United Kingdom coincides with the presence of Anglo-American troops patrolling streets in Muslim lands. The Defense Science Board (2004) made a very relevant point:

> Muslims do not hate our freedom, but rather they hate our policies. The overwhelming majority voice their objections to what they see as one-sided support in favour of Israel and against Palestinian rights, and the long-standing, even increasing, support for what Muslims collectively see as tyrannies, most notably Egypt, Saudi Arabia, Jordan, Pakistan and the Gulf states. Thus, when American public diplomacy talks about bringing democracy to Islamic societies, this is seen as no more than self-serving hypocrisy.

Shall we say that terrorists in Chechnya, Kashmir and Sri Lanka are also against Anglo-American freedom and democracy? These countries are hardly free in the Western sense of freedom and democracy.

President Bush and former Prime Minister Blair pose to the world that they want to promote freedom and democracy in the Muslim world. This argument is not convincing for two main reasons. First, the Anglo-Americans never promoted genuine democratic processes in the Muslim world. They sustain dictatorship and dynastic regimes, such as Saudi Arabia, Jordon, Kuwait, Pakistan, and other Gulf states (see Lawrence, 2005). Conversely, Iran is a stable democracy, but America does not consider Iran a democracy. "Let me speak directly to the citizens of Iran: America respects you, and we respect your country. We respect your right to choose your own future and win your own freedom. And our nation hopes one day to be the closest of friends with a free and democratic Iran" (Bush, January 31, 2006). Iran, like other countries in the region, has a poor human rights record and follows harsh interpretation of Islamic law, but that does not make Iran un-democratic. Neither Bush nor Blair addressed the citizens of Saudi Arabia or Pakistan by saying that one day these countries will become free and democratic. Second, they promote ghost opposition figures, such as Ahmed Chalabi of Iraq, abroad and support those having no roots in public or track record of public service whatsoever. Hamid Karzai of Aghanistan is good example. Would the United

States or the United Kingdom elect someone as President or Prime Minster who had lived outside the country and had no record of public service? This does not seem probable. They provide safe havens to fugtives from the law, such as the late former Prime Minister of Pakistan Banezir Bhutto, or Russian tycoon Boris Berezovsky (*Guardian*, April 13, 2007). If Anglo-Americans are sincerely interested in promoting democracy in the Muslim world, they should focus on education, empower people economically, not politicians of their choice, and help establish the rule of law. This process should be stretched over decades. Any short-term arrangment will not bear the results needed for stable civic society and democracy. However, the Anglo-American does not seem to be engaged in any such programs.

3.4.5 Theory of "Reactive Terror"

None of the previously discussed reasons fully or convincingly explain why terrorists are terrorists. The most plausible interpretation for terrorism seems to be that terrorists strongly believe that their land and faith are under attack, and they are reacting to repel the attacker. The evidence from the statements of terrorist groups, suicide videos, statements from detainees, and origin of current and past conflicts supports the theory of "reactive terror." Nothing comes out of nothing. Everything seems to be a reaction to something. Bin Laden (March 1997) says:

> We declared jihad against the US government, because the US government is unjust, criminal and tyrannical. It has committed acts that are extremely unjust, hideous and criminal whether directly or through its support of the Israeli occupation of . . . (Palestine). And we believe the US is directly responsible for those who were killed in Palestine, Lebanon and Iraq. The mention of the US reminds us before everything else of those innocent children who were dismembered, their heads and arms cut off in the recent explosion that took place in Qana (in Lebanon). (see Lawrence, 2005)

In another statement, Bin Laden (24 November 2002) says:

> Because you attacked us and continue to attack us. Under your supervision, consent and orders, the governments of our countries which act as your agents, attack us on a daily basis. You steal our wealth and oil at paltry prices because of your international influence and military threats. Your forces occupy our countries; you spread your military bases throughout them; you corrupt our lands, and you besiege our sanctities, to protect the security of the Jews and to ensure the continuity of your pillage of our treasures. You have starved the Muslims of Iraq, where children die every day. It is a wonder that more than

> 1.5 million Iraqi children have died as a result of your sanctions, and you did not show concern. Yet when 3000 of your people died, the entire world rises and has not yet sat down. (see Lawrence, 2005:162)

Khalid Shiekh Muhammad (March 15, 2007), in his testimoney to the U.S. military tribunal, said that Islam did not give him the "green light to kill people." He calls himself a revolutionary and claims he is at war with Anglo-Americans. He thinks killing people in war is the langauge of war: "If now we were linving in the Revolutionary War and George Washington [was] being arrested through Britian. For sure . . . they [British] consider him enemy combatant. But Americans, they consider him as hero." The ring leader of the July 7, 2005 bombing in London, Sadique Khan, said in his video that Britain was punished because its "democratically elected governments continuously perpetrate atrocities on my people all over the world. . . . Until you stop the bombing, gassing, and imprisonment of my people, we will not stop this fight" (*BBC*, September 2, 2005). Al-Zarqawi (cited in Pape, 2005:259) said that Jordon was attacked in the summer of 2005 because it had become a "rearbase camp for the Crusader army."

It is not only Muslims and Muslim sources that say that terrorism is a reaction to the killing and atrocities of Muslims. Independent works, mainly Western works, on terrorism show that militant organizations see themselves as the defenders of their lands and faith, which they intensely believe are under attack from un-Islamic forces. These forces come with a hidden agenda: getting control of the region and changing the Islamic way of life. "They see themselves as defending sacred territory or protecting the rights of their coreligionists . . . because the true faith is purportedly in jeopardy" (Stern, 2004:xviii). It is not surprising that terrorism typically begins with the arrival of foreign troops in Muslim lands. "There is a simple *reason* why [Bin Laden] attacked the US: American imperialism. As long as America seeks to control the Middle East [and Muslim world at large], he and people like him will be its enemy" (Mann, 2003:169; Scheuer, 2004). "The taproot of suicide terrorism is nationalism—the belief among member of a community that they . . . are entitled to govern their national homeland without interference from foreigners" (Pape, 2005:79). The examination of Al-Qaeda terrorists shows that they are ten times more likely to come from Muslim countries where U.S. troops are present (Pape, 2005:104).

It is vital for the plausibility of theory of "reactive terror" to establish how and when the terrorism of Al-Qaeda started. Former Prime Minister Blair (July 6, 2006) said: "It is non-sense to say that the United States attacked Al-Qaeda. The United States was attacked first." However, the evidence proves the contrary. It is important to establish the beginning of Al-Qaeda's terrorism against the West. As indicated above, the Russians invaded Afghanistan in 1979. The war lasted until 1989. During this period, the West and the Muslim world supported the Afghan Jihad. Abdullah Azzam and Bin Laden led the Afghan Jihad. The *Encyclopedia of Afghan Jihad* is dedicated to both of them. The West and Bin Laden were in alliance against the Russian and the pro-Communist regime of Afghanistan. In Afghanistan the civil war started after the defeat of the Russians. In the meantime the Anglo-Americans and Pak-Saudi alliance gave birth to an illegitimate child called Taliban. Taliban were able, with the active support of these countries, to capture most of the Afghan provinces by force. They were not elected democratically but still the Anglo-Americans supported them. In 1990, Iraq captured Kuwait claiming it to be one of her provinces. The Anglo-American forces came to the collective defense of Kuwait but never left after liberating Kuwait. Until 1990, there is no evidence of Al-Qaeda terrorists attack against the West. Al-Qaeda's terrorism started when Bin Laden was expelled from Saudi Arabia, Somalia, and was then chased into Pakistan after 1990. In 1998, President Clinton fired a missile at Bin Laden's base in Afghanistan (Lawrence, 2005:33; AbuKahlil, 2002). The "Counter Terrorism Strategy" of the United Kingdom (2006:6) lists several terrorist incidents, but none of them occurred before 1990. The U.S. documents studied also do not provide evidence that Al-Qaeda's terrorism started before 1990. The absence of evidence of terrorism before the arrival of Anglo-Americans in the Middle East, that is, 1990 and other Muslim lands supports the theory of "reactive terror."

3.4.5.1 Examples of Al-Qaeda's Type Jihad

It throws further light on the plausibility of the theory of "reactive terror" if we briefly look at the history of Islam when Al-Qaeda style declarations of Jihad were issued. It will be more approriate to say that Al-Qaeda's declaration of Jihad is based on the style of these declarations of Jihad. Three instances are discussed further in this chapter: declaration of Jihad against Tartars, the Portuguese, and the Kashmir Jihad. One of the most prominent examples of the delcaration of Jihad is that of Ibn Taymiyyah's (1268–1328) against the Tartars. Ibn Taymiyyah joined the war against Tartars as he believed in self-defense (Streusand, 1997; Selvirman, 2002; see 2.3). Another important but less celebrated example is the declaration of Jihad against Portuguese in the Asian regions, such as Malabar, Atjeh, and the Philippines at the end of sixteenth century. Zayn al-Din al-Ma'bari issued a declaration of Jihad: "The Gift to the Holy Warriors in Respect to Some Deeds of the Portugese." "In [this declaration] Zayn al-Din called upon Muslims to conduct [J]ihad . . . in order to galvanise Muslims to counter the Portuguese usuerpation of Muslim trade and their assault on the Muslim community" (Dale, 1988:46). He "supported his call to arms with hsitorical evidence and Islamic legal doctrine" (Dael, 1988:46).

The Kashmir Jihad started mainly in the 1980s, but its roots lie in the 1947 division of the Indian subcontinent into the two independent state of India and Pakistan. Muslims and Hindus were given the choice to join either India or Pakistan. Naturally, the Muslims joined the Muslim majority state of Pakistan and Hindus remained in the Hindu majority state of India. Kashmir was a Muslim majority state, but its ruler was a Hindu who joined India against the wishes of his Muslim subjects. Kashmiris started agitation against this decision. Some Muslim tribes came to support Kashmiri Muslims, which alarmed the Indian government, hence invaded Kasmir. India captured a big chunk of Kashmir called Indian held Kashmir. Pakistan also joined the Kashmiris and occupied some part of Kashmir known as Pakistan held Kashmir. In 1948, the United Nations Security Council passed resultion number 47 (April 21, 1948) urging India to hold plebescite: "The Government of India should undertake that there will be established in Jammu and Kashmir a Plebiscite Administration to hold a plebiscite as soon as possible on the question of the accession of the State to India or Pakistan." India, however, did not observe resolution 47. The Indian apprehension is that Kashmir is a Muslim majority state and Muslims will opt for joining Pakistan. The Kashmiri waited for decades for India to settle the issue peacefully, but they waited in vain. After losing hope in India and the United Nations' commitment to hold plebiscite, some Kashmiri groups started militant actions for the liberation of Kashmir from India. This is what India and others call Kashmiri militancy/terrorism. On the contrary, Kashmiris consider themselves freedom fighters. Kashmir militancy is a a reaction to what Kashmiris consider Indian occupation of their land.[13]

The common feature of these declarations of Jihad is that they claim to be in self defense. They are against non-Muslims and happened at a point of history when non-Muslims troops were either in a Muslim land or touching its borders. "They represent essentially the same phenomenon, protests against Western hegmoney or colonial rule by Muslims who felt that they had no other means of fighting against superior European or American power" (Dale, 1988:39). The invaders invariably called as fanatics those Muslims who resisted the Americans or Europeans (Dale, 1988:45). Another common element is the political circumsatnces where a group of devout Muslims often believe that the incumbent rulers are corrupt or on the side of the invaders. These individuals regard themselves as the true followers and defenders of Islam and Muslim lands. For them, corrupt Muslim governments are legitimate targets like the invaders. It is hard to find an example in Muslim history where Jihad has been declared without citing self-defense. Al-Qaeda (1998) says that its declaration is in self-defense against "the crusader armies spreading in [the Arabian Peninsula] like locusts, eating its riches." Similarly, if we want to understand the Palestinian militancy, or what some would describe as terrorism, we need to start from the creation of Israel in 1948 and Israel's war with her neigbors.

The study of the Koran and the mounting reaction of Muslims to the presence of foreign troops in Muslim countries demonstrates that the main reasons for the rise of terrorism is the direct and indirect intervention of un-Islamic forces—chiefly Anglo-Americans—in Muslim countries. Muslims are disenchanted by the Anglo-American support for corrupt Muslim polities and double standards on democracy and human rights. Those who did not see sense in Al-Qaeda's claims initially, may now be listening more carefully and probably sympathize with Al-Qaeda. Terrorism may not be the right means to an end but the theory of "reactive terror" provides plausible explanation for terrorism.

3.6 Conclusion

According to Islamic law, non-state actors such as Al-Qaeda are not allowed to declare Jihad in self-defense. The declaration of defensive Jihad shall come from the head of a Muslim state unless the ruler is on the side of invaders and working against Muslims. The nature of conflicts in Afghanistan and Iraq is worsening every day. The loss of Muslim lives and damage to their properties is enormous. The Anglo-Americans and pro-Western governments of Iraq and Afghanistan failed to protect Muslims. The frustration of Muslims is rising day by day. If the occupation of Muslim lands continues, it is probable that Muslims leaders, not Al-Qaeda or pro-Western Muslims rulers, by consensus, may declare Jihad. If such a consensus declaration is made, it will be Koranic (legitimate). International law will also be on the side of Mujahidin.

References

AbuKhalil, A. (2002) *Bin Laden, Islam and America's new "war on terrorism."* New York: A Seven Stories Press & Open Media Book.

Afghanistan Independent Human Rights Commission (2007) Report on VBIED Attack in Nangahar Province on March 4, 2007. Available at: http://www.aihrc.org.af/Investigatoin.pdf.

——— (2007b) Violation of International Humanitarian Law in Afghanistan Practices of Concern and Example Cases. Available at: http://www.aihrc.org.af/IHL_practices_and_examples_final_Coalition_Vioalatioin.pdf.
Ali, Y.(1989) *The meaning of the holy Qur'an.* Maryland: Amana Corporation.
Al-Qardawi, Y. (2004) Controversial preacher with 'star status. July 7. Available at: http://news.bbc.co.uk/1/hi/uk/3874893.stm.
Al-Skeini & Others [2007] UK House of Lords 26.
Amnesty International (2006) Israel/Lebanon Out of all proportion—civilians Bear the brunt of the war. Available at: http://web.amnesty.org/library/Index/ENG MDE020332006.
——— (2006) 2006 Elections to the Human Rights Council. Available at: http://web.amnesty.org/library/index/engior410062006.
——— (2004) "Killings of civilians in Basra and al-'Amara." May 11. Available at: http://web.amnesty.org/library/index/engmde140072004.
——— (2004) An open letter to President George W. Bush on the question of torture and cruel, inhuman or degrading treatment. May 4. Available at: http://web.amnesty.org/library/index/engamr510782004.
——— (2001) Annual Report. Available at: http://web.amnesty.org/report2001/regMDE/regMDE?OpenDocument.
Arbour, L. (2006) UN warning on Mid-East war crimes. *BBC*, July 20. Available at: http://news.bbc.co.uk/2/hi/middle_east/5197544.stm.
Azzam, A. (1985) Defence of Muslim lands: The first obligation after Iman [Faith]. Available at: http://www.religioscope.com/info/doc/jihad/azzam_defence_1_table.htm.
BBC (2007) Karzai anger over civilian deaths. May 2. Available at: http://news.bbc.co.uk/1/hi/world/south_asia/6615781.stm.
——— (2006) Blair defends Saudi probe ruling. December 15. Available at: http://news.bbc.co.uk/1/hi/uk_politics/6182125.stm.
——— (1991) Saddam's Iraq: Key events." Available at: http://news.bbc.co.uk/1/shared/spl/hi/middle_east/02/iraq_events/html/collateral_damage.stm.
Benn, T. (2006) *BBC Question Time.* March 22. Available at: http://news.bbc.co.uk/1/hi/programmes/question_time/6478409.stm.
Berezovsky, B. (2007) I am ploting a new Russian revolution. April 13. Availabe at: http://www.guardian.co.uk/russia/article/0,,2056321,00.html.
Bin Laden, O. (1996) Declaration of war against the Americans occupying the land of the to holy places. August. Available at: http://www.pbs.org/newshour/terrorism/international/fatwa_1996.html.
Blair, T. (2006) Conform to our society. December 8. Available at: http://news.bbc.co.uk/1/hi/uk_politics/6219626.stm.
———. (2006) Prime Minister speech in Los Angles. July 6. Available at: http://www.pm.gov.uk/output/Page9948.asp.
———. (2003) Prime Minister's address to the nation. March 20. Available at: http://www.number10.gov.uk/output/Page3327.asp.
———. (2001) Prime Minister's statement at 10 Downing Street. Available at: http://www.number10.gov.uk/output/Page1604.asp.

———. (2001) Prime Minister's statement to the House of Commons following the September 11 attacks. Available at: http://www.number10.gov.uk/output/Page 1598.asp.

Bloom, M. (2005) *Dying to kill: The allure of suicide terror.* New York: Columbia University Press.

Bush, G. W (2006) President Bush addresses American Legion National Convention. August 31. Available at: http://www.whitehouse.gov/news/releases/2006/08/print/ 20060831-1.html.

———. (2006) President Bush delivers State of the Union Address. January 31. Available at: http://www.whitehouse.gov/news/releases/2006/01/20060131-10 .html.

———. (2006) Press Conference by President. 26 Ocotber. Available at: http:// www.whitehouse.gov/news/releases/2006/10/.

———. (2005) President addresses nation, discusses Iraq, war on terror. Fort Bragg, North Carolina. June 28. Available at: http://www.whitehouse.gov/news/releases/ 2005/06/print/20050628-7.html.

———. (2003) President Bush addresses to the nation. March 19. Available at: http://www.whitehouse.gov/news/releases/2003/03/20030319-17.html.

———. (2003) President says Saddam Hussein must leave Iraq within 48 hours. March 17. Available at: http://www.whitehouse.gov/news/releases/2003/03/20030 317-7.html.

———. (2001) Statement by the President in his address to the nation. September 11. Available at: http://www.whitehouse.gov/news/releases/2001/09/20010911-16 .html.

———. (2001) Address to a joint session of Congress and the American people. September 20. Available at: http://www.whitehouse.gov/news/releases/2001/09/ 20010920-8.html.

Christian Aid, (2007) Memorandum to UK Parliamentary Defence Committee. April 12. Available at: http://www.publications.parliament.uk/pa/cm200607/ cmselect/cmdfence/memo/408/ucm09.htm.

Coll, S. (2005) *Ghost wars: The secret history of the CIA, Afghanistan and Bin Laden.* London: Penguin Books Ltd.

Council of Europe (2007) Dick Marty's Report "Alleged Secrete Detentions Flights in the Council of Europe Member States." June 8. Available at: http://assembly .coe.int/CommitteeDocs/2006/20060124_Jdoc032006_E.pdf.

Daily Mail, (2006) Sir Richard Dannat: A very honest general. September 12. Available at: http://www.dailymail.co.uk/pages/live/articles/news/news.html?in_ article_id=410175&in_page_id=1770.

Dale, S. F. (1988) Religious suicide in Islamic Asia: Anticolonial terrorism in India, Indonesia, and the Philippines. *The Journal of Conflict Resolution*, March, pp.37–59.

Guardian, (2007) "Up to 80 civilians dead after US air strikes in Afghanistan. July 1. Available at: http://observer.guardian.co.uk/world/story/0,,2115846,00.html.

———, (2006) National interest halts arms corruption inquiry. December 15. Available at: http://www.guardian.co.uk/armstrade/story/0,,1972749,00.html.

———, (2006) Iraq war was terrorism recruiting sergeant. September 28. Available at: http://www.guardian.co.uk/Iraq/Story/0,,1882713,00.html.

Hilsum, L. (2006) Collective punishment, collective suffering. July 17. Available at: http://www.channel4.com/news/articles/politics/international_politics/collective%20punishment%20collective%20suffering/168255.

Hoffman, B. (2003) The logic of suicide terrorism. *The Atlantic Monthly*, June. Available at: http://www.theatlantic.com/doc/200306/hoffman.

Human Rights Watch (2005) Annual Report: Saudi Arabia. Available at: http://hrw.org/english/docs/2005/01/13/saudia9810.htm.

——— (2004) The road to Abu Ghraib. Available at: http://hrw.org/reports/2004/usa0604/usa0604.pdf.

——— (1991) Needless deaths in the Gulf War. Available at: http://www.hrw.org/reports/1991/gulfwar/.

ICRC (2004) Report on the treatment by the coalition forces of prisoners of war and other protected persons in Iraq. Available at: http://www.globalsecurity.org/military/library/report/2004/icrc_report_iraq_feb2004.htm.

Khan, S. (2005) London bomber video aired on TV. September 2. Available at: http://news.bbc.co.uk/1/hi/uk/4206708.stm.

Lawrence, B. (2005) *Messages to the world: The statements of Bin Laden*. (Howarth, J.). London: Verso.

Lewis, B. (2004) *The crises in Islam: Holy war and unholy terror*. London: Phoenix.

———. (1998) License to kill. *Foreign Affairs*. November–December.

Mann, M. (2003) *Incoherent empire*. London: Verso.

Muhammad, K. S. (2007) Testimony to military tribunal at Guantanamo. Available at: http://news.bbc.co.uk/1/shared/bsp/hi/pdfs/15_03_07_mohammed_transcript.pdf.

Nelson, B. (2007) Oil a factor in Iraq conflict. July 5. Available at: http://www.guardian.co.uk/australia/story/0,,2119110,00.html.

New York Times (2007) Desperate Iraqi refugees turn to sex trade in Syria. May 19. Available at: http://www.nytimes.com/2007/05/29/world/middleeast/29syria.html?ex=1338177600&en=8caf56b484d2ebb9&ei=5124&partner=digg&exprod=digg.

New York Times (2007) Iraqi premier orders work stopped on wall. April 23. Available at: http://www.nytimes.com/2007/04/23/world/middleeast/23iraq.html?ex=1334980800&en=bd7b50d6c2b2d2c8&ei=5088&partner=rssnyt&emc=rss.

New York Times (2007) Israel's protests are said to stall gulf arms sale. April 5. Available at: http://select.nytimes.com/gst/abstract.html?res=F40F10FA3D5B0C768CDDAD0894DF404482&n=Top%2fNews%2fWorld%2fCountries%20and%20Territories%2fSaudi%20Arabia.

——— (2007) With Korea as model, Bush team ponders long support role in Iraq. June 3. Available at: http://select.nytimes.com/gst/abstract.html?res=F00B14FB3B540C708CDDAF0894DF404482.

——— (2006) British drop inquiry into Saudi arms deal. December 15. Available at: http://query.nytimes.com/gst/fullpage.html?res=9E01EFDD1231F936A25751C1A9609C8B63.

——— (2006) President Bush's reality (Editorial). September 12. Available at: http://www.nytimes.com/2006/09/12/opinion/12tue1.html?ex=1315713600&en=59d7e29c6efe7298&ei=5088.

——— (2006) Spy agencies say Iraq War worsens terrorism threat. September 24. Available at: http://www.nytimes.com/2006/09/24/world/middleeast/24terror.html?ex=1316750400&en=da252be85d1b39fa&ei=5088&partner=rssnyt&emc=rss.

Pape, R. (2005) *Dying to win: The strategic logic of suicide terrorism*. New York: The Random House Publishing Group.

Rapoport, D. C. (1984) Fear and trembling: Terrorism in three religious traditions. *American Political Science Review*, 78(3), pp.668–72.

Rashid, A. (2002) *Taliban: Militant Islam, oil and fundamentalism in Central Asia*. New Haven: Yale University Press.

Reese, C. (2003) Baghdad George. Available at: http://reese.king-online.com/Reese_20031107/index.php.

Reuter, C. (2004) *My life is a weapon: A modern history of suicide bombing*. New Jersey: Princeton University Press.

Scheuer, M. (2004) *Imperial hubris: Why the West is losing the war on terror*. Potomac Books.

Senlis Council, (2007) Memorandum to UK Parliamentary Defence Committee. March 15. Available at: http://www.publications.parliament.uk/pa/cm200607/cmselect/cmdfence/memo/408/ucm03.htm.

Shakespeare, W. (2007) *King Lear*. London: Penguin Classics.

———. (1981) *The merchant of Venice*. London: Penguin Classics.

Stern, J. (2004) *Terror in the name of God: Why religious militants kill*. New York: Happer Colins.

Stone, R. (2006) *Civil liberties and human rights*. Oxford: Oxford University Press.

Streusand, D. (1997) What does Jihad mean? *Middle East Quarterly*. September.

Suellentrop, C. (2002) Abdullah Azzam, the godfather of Jihad. April 16. Available at: http://www.slate.com/?id=2064385.

The Sun, (2007) Fury at RAF kamikaze plan. April 3. Available at: http://www.thesun.co.uk/article/0,,2007150271,00.html.

Taguba, A. (2004) Hearing of Article 15–16 16 Investigation of the 800th Military Police Brigade (known as Taguba report, United States). Available at: http://news.findlaw.com/hdocs/docs/iraq/tagubarpt.html#ThR1.18.

Taylor, M. (2007) Taylor's presentation on terrorism in the UK, conference titled "Faces of Terrorism" organised by the Centre for Investigative Psychology, Liverpool University. April 25–26.

United Kingdom (2007) Foreign and Commonwealth Office's Annual Report 2006. Available at: http://www.fco.gov.uk/Files/kfile/hr_report2006.pdf.

——— (2006) Countering International Terrorism: the United Kingdom's Strategy, 2006.

——— (2005) Intelligence and Security Committee: The Handling of Detainees by UK Intelligence Personnel in Afghanistan, Guantanamo Bay and Iraq. 1 March.

Available at: http://www.cabinetoffice.gov.uk/publications/reports/intelligence/treatdetainees.pdf.

United Nations High Commissioner for Refugees (2007) Statistics on displaced Iraqis around the world. Available at: http://www.unhcr.org/cgi-bin/texis/vtx/home/opendoc.pdf?tbl=SUBSITES&id=461f7cb92.

United Nations, Human Rights Council (2006) Report of the Human Rights Council on its Second Special Session. August 11. Available at: http://www.ohchr.org/english/bodies/hrcouncil/docs/specialsession/A.HRC.S-2.2_en.pdf.

United Nations (Iraq Mission) (2007) Human Rights Report January 1–March 3, 2007. Available at: http://www.uniraq.org/FileLib/misc/HR%20Report%20Jan%20Mar%202007%20EN.pdf.

——— (Iraq Mission) (2006) Human Rights Report November 1–December 31, 2007. Available at: http://www.uniraq.org/FileLib/misc/HR%20Report%20Nov%20Dec%202006%20EN.pdf.

United Nations Security Council (1948). India–Pakistan Situation, Resolution No 47.

United States, (2007) National intelligence estimate: Prospects for Iraq's stability: A challenging road ahead. January. Available at: http://dni.gov/press_releases/20070202_release.pdf.

———, (2007) Pentagon's Mental Health Advisory Team IV: Operation Iraqi Freedom 05–07. Available at: http://i.a.cnn.net/cnn/2007/images/05/04/mhat.iv.report.pdf.

———, (2007) The terrorist threat to the U.S. Homeland Security (National Intelligence Estimate). July 2007. Available at: http://www.dni.gov/press_releases/20070717_release.pdf.

———, (2004) Report of the Defense Science Board Task Force on Strategic Communication. September. Available at: http://www.fas.org/irp/agency/dod/dsb/commun.pdf.

———, (2004) The 9/11 Commission Report (Congress). July 22. Available at: http://www.9-11commission.gov/report/911Report.pdf.

United States Department of State, (2001) Country Reports on Human Rights Practices (Saudi Arabia). Available at: http://www.state.gov/g/drl/rls/hrrpt/2001/nea/8296.htm.

United States, National Intelligence Council (2005) Mapping the global future Available at: http://www.dni.gov/nic/NIC_globaltrend2020.html#contents.

Woodward, B. (2006) *State of denial: Bush at war, Part III*. Cambridge: Simon & Schuster Ltd.

World Bank Technical Team (2007) Movement and Access Restriction in the West Bank. Available at: http://siteresources.worldbank.org/INTWESTBANKGAZA/Resources/WestBankrestrictions9Mayfinal.pdf.

World Islamic Front, (1998) Jihad against Jews and Christians. February 23. Available at: http://www.fas.org/irp/world/para/docs/980223-fatwa.htm.

PART II

CHAPTER 4

Self-defense in International Law[1]

The right to self-defense is a natural right known and recognized since time immemorial. It is available to individuals and, after the emergence of states, to states as sovereign entities. Individual actors have historically reserved the right to use force unilaterally to protect and vindicate legal entitlements (Reisman, 1985). "It is admitted that a just right of self-defence attaches always to nations as well as to individuals, and is equally necessary for the preservation of both" (Webster, 1841). It was a common practice for centuries to use force to settle disputes among individuals, tribes, and later on states. "Men rush to arms for slight causes or no causes at all, and . . . when arms have once been taken up there is no longer any respect for law; divine or human" (Grotius, 1625). There are two fundamental limitations, necessity and proportionality, on the use of force under customary law since the classic case of *Caroline* of 1837 (see Jennings, 1938; Waldock, 1952). In the past century, efforts were made to codify restrictions on the use of force: the 1928 General Treaty for the Renunciation of War (Kellogg-Briand Pact), the 1919 Covenant of the League of Nations, and so on. However, agonized by the horrors of World War II, the international community codified the rules on the peaceful settlement of disputes and the use of force in the form of the Charter of the United Nations.

The constitutive purpose of the United Nations was "to save the succeeding generations from the scourge of war" (Charter, 1945, preamble, paragraph, 1). To realize this lofty ideal, the Charter laid down that "All Members shall settle their international disputes by peaceful means" (Art. 2(3)) and that "All Members shall refrain in their international relations from the threat or use of force against the territorial integrity or political independence of any state, or in any other manner inconsistent with the Purposes of the

United Nations" (Art. 2(4)). The Charter, however, recognizes two exceptions to this rule: (a) the Security Council may authorize the use of force as an enforcement measure (article 42) and (b) the use of force in self-defense when there is an armed attack against a state (article 51).

The purpose of this chapter is to examine the right to the use force in self-defense as an exception to the general proscription on the use of force. It addresses two questions: When does the right to self-defense begin? and When does the right to self-defense end? The first question involves issues such as what constitutes an "armed attack," the legal status of anticipatory self-defense with a focus on the "Bush doctrine of preemption." In substance, this is a question of "necessity": when resort to force is permissible. The second question involves issues such as when self-defense ends: Does it end after the Security Council takes action or does it continue until the state achieves the objective for using force? This question centers on "who decides" and is in substance a decision on the principle of proportionality. The ultimate aim is to find out whether international terrorism can be dealt with effectively under articles 51 and 39 or whether we need new rules.

4.1 Self-defense under Article 51

A great deal has been written on the scope of article 51, but the recent terrorist attacks of September 11, 2001, in the United States and its response thereto, have reignited the debate on how to deal with this new wave of terrorism under the cloak of self-defense. Article 51 of the Charter reads:

> Nothing in the present Charter shall impair the inherent right of individual or collective self-defence if an armed attack occurs against a Member of the United Nations, until the Security Council has taken measures necessary to maintain international peace and security. Measures taken by Members in the exercise of this right of self-defence shall be immediately reported to the Security Council and shall not in any way affect the authority and responsibility of the Security Council under the present Charter to take at any time such action as it deems necessary in order to maintain or restore international peace and security.

The simple and traditional interpretation of article 51 seems to be that it allows the use of force in self-defense as an exception to the general prohibition (Art. 2(4)) when there is an armed attack against a state. It does not state that the armed attack must come from another state but the traditional understanding is that usually one state attacks another state (*Democratic*

Republic of Congo case, 2005; ICJ Israel Wall Opinion, 2004). Article 51 requires the victim state to report its use of force in self-defense to the Security Council, which would take necessary measures. It seems that the right to self-defense is available until the Security Council comes into action (Cassese, 2001). In addition, article 51 states that any self-defense measure of the victim state shall not affect the authority of the Security Council to take any action it may deem necessary either to maintain or restore peace and security. It suggests that the Security Council has the power to take measures whether the victim state reports or does not report its use of force in self-defense. The Security Council may add to the measures already taken by the victim state or restrain the victim state from further action if it serves the purpose of maintaining or restoring peace and security.

Article 51 contains more than what this simple interpretation presents. Scholars of international law are divided on its scope. There are two schools of thought: The first follows a restrictive interpretation, while the second argues for an expanded interpretation. Most of the arguments of both schools focus on the semantics of article 51.

4.1.1 Restrictive Interpretation

Those who argue for the restrictive interpretation of article 51 focus on the qualifying phrase "if an armed attack occurs" and what constitutes an "armed attack." They maintain that the use of force is expressly limited to situations where an armed attack has already commenced or occurred. They believe, in general, that an armed attack means once the armed forces of one state have crossed the border into another state. They argue that while customary international law, prior to the United Nations Charter, might have allowed self-defense in anticipation of an armed attack in certain circumstances, article 51 limits the scope of that right. Self-defense is now only allowed in response to an "armed attack" against a state and does not include anticipatory self-defense. Any use of force in self-defense shall be reported to the Security Council immediately, which shall take necessary measures. On this interpretation, the right to use force in self-defense seems an independent but transitory right—until the Security Council comes into play and hinges on the occurrence of an armed attack. Apparently, article 51 exhausts the customary right to self-defense.

Kunz (1947:877–78) argues that article 51 "constitutes an important progress by limiting the right of . . . self-defense to the one case of armed attack against a member of the U.N." He adds: "This right does not exist against any form of aggression which does not constitute 'armed attack' and it 'means something which has taken place'" (Kunz, 1947:877–78). Kelsen

(1948) contends that article 51 restricts the right of self-defense to instances when an armed attack against members of the United Nations occurs until the time the Security Council intervenes. "This provision restricts the right of self-defense to the case of an 'armed attack.' . . . As soon as the Council takes the measures necessary to restore peace, the competence to interpret the term 'armed attack' and to ascertain whether an armed attack exists in a concrete case, is transferred to the Council. The member states acting under Article 51 are, according to Article 25, obliged 'to accept and carry out the decisions of the Security Council' in this respect" (Kelsen, 1948:791–92). Glennon (2003:20) submits that article 51 of the Charter permits the use of force in self-defense and only "if an armed attack occurs against a Member of the United Nations." Wehberg (cited in Hole, 2004:81) describes the exception for self-defense as "substantially limited" and says that parties may not invoke the exception except in cases of "armed aggression." Gross (2001:213) argues that "the wording of Article 51 requires an armed attack using weapons and that mere threats or declarations are insufficient. . . . The indispensable condition for the exercise of the right of . . . self-defense under Article 51 of the Charter is that 'an armed attack occurs.'"

4.1.2 Expanded Interpretation

Contrary to what the restrictive school believes, a significant number of publicists argue that force may not only be used in self-defense as response to an armed attack but it may also be used as a response to an "imminent threat" of an armed attack. They reason that self-defense is a customary right as well as recognized by the Charter. Customary law lives side by side with conventional law. Under customary law, anticipatory self-defense is permissible when the threat of an armed attack is "imminent." The Charter codifies the preexisting customary rule of self-defense but does not exhaust it. Hence, the right to anticipatory self-defense exists and states may rely on customary rule or Charter or both of them.

Waldock (1952) argues that to say that self-defense begins only "if an armed attack occurs" is to go beyond the necessary meaning of the word. It was not the intention of the drafters to cut down the right of self-defense beyond the narrow doctrine of the *Caroline* (1837) incident. In the *Corfu Channel* (1949) case, the International Court of Justice "did not take a narrow view of the inherent right of self-defense reserved by Article 51" (Waldock, 1952:501). Bowett (1958) argues that article 51 does not preclude an action taken against imminent danger.

> It is a fallacy of the first order to assume . . . that the right has no other content than the one determined by Article 51. Such a view produces a restricted interpretation of the right not warranted by the Charter. Not least of the restrictions involved in this view is the construction of Article, which limits the right of individual or collective self-defence to cases where an "armed attack" occurs. This is a restriction certainly unrecognized by general international law, which has always recognized an "anticipatory" right of self-defence. (Bowett, 1955–56:131)

McDougal and Feliciano (1961), after digging through the preparatory history of the Charter, conclude that member states did not draw article 51 to narrow down the right of self-defense under customary law. Schachter (1986) cautiously says that it is erroneous to say that article 51 completely excludes anticipatory self-defense as it is not clear whether it was intended to cut down the inherent right to self-defense under customary law.

> In light of the preoccupation with increased but limited autonomy for regional organisations it is difficult to argue that Article 51 in its final draft form was intended to be a restriction of the customary right of self-defence in existence before the Charter or that the drafters were attempting to determine new limits to the circumstances in which a State could legitimately use force in self-defence. (McCormack, 1991:31–32)

The International Court of Justice invariably shied away from addressing the question of anticipatory self-defense despite the fact that such opportunities were present. In the case of *Nicaragua* (1986, paragraph 194), the court refrained from extending its discussion to anticipatory self-defense:

> In view of the circumstances in which the dispute has arisen, reliance is placed by the parties only on the right of self-defence in the case of an armed attack, which has already occurred, and the issue of the lawfulness of a response to the imminent threat of armed attack has not been raised. Accordingly the court expresses no view on that issue.

However, in his dissenting opinion, Judge Schwebel (paragraph 173) says:

> I do not agree with a construction of the United Nations Charter which would read Article 51 as if it were worded: "Nothing in the present Charter shall impair the inherent right of individual of collective self-defence if, and only if, an armed attack occurs." I do not agree that the terms or intent of Article 51 eliminate the right of self-defence under customary international law, or confine its entire scope to the express terms of Article 5.

In the case of *Democratic Republic of Congo* (2005, paragraph 134), again the International Court of Justice did not extend its discussion to the question of "imminent threat." The court should have done so because its guidance would have been informative and timely given the fact that self-defense is used as a main argument in the current "war on terror." The court referred to its position in the *Nicaragua* (1986) case that the parties had not raised the issue of a response to an "imminent threat" so it expressed no view on that issue and "so it is in the present case." Several judges, however, expressed dissenting opinions arguing that the court should have picked up the opportunity and discussed the question of anticipatory self-defense (see Judge Kooijmans, paragraphs 25–34; Judge Simma, paragraphs 7–15).

The views of different publicists suggest that the Charter codifies the right of anticipatory self-defense available under customary international law. The intention of article 51 seems to be to make anticipatory self-defense a statutory right, not to limit it. What was considered a common practice before acquired the shape of statutory law after the adoption of the Charter without diminishing it. The inclusion of the word "inherent" and no objection to it by the states strongly points toward this interpretation. Another plausible interpretation seems to be that article 51 was designed to accommodate the concerns of Latin American states regarding regional security arrangement under the Inter-American Reciprocal Assistance and Solidarity (Act of Chapultepec), 1945. It was neither intended to limit or deny the customary right of self-defense. The focus was rather something else: regional security arrangement of the Latin American states (see Halberstam, 1996). Therefore, in my opinion, the customary right remains unaffected and anticipatory self-defense together with its limits does exist today.

4.2 What Constitutes an "Armed Attack?"

Central to the understanding of views of the two schools discussed above is the question, what constitutes an "armed attack?" The discussion on the nature and meaning of an "armed attack" raises further two crucial questions: Does an armed attack comprises an "imminent threat" of attack and can the acts of non-state actors amount to an armed attack? These questions are discussed later in this chapter, but first what is an armed attack? The Charter does not define the term "armed attack" nor does any discussion of the term appear in the records of the San Francisco Conference (Baker, 1987–88). The meaning of this phrase, however, has generated a vast literature with little consensus on its definition. There is even less consensus in the context of activity by international terrorists (Travalio, 2000). The restrictive school follows the argument that armed attack means the physical occurrence of the attack when the forces of one state cross the border into another state.

4.2.1 Does an Armed Attack Include "Imminent Threat"?

In contrast to the view of the restrictive school, the liberal school believes that an "imminent threat" is included in the notion of an armed attack and states are allowed to resort to the use of force in self-defense in anticipation for when the threat is real and imminent. There are two main arguments for the justification of the use of force in self-defense in the case of an "imminent attack" or anticipatory self-defense.

The main argument is that article 51 preserves the customary right of self-defense, which recognizes anticipatory self-defense.

> Where there is convincing evidence not merely of threats and potential danger but of an attack being actually mounted, then an armed attack may be said to have begun to occur, though it has not passed the frontier. . . . If an armed attack is imminent within the strict doctrine of the Caroline, then it would seem to bring the case within Article 51. To read Article 51 otherwise is to protect the aggressor's right to first strike. (Waldock, 952:498)

Bowett (1955–56:131) says that any construction of article 51 limiting self-defense to occurrence of an armed attack is "a restriction certainly unrecognized by general international law, which has always recognized an 'anticipatory self-defense.'" Schachter (1984:1633–34) sums up this position thus:

> On one reading [of Article 51] this means that self-defense is limited to cases of armed attack. An alternative reading holds that since the article is silent as to the right of self-defense under customary law (which goes beyond cases of armed attack) it should not be construed by implication to eliminate that right. . . . It is therefore not implausible to interpret article 51 as leaving unimpaired the right of self-defense as it existed prior to the Charter.

The development in weaponry and its delivery system has buttressed the main argument.

> The introduction of vastly more destructive and rapidly delivered weapons began to undercut the cogency of that legal regime [in which self-defence was restricted to an armed attack]. The reason was simple: a meaningful self-defense could be irretrievably lost if an adversary with much more destructive weapons and poised to attack had to initiate (in effect, accomplish) its attack

> before a right of self-defense came into operation. This development prompted a claim to expand the right of reactive self-defense . . . to "anticipatory' self-defense. (Reisman, 2003:142)

Higgins (1994:242) says:

> In a nuclear age, common sense cannot require one to interpret an ambiguous provision in a text in a way that requires a state passively to accept its fate before it can defend itself. And, even in the face of conventional warfare, this would also seem the only realistic interpretation of the contemporary right of self-defence. It is the potentially devastating consequences of prohibiting self-defence unless an armed attack has already occurred that leads one to prefer this interpretation—although it has to be said that, as a matter of simple construction of the words alone, another conclusion might be reached.

Frank (2001) argues that in San Francisco, the founders deliberately closed the door to any claim of "anticipatory self-defense" but that posture was soon challenged by the exigencies of a new age of nuclear warheads and long-range rocketry. The "transformation of weaponry to instruments of overwhelming and instant destruction" and the first strike capabilities "begat a doctrine of 'anticipatory self-defense.'" After reading the practices of the organs of the United Nations, Frank (2001:68) concludes: "the use of force by a state or regional or mutual-defense system is likely to be tolerated if there is credible evidence that such first-use was justified by the severe impact of another state's indirect aggression or by clear evidence of an impending, planned, and decisive attack by a state."

These arguments seem plausible. As previously demonstrated, the customary right of anticipatory self-defense is preserved and coexists side by side with the Charter rule; this brings "imminent threat" into the meaning of an armed attack. However, it must meet the criterion that the threat should be real, verifiable, and leave no choice of other means to deflect it. Only then may the use of force in anticipatory self-defense within the strict limits of proportionality be justified. The burden of proof lies on the potential victim state to provide justification for its use of force in anticipation under article 51. The argument that states cannot be "sitting ducks"—to borrow the phrase from McDougal (1963:601)—keeping in view the advancement in weaponry is understandable, but it is not totally free from the danger of being abused. Therefore, I believe that the above criterion must be strictly adhered to. The mere possession of these dangerous weapons should not in itself be a ground for reaching a conclusion that the attack is imminent. There must be a clear intention and some sort of mobilization for using these weapons against the target state to justify the use of force in anticipation. Resorting to the use of force on unfounded fear of imminent attack could be disastrous. The case of India and Pakistan is very relevant. Both India and Pakistan are nuclear powers and always seem to pose a serious threat to each other. Border skirmishes are a routine and on many occasions border military build-ups have been seen. The 2002 military build up and the concern of the international community is a good example. Pakistan's nuclear capability is focused on India's nuclear capacity, and India's nuclear capability competes with China and Pakistan. Loosening the criterion from the strict limits of the *Caroline* doctrine will give any one of them an excuse to use force in anticipation, which might engulf the region and disturb international peace and security.

4.2.2 Can Acts of Non-state Actors be an "Armed Attack?"

The answer to this question depends on two further questions: Do the Charter rules apply to non-state actors, and does a terrorist attack meet the "scale and effect" test of the *Nicaragua* (1986) case?

First, it has been understood for a long that an armed attack is carried out by one state against another state. This is why some publicists tend to interpret article 51 narrowly despite the fact that it does not say that an armed attack must come from one state against another state. It only says that "if an armed attack occurs against a Member of the United Nations" leaving open the question of who carried out the attack. The attack may come from one member state against another or non-member or non-state agents, such as a terrorist network. "While the notion of 'armed attack' in 1945 no doubt was closely associated with the idea of armies crossing borders, the Nicaragua Court recognized in the 1980s that an armed attack could arise in other ways, such as the sending of armed groups into a state" (Murphy, 2002:51). The Security Council Resolutions 1368 (2001, preamble) and 1373 (2001, preamble), adopted immediately after the September 11, 2001, terrorist attacks, confirmed the inherent right of individual and collective self-defense against terrorist attacks without mentioning the perpetrators. Resolution 1368 (2001, paragraph 3) called on states "to bring to justice the perpetrators, organizers and sponsors of these terrorist attacks." Resolution 1373 called on states "to prevent and suppress terrorist acts" and to "take all necessary steps" to implement this resolution (2001, paragraph 8). "Necessary steps" are usually interpreted to include the use of force. These resolutions support the interpretation that a state as well as non-state agents may carry out an armed attack and in some cases a terrorist attack might amount to an "armed attack" against which force may be used in self-defense. Murphy (2002:50) contends:

> There is nothing in Article 51 of the U.N. Charter that requires the exercise of self-defense to turn on whether an armed attack was committed directly by another state. Indeed, the language used in Article 2(4) (which speaks of a use of force by one "Member" against "any state") is not repeated in Article 51. Rather, Article 51 is silent on who or what might commit an armed attack justifying self-defense.

This indicates that the Charter rules cover the activities of non-state actors in the case of an armed attack.

The second requirement is that any attack carried out by the non-state actors must be of such a *scale* and have such *effect* that it would amount to an "armed attack" had it been carried out by the regular armed forces of a state. This will require a case-by-case assessment. In the case of *Nicaragua* (1986, paragraph 195), the court said that self-defense could include responses to the "sending by or on behalf of a State of armed bands, groups, irregulars or mercenaries, which carry out acts of armed forces against another State of such gravity as to amount to (*inter alia*) an actual armed attack conducted by regular armed forces, or its substantial involvement therein." If a terrorist attack touches the required scale of gravity, it can amount to an "armed attack."

The literature on terrorism is immense and ever expanding. It is not surprising that scholarly opinion has varied substantially. Beck and Arend (1994) identify three trends in the current literature: lack of common analytical framework, no consensus on the parameters of terrorist behavior giving rise to the right of states using force in self-defense, and how to respond legally with force to terrorist acts. Three thresholds for using force in self-defense against terrorists may be discerned from a survey of current scholarship in the field: high threshold, low threshold, and moderate threshold.

Boyle (1987) believes in the high threshold. He argues that self-defense under article 51 could only be exercised in the event of an armed attack or perhaps at least an imminent attack against a state itself. Henkin (1979:142) notes that the United Nations recognizes the exception of self-defense in emergency but limits it to actual armed attack, which is clear, unambiguous, subject to proof; and not easily open to misinterpretation or fabrication. Lobel (1999:543) argues:

> When one nation attacks another, the factual predicate for self-defense is clear and observable. That is usually not the case where a nation claims the right to

> use force in response to alleged terrorist attacks and imminent threats thereof. It is untenable for international law to permit one nation to attack another merely because it alone claims that a group operating in the other country is launching terrorist attacks against it. Such a rule would obliterate the prohibition against the use of force, as unsubstantiated claims by a single state would become the new legal predicate for the use of force. Those who urge a looser interpretation of Article 51 have yet to prescribe a viable method of ensuring that self-serving characterizations of facts are subject to some clear legal standard and international oversight.

It can be discerned from the *Nicaragua* (1986) case that a military response to a terrorist attack should at a minimum require that the nation carefully evaluate the evidence to ensure a high degree of certainty that it has identified those responsible for an attack and that more attacks are imminent; that the facts relied upon be made public; and that the facts are subject to international scrutiny and investigation. Charney (2001:836) contends:

> Any state that seeks to invoke the right of self-defense should be required to furnish the international community with credible evidence that it has suffered an attack, that the entity against which the right of self-defense is exercised was the source of the attack, that the attack or threat of attack is continuing, and that the use of force is necessary to protect the state from further injury.

On the other hand, Coll (1987) argues for a low threshold. Challenging the views of Boyle, he contends that self-defense need not be viewed as a "straitjacket." The self-defense provision of the Charter does not address the subtler modes of international violence. According to Coll, self-defense essentially consists of those measures, which is necessary to protect the state and its people from outside armed attack in its conventional and non-conventional forms, including terrorism. O'Brien (1990) contends that article 51 should not be interpreted narrowly. Terrorist actions such as armed attack against state territory, hostage taking, and armed attacks on nationals abroad might amount to an armed attack. Sofaer (1989:96) claims that the United States must use force when responding to terrorism even if our claims cannot "be proved in a real court or in the court of public opinion." Wedgwood (1999:563) argues that military force should be used prudently to prevent terrorist attacks and to degrade terrorist infrastructure. Murphy (2002:45) describes the two positions in the following words:

> In an analysis under Article 51, one must consider the scale of actions that might constitute an armed attack. At the low end of the scale (below the "armed attack" thresh-old) are actions such as the provision of arms to the

> nationals of a state who are seeking to overthrow their government. At the high end of the scale (above the threshold constituting an "armed attack") are actions such as armies crossing borders, as well as a state sending armed irregulars who 'carry out acts of armed force against another State of such sufficient gravity as to amount to an actual armed attack by regular forces."

Between these high and low thresholds lies a middle ground: a moderate threshold. Rowles (1987) suggests that a military response to terrorist acts would be lawful if those acts are on a scale equivalent to what would be an armed attack had it been carried out by the forces of government. Large scale and continuous terrorist attacks could give rise to the use of force in self-defense but an isolated attack would not justify the use of force. Cassese (1989:596) contends that "to qualify as an armed attack, international law requires that terrorist acts form part of a consistent pattern of violent terrorist action rather than just being isolated or sporadic attacks . . . sporadic or minor attacks do not warrant such a serious and conspicuous response as the use of force in self-defense."

I submit that the standard should be the moderate threshold if terrorist acts amount to an armed attack. However, I disagree with the argument that an isolated terrorist attack may not be a ground for the use of force against terrorists because there is and certainly will be situations where a single attack may be characterized as an armed attack, such as September 11, 2001. Commenting on the nature of these attacks, Tony Rogers (2001) says that "given the sheer scale of the recent attack, which puts it on a completely different level from previous terrorist acts and despite the unusual 'weapons' used, it can be argued that it amounts to an armed attack, giving rise to the right of self-defense." I agree with Rogers' assessment. The reaction of this event and the support of the international community for the actions of the United States against the perpetrators of September 11, 2001, confirm this interpretation. The events of September 11, 2001, might compel publicists to think differently, including Rowles and Cassese who expressed their views in the late 1980s.

4.2.3 Military Force Used Against Non-state Actors

It is demonstrated above that the Charter rules are applicable to non-state actors and their acts might amount to an armed attack if certain conditions are met. The next logical question follows: Is the use of military force permissible against non-state actors? The answer is that military force may be justified against terrorists if three conditions are met.

First, the terrorist act either inside or outside the state must amount to an "armed attack." The severity and scale of damage caused must be such that it would amount to an armed attack had it been carried out by the regular forces of a state. Anything illegal but less than amounting to an armed attack would require countermeasures. It was held in the *Nicaragua* (1986, paragraphs 201; 211) case that although the provision of arms or other forms of aid by one government to guerrillas could be considered an unlawful use of force, it would not necessarily constitute an armed attack upon the other. The court suggested that the attacked state—though not its allies—could take proportionate and necessary countermeasures. The violation of international obligations does not justify the use of force. In the *Corfu Channel* (1949) case, the International Court of Justice found that Albania's actions violated its international obligations but that it did not justify the use of military force by the United Kingdom against Albania by itself.

Second, the acts of terrorists must be attributable to a host state. When a state becomes responsible for the wrongful act of its non-state agents is a question, which remains unsettled under international law. This is because "international case law is contradictory, no treaty in force addresses the subject, and rules of attribution have not risen to the level of customary international law" (Townsend, 1997:635). The emerging norm can be gleaned from the declarations of different United Nations organs, jurisprudence of the International Court of Justice and scholarly writings. Article 8 on State Responsibility of the International Law Commission directly deals with the issue:

> The conduct of a person or group of persons shall be considered an act of a State under international law if the person or group of persons is in fact acting on the instructions of, or under the direction or control of, which State in carrying out the conduct.

Crawford (2003:110–13) contends that, as a general principle, a state is not responsible for the conduct of private persons. However, in certain situations where a factual relation exists between a person and the state, such conduct may become attributable to the state. It is necessary to establish the existence of a "real link" between the state and non-state agents. Such a conduct will be attributable if the state directed or controlled the specific operation and the conduct complained of was an "integral part" of that operation. Peripheral or incidental conduct falls beyond the scope of article 8. Crawford further argues that the three terms "instruction," "direction," and "control" in the text of article 8 are disjunctive and to attract attribution it is sufficient to establish any one of them.

The *degree of control* exercised by the state in order for conduct to be attributable to a state was a crucial question in the *Nicaragua* (1986) case. The question was whether the support given by the United States to the *Contras* was attributable to the United States and whether it would be held responsible for breaches of international humanitarian law by the *Contras*. The court held the United States responsible for "planning, direction and support" to the *Contras* but rejected the claim of Nicaragua that all the conduct of *Contras* was attributable to the United State because of its control over *Contras*. The court (paragraph 115) held:

> For this conduct to give rise to legal responsibility of the United States, it would in principle have to be proved that that State had effective control of the military or paramilitary operations in the course of which the alleged violations were committed.

The court thus set a high threshold of *effective control* for attribution of a conduct to a state and confirmed that "a general situation of dependence and support would be insufficient to justify attribution of the conduct to the state" (Crawford, 2003:111). Judge Jennings (1986:533), however, disagreed with the majority view on this point. He said that it may be agreed that the mere provision of arms might not amount to an armed attack. But the provision of arms if coupled with other kinds of involvement may be considered an armed attack: "It seems to me that to say that the provision of arms, coupled with 'logistical or other support' is not an armed attack is going too far."

The question of *degree of control* was also an issue in the case of *Tadic* (1997) before the Appeals Chamber of the International Criminal Tribunal for the Former Yugoslavia. The majority Judges seem to disagree with the threshold set out in the *Nicaragua* (1986) case. The Appeal Chamber (paragraph 117) held that "the requirement of international law for the attribution to States of acts performed by private individuals is that the State exercises control over the individuals. The degree of control may, however, vary according to the factual circumstances of each case." The Appeal Chamber (paragraph 147) held that the required degree of control is the "*over all control* going beyond the mere financing and equipping of such forces and involving also participation in the planning and supervision of military operations" (emphasis in original).

It seems that the high threshold of *effective control* laid down in *Nicaragua* (1986) was lowered to the *over all control* in *Tadic* (1997) case. "Although the 'overall control' test applied in *Tadic* (1997) did indeed lower the threshold for imputing private acts to states when compared to the ICJ rule, the touchstone of both approaches is that states must direct or control, not simply support, encourage or even condone, the private actor" (Jinks, 2003:145). These two cases indicate that the mere belonging to or presence of non-state actors in a particular state would not make that state liable for the wrongful acts of non-state agents. There must be a "real link" between a state and non-state actors and there must be strong evidence suggesting *effective control* or *overall control.* Mere support or tolerance by a state of non-state actors would not suffice to attract attribution and adverse action under international law.

Third, the use of force must be proportionate. "Acts done in self-defense must not exceed in manner or aim the necessity provoking them," (Schachter, 1986:132) and they should not be "unreasonable or excessive" (Webster, cited in Knauft, 1996:774). Military force should be used only to eliminate the source of attack or to prevent reoccurrence.

> Terrorists are in a way "modern enemies of mankind," and every State should endeavor to search for, try and punish them on its own territory. This, however, does not entail a license to use force in the territory of other States or against ships or aircraft of other States. If such a license were given by international law, our present condition of relative anarchy would be at risk of turning into one of absolute anarchy. (Cassese, 1989:606)

Armed attacks by non-state, non-nation, non-belligerent, non-insurgent actors such as members of Al-Qaeda may trigger the right of selective and proportionate self-defense under the United Nations Charter against those directly involved in processes of armed attack (Puast, 2002). Force may be used in self-defense against non-state actors when these three conditions are met.

4.3 Anticipatory Self-defense and Terrorism

It is established in this chapter that the concept of armed attack includes an imminent attack, and, therefore, anticipatory self-defense is a credible rule of international law. It is also argued that the rules of the Charter are applicable to the acts of non-state actors and, in some cases, their acts might amount to an armed attack justifying the use of force both in the case of reactive self-defense and anticipatory self-defense. However, there is a need for a mechanism to verify the evidence of a real and imminent threat and define limits on the anticipatory use of force to avoid the danger of being misused or abused. The risk and uncertainty involved in the use of force in anticipation and recent several intelligence failures in the war against Afghanistan and Iraq teaches us to be very careful in the verification and evaluation of evidence.

However, a consensus seems to be emerging that if cogent and verifiable evidence of terrorist attack is available, limited use of force should be allowed. In my opinion, military force should be used if: (a) the threat is real and imminent; (b) a "real link" and the required "degree of control" is established between the state and terrorist organization, which allegedly intends to carry out the attack; and (c) the response is limited and measured.

4.4 Preemptive Self-defense

Before proceeding to the arguments regarding the legal status of preemptive self-defense, it is important to note the difference between anticipatory and preemptive self-defense. The Chambers dictionary's (2001:30) meaning of the word "anticipate" is "to predict something and then acts as though it is bound to happen." It connotes that something is certain and bound to happen, which must be responded to. The degree of certainty is greater so there is a lesser chance of miscalculations. The Chambers dictionary's (2001:465) meaning of the word "pre-emptive," on the other hand, in military sense, is "effectively destroying the enemy's weapons before they can be used." It connotes a military tactic during the war rendering the enemy less capable of fighting. It does not involve an action against a sovereign nation's weaponry installations without being in a state of war. Reisman (2003:143) defines preemptive self-defense as "claim of authority to use, unilaterally and without international authorization, high levels of violence in order to arrest a development that is not yet operational and hence is not yet *directly* threatening, but which, if permitted to mature, could be neutralized only at a high, possibly unacceptable, cost" (emphasis in original). Making a distinction between anticipatory and preventive self-defense, O'Connell (2002:2) states that preemptive self-defense refers to cases where a party uses force to quell any possibility of future attack by another state, even where there is no reason to believe that an attack is planned and where no prior attack has occurred. Anticipatory self-defense is a narrower doctrine that would authorize armed responses to attacks that are on the brink of launch or where an enemy attack has already occurred and the victim learns that more attacks are planned.

Reisman (2003) has given thresholds for different kinds of self-defense. The requisite threshold for reactive self-defense is "actual armed attack," for anticipatory self-defense "palpable and imminent threat of attack" and for preemptive self-defense a "conjectural and contingent threats of possible attack." The goal of pre-emptive self-defense is to prevent "more generalised threats from materializing" rather than trying to "preempt specific, imminent threat" (Sapiro, 2003:599). It is reminiscent of the notion of strategic preemption that animated the German policy in the early years of the twentieth century. Its key idea is the political justification of assaulting another state so as to block any unfavorable shift in the balance of power (Farer, 2002:359).

4.4.1 Permissibility of Preemptive Self-defense

Three trends can be gleaned from the current debate on the preemptive use of force: (a) states such as the United States and scholars that strongly argue for the justification of pre-emptive use of force under the broader interpretation of article 51, (b) those publicists who recognize the gravity of the threat terrorism poses and argue for reasonable interpretation of rules on the use of force, and (c) publicists and states aware of the dangers and abuse involved in the preemptive use of force that strongly argue against it.

4.4.1.1 Argument for Preemptive Self-defense

Reisman (2003) explains that the introduction of vastly destructive and rapidly delivered weapons prompted a claim to expand the right of reactive self-defense to anticipatory self-defense. However, the proliferation of atomic, biological, and chemical weapons and their diffusion into the hands of non-state actors has given impetus to a new claim of "preemptive" self-defense. The arch proponent, besides Israel, of the preemptive doctrine is the United States. Soon after the September 11, 2001 attacks, the United States spelled out its National Security Strategy (2002, revised in 2006) stating that "the war against terrorists of global reach is a global enterprise of uncertain duration" and "as a matter of common sense and self-defense, America will act against such emerging threats before they are fully formed." The United States clarified its position on the relationship between terrorists and those who supports terrorism: "We make no distinction between terrorists and those who knowingly harbour or provide aid to them." We will disrupt and destroy terrorist organizations:

> By direct and continuous action is using all the elements of national and international power . . . defending the United States, the American people, and our interests at home and abroad by identifying and destroying the threat before it reaches our borders. While the United States will constantly strive to enlist the support of the international community, we will not hesitate to act alone, if necessary, to exercise our right of self-defense by acting preemptively against such terrorists, to prevent them from doing harm against our people and our country, and denying further sponsorship, support, and sanctuary to terrorists by convincing or compelling states to accept their sovereign responsibilities. (National Security Strategy, 2002:6)

The United States National Security Strategy (2002:15) offers an interpretation of the right to self-defense and the reasons to strike preemptively:

> For centuries, international law recognized that nations need not suffer an attack before they can lawfully take action to defend themselves against forces that present an imminent danger of attack. . . . Legal scholars and international jurists often conditioned the legitimacy of preemption on the existence of an imminent threat—most often a visible mobilization of armies, navies, and air forces preparing to attack. We must adapt the concept of imminent threat to the *capabilities and objectives* of today's adversaries. Rogue states and terrorists do not seek to attack us using conventional means. They know such attacks would fail. Instead, they rely on acts of terror and, potentially, the use of weapons of mass destruction.

The United States National Security Strategy (2002:15) justifies the notion of preemptive action in the following words:

> Given the goals of rogue states and terrorists, the United States can no longer solely rely on a reactive posture as we have in the past. The inability to deter a potential attacker, the immediacy of today's threats, and the magnitude of potential harm that could be caused by our adversaries' choice of weapons, do not permit that option. We cannot let our enemies strike first. . . . The purpose of our actions will always be to eliminate a specific threat to the United States or our allies and friends. The reasons for our actions will be clear, the force measured, and the cause just.

Taft and Buchwald (2003:557)[2] argue:

> In the end, each use of force must find legitimacy in the facts and circumstances that the state believes have made it necessary. Each should be judged not on abstract concepts, but on the particular events that gave rise to it. While nations must not use preemption as a pre-text for aggression, to be for or against preemption in the abstract is a mistake. The use of force preemptively is sometimes lawful and sometimes not.

Ruth Wedgwood (2003) strongly argues that "deterrence and containment were the core doctrines of the Cold War. These do not translate easily to a brave new world of non-state terror networks. . . . To a strategist; September 11 thus teaches that the keystone doctrines of the Cold War confrontationn . . . have ceased to be reliable. Rather, one must consider acting against terrorist *capability* before it is employed and, better yet, before it is acquired" (emphasis in original). John Yoo (2004) believes that the emergence of rogue states, international terrorism, and the easy availability of weapons of mass destruction have placed enormous strain on the bright line rules of the Charter system. He (2004:730) makes a strong argument that "a more flexible standard should govern the use of force in self-defense, one that focuses less on temporal imminence and more on the magnitude of the potential harm and the probability of an armed attack."

> The test for determining whether a threat is sufficiently "imminent" to render the use of force necessary at a particular point has become more nuanced than Secretary Webster's nineteenth-century formulation. Factors to be considered should now include the probability of an attack; the likelihood that this probability will increase, and therefore the need to take advantage of a limited window of opportunity; whether diplomatic alternatives are practical; and the magnitude of the harm that could result from the threat. If a state instead were obligated to wait until the threat were truly imminent in the temporal sense envisioned by Secretary Webster, there is a substantial danger of missing a limited window of opportunity to prevent widespread harm to civilians. (Yoo, 2003:574)

I do not agree with the reasoning of Wedgwood and the National Security Strategy of the United States for using force against *acquiring capabilities*. I also disagree with the proposed test of Yoo for using force if the attack is probable and the expected harm is enormous for the reasons given at the end of section 4.4.1.2.

4.4.1.2 Argument against Preemptive Self-defense

The majority of international law scholars oppose the notion of preemption. They argue that it breaches the core principles of international law. The thrust of the Charter is to prohibit the use of force, it should be used when extremely necessary and all peaceful means are exhausted. Damrosch (2000:68) argues that "force should ordinarily be a last rather than a first resort." Use of force in self-defense is an exception to the general proscription and should be interpreted very narrowly. Paust (2004:1343) contends that absent an actual armed attack on a state triggering the right of self-defense under article 51 and absent an authorization to use armed force from the UN Security Council or an appropriate regional organization, no state can lawfully engage in what some term preemptive self-defense.

> While I reject the notion of preemptive self-defense, in my judgment, when an armed attack can be categorized as incipient, the target state need not wait until the first shot is fired but can respond to intercept it at an early stage. That

> is to say, there is nothing preemptive about nipping an armed attack in the bud. The point is that you need a bud. Self-defense cannot be exercised merely on the ground of expectations, anticipations, and fear. You have to prove that the other side is already embarked on an inevitable course of action. (Dinstein, 2003:148)

Greenwood (2002) argues:

> The right of anticipatory self-defense is quite narrowly defined. Ever since the United Kingdom-US exchange in what has become known as the Caroline case in 1837–38, the right has been confined to instances where the threat of armed attack was imminent. In my opinion, that still reflects international law and, in so far as talk of a doctrine of "pre-emption" is intended to refer to a broader right to respond to threats, which might materialise some time in the future, I believe that such a doctrine has no basis in law.

In his legal opinion to former Prime Minister Blair, Attorney General Lord Goldsmith (March 7, 2003) argues:

> Force may be used in self-defense if there is an actual attack or imminent threat of an armed attack; the use of force must be necessary . . . and the force used must be a proportionate response . . . I am aware that the USA has been arguing for recognition of a broad doctrine of a right to use force to pre-empt danger in the future. If this means more than a right to respond proportionately to an imminent attack (and I understand that the doctrine is intended to carry that connotation) this is not a doctrine which, in my opinion, exists or is recognized in international law.

The reaction of "the Security Council . . . [to the attacks of] September 11, 2001, can be cited to support anticipatory self-defense in cases where an armed attack has occurred and convincing evidence exists that more attacks are planned, though not yet underway. By contrast, international law prohibits pre-emptive and even anticipatory self-defense if that is understood to be different from responding to incipient or ongoing campaigns" (O'Connell, 2002:11). In the history of the United Nations, there have been authoritative condemnations of both preemptive and retaliatory actions so it seems to be against the purposes of the Charter (Paust, 1986:717). Bothe (2003) argues that the doctrine of preemptive strikes formulated in the recent U.S. National Security Strategy proposes to adapt this concept to new perceived threats in a way that would constitute an unacceptable expansion of the right of anticipatory self-defense. Byers (2002) argues that the Bush doctrine of preemption is to make a new law. It is unprecedented in that it argues for a right to take preemptive action against potential threats and future threats. It is a way of effectively closing down dangerous regimes before they become imminent threats. It is clearly illegal. Brownlie (1963:275) says:

> It is believed that the ordinary meaning of the phrase precludes action which is preventive in character. . . . There is no further clarification of the phrase to be gained from study of the travaux preparatoires. However, the discussions at San Francisco assumed that any permission for the unilateral use of force would be exceptional and would be secondary to the general prohibition in Article 2, paragraph 4. There was a presumption against self-help and even action in self-defense within Article 51 was made subject to control by the Security Council. In these circumstances the precision of Article 51 is explicable.

The arguments for pre-emptive self-defense are not persuasive and the notion seems to be too broad and fraught with risks to be accepted as a norm of international law. To use military force for preventing the states from gaining *capabilities* that may pose a threat to a target state or international peace and security in the future, as Wedgwood and National Security Strategy suggest, is a very loose ground and several situations would require action today. The Arab states may join hands to attack Israel because it is building its nuclear arsenal and is becoming a growing threat to Muslim states in the region. Iran's current nuclear program would entitle Israel, if not America, to attack and destroy Iran's nuclear capabilities. India may attack Pakistan because Pakistan supports the Kashmir freedom fighting movements and its nuclear capability is India specific. This will breach international peace and security.

4.4.1.3 Preemptive Self-defense: A Cautious Approach

The above pro and contra positions seem to be going too far in either case. The opponents of preemption fail to take into account the changes in weaponry and the rise of international terrorism. The proponents of preemption are stretching the notion of self-defense to an extent that the distortion seems beyond legal recognition. It is the creation of a new rule, not an extended interpretation of an existing rule as an exception to general prohibition on the use of force under the Charter. However, there are scholars who argue for a more cautious approach: Terrorism must be eliminated but within the well demarcated boundaries of law. "In the fight against terrorism the rule of law must not be part of the collateral damage" (Dickson, 2005).

The better argument in the debate appears to support a cautious view of anticipatory self-defense recognizing that the concept must be interpreted consistently with the Charter's goal of limiting the use of force. Today it is more likely to be foolish, if not suicidal, for a state to believe that its fundamental security interests are at risk to wait until the first attack. It is simply to recognize that the meaning of a document meant to be universally accepted and to remain relevant must also be flexible enough to adapt to changing circumstances. The requirement of imminence should mean that there is no time for deliberation and no time to choose an alternative course of action. However, the danger should be imminent in that it can be identified credibly, specifically, and with a high degree of certainty. Further, the requirement of necessity should continue to mean that time has run out because peaceful efforts to avoid a resort to force have been exhausted. Ideally, this requirement would include an appeal to the Security Council to resolve the problem, although there may be cases where the urgency of the threat makes resort to the Council impractical.

Frank (2002) follows a middle way approach. He says to insist that a small country wait for a neighbor to attack it with nuclear weapons before responding and to say that that's what the law requires, everybody would just say well the law is "an ass." On the other hand, if there is a law, which says that any time a country feels threatened, it is free to attack any country from which it feels the threat is emanating, then you don't have a law at all and the "law is an ass again." The law has to try to find very narrow exceptions to itself that can be applied in a sensible way on the basis of rigorously demonstrated evidence that meets a reasonable test. The law on self-defense has to be interpreted reasonably but that is not the same as saying the law can be interpreted unilaterally by a party at interest. If the process is an entirely unilateral one in which the strong do as they will and the weak have to accept it, then we are right back to the Peloponnesian wars, which most countries would resist. Similarly, Judge Sofaer (2003) examines the background of the requirement that preemption is restricted to imminent attacks, and argues that the narrow standard properly applies only when a potential victim state can rely on the police powers of the state from which a prospective attack is anticipated. A more flexible standard for determining necessity is appropriate for situations in which the state from which attacks are anticipated is either unwilling or unable to prevent the attacks or may even be responsible for them.

The Charter of the United Nations is neither a "suicidal pact" nor a "free license" to use force in self-defense. To expect a state to wait for an actual attack when there is credible and verifiable evidence would render the Charter a suicidal pact, but to interpret article 51 as covering a perceived threat based on uncertain evidence would be providing a license to use force for any reason, such as in hidden and in some cases parallel agendas. In my view, the current norms of international law on self-defense and anticipatory self-defense provide an effective legal framework to deal with the threat of terrorism. If there is an armed attack, we will see it and proportionate force may be used. If the threat is imminent and there is no time for relying on peaceful means or no alternative mean is available to deter it, then force may be used in anticipation in a proportionate way. All other threatening situations shall be referred to the Security Council for determination under article 39:

> The Security Council shall determine the existence of any threat to the peace, breach of the peace, or act of aggression and shall make recommendations, or decide what measures shall be taken in accordance with Articles 41 and 42, to maintain or restore international peace and security.

The plain meaning of article 39 suggests that the Security Council has to determine three issues: whether there is any threat to peace, whether there is breach of peace, and whether there is an act of aggression. After determining the existence of any one of these issues, the Security Council might recommend measures. Paust (2002:538) contends that article 39 of the Charter appears to preclude the use of preemptive armed force against perceived threats that do not amount to an armed attack under article 51 by requiring the Security Council to determine whether a threat exists and what measures, if any, it chooses to authorize. I agree with Paust. Article 39 uses the word "restore," which indicates that peace is breached and now there is need to restore it. Article 39 also uses word "maintain," which suggests that an action may be taken before peace is breached. This brings in the notion of an action beforehand. The word "restore" explains the conception of reactive self-defense whereas the word "maintain" entails prejudging and, therefore, requires that any situation threatening peace and security may be referred to the Security Council.

In a nutshell, international law provides three mechanisms to deal with the threat of attack or armed attack by the non-state actors: the use of force in self-defense in a case of an armed attack, the use of force in anticipation when the attack is imminent, and referring the matter to the Security Council for determination under article 39 when the threat is remote and uncertain. There is no room for preemptive self-defense in the presence of article 39. If the Security Council fails to determine or take effective measures because of veto or any other reason and the threat becomes imminent, the right of anticipatory self-defense provides a narrow window to use force in self-defense.

4.5 When Self-defense Ends

The victim state is not totally free to use any amount of force in self-defense indefinitely. Conventional and customary law imposes certain limits both as to the amount of force and period of time for any use of force in self-defense. The question of termination of self-defense centres on two things: the interpretation of the "until clause" in article 51 and a proportionate response.

4.5.1 Article 51: The "Until" Clause

One of the requirements of article 51 is that any action taken in self-defense shall be reported to the Security Council immediately. Apparently, it seems that the right to self-defense continues until the matter is reported to the Security Council and it has taken necessary measures in response to the matter referred. This raises an important question: Does the victim state retain the right of self-defense once the Security Council takes notice of the matter? There is no simple answer to this question. Different scholars take different lines of argument as to whether and to what extent the use of force is allowed in self-defense once the matter is reported to the Security Council. The first argument is that self-defense is a temporary right. Once the matter is reported to the Security Council, it is the primary responsibility of the Security Council to take necessary measures under chapter VII. The state's right to self-defense ends here. The second argument is that self-defense is an "inherent" right and continues until the Security Council has taken necessary measures, and those measures are adequate and effective in the opinion of the victim state. Otherwise, the state retains the right to self-defense despite reporting to the Security Council.

Chayes (1991) argues that the right of self-defense ends once the Security Council is seized of the matter. The right of state is subject to limit of time "until the Security Council has taken the measures necessary to maintain international peace and security." He contends that "Article 51 is not an affirmative grant of a right of self-defense but a statement of the situations in which the exercise of an 'inherent right' is not precluded by the Charter." He argues that it is the primary responsibility of the Security Council to maintain international peace and keep in view the proscription on the use of force under article 2(4). The use of force under article 51 should be confined to the narrowest possible range. Greig (1991:389) states that the common sense of the situation suggests that a state is not obliged to cease acting in self-defense against an aggressor that is continuing with its offensive until the measures, its own or those employed by the Security Council, prove effective.

The use of the word "necessary" in article 51 would seem to reinforce such an interpretation. Schachter (1991), following the same line of argument, contends that the Security Council has the authority to replace collective self-defense with enforcement measures under chapter VII if it intends to do so. It is inconsistent with the Charter to say that "self-defense as an inherent right cannot be taken away." Article 51 not only requires states to report the claims of self-defense to the Security Council but also says that such measures shall not "in anyway affect the authority and responsibility of the Security Council." However, Schachter (1991) rejects the interpretation that the right of self-defense is "overridden whenever the Security Council adopted measures considered necessary in case of an armed attack." Frank (2001) takes the position that once the Security Council has taken action, the target state is barred from using force as self-defense.

> If states use armed force under the self-defense rubric of Article 51, their individual activities are subsumed by, or incorporated into, the global police response once it is activated. That is, the old way is licensed only until the new way begins to work: "until," in the words of Article 51, "the Security Council has taken the necessary measures to maintain international peace and security. (Frank and Patel, 1991:63)

However, they add a caveat that it is sensible to assume that the right of self-defense revives if the Security Council fails, for whatever reason, to take action.

Other scholars such as Reisman (1991) argue that article 51 is not intended to take away the right to use force in self-defense once the Security Council acts. It is counterproductive to interpret article 51 barring the use of force in self-defense once the Security Council takes action:

> An interpretation of the Charter according to which individual states reserve the right of individual and collective self-defense keeps the pressure on an aggressor nation . . . an interpretation that says that states no longer have that right bleeds that pressure off. (Reisman, 1991:43)

Rostow (1991) rejects the interpretation that article 51 bars the use of force in self-defense after the Security Council comes into motion on the matter. It would be fatal to subordinate states' right of self-defense to the prior permission of the Security Council. He contends that the Charter intends the opposite of this position: The victim or targeted state and, in some case, its allies may decide for themselves when to use force in self-defense until the Security Council restore peace or decides that self-defense has gone too far and has become a threat to peace itself. Kelsen (1950) contends that a state has the right to use force in self-defense until the Security Council takes action and that action is adequate in the opinion of the claimant state.

The right to self-defense is a natural and independent right. The state neither requires the prior permission of the Security Council for its exercise nor does reporting to the Security Council exhaust it. This right continues until the Security Council takes effective measures either to throw out the aggressor or deter an imminent attack and prevent the recurrence of such attacks. In the case of effective action by the Security Council, the state "willingly suspends" its right of self-defense but is not diminished. It remains in willing suspension only and can be revived any time if the Security Council fails to sustain its effective treatment of the matter. It is the belief of a state in the collective security system under the Charter, which makes a state suspend its right of self-defense as the Security Council is expected to act on its behalf. Otherwise, the state is the natural wielder of the right. As with the case of an individual's right of self-defense, no state would surrender its security without effective measures of protection provided by the Security Council. This seems to be the intention of the Charter, as it cannot be imagined that its drafter would make a rule that would put in jeopardy the security and, in some cases, the very existence of a state.

The interpretation that the right of self-defense ends after the Security Council takes necessary action would have some weight if the Security Council had a record of taking swift and effective measures in response to situations requiring individual use of force in self-defense. However, the history of the Security Council provides the opposite picture. In such a state of affairs, the wisdom of a policy relying on a body that has failed constantly to offer an effective alternative to the use of force may be questioned. No one will wholeheartedly entrust their personal security to a police force in a state where it is believed the police cannot respond to a threat in time or it has a record of failures in protecting individuals. There is no suggestion that the Security Council should be shunned, but states would be very cautious in laying down their security at the mercy of such a body. Moreover, the Security Council suffers from a serious systemic flaw: It is founded on the notion of an oligarchy where the permanent five members decide on the security of states that might not even have a vote in some cases. The veto of one oligarch can render the body impotent. The history of the Security Council is replete with such instances.

4.5.2 Proportionality

There exists a rule that any use of force in self-defense must be proportionate (see *Nicaragua*, paragraph 194). "Any state attempting to justify a forceful action as self-defense would be expected to show that the amount of force used was not disproportionate to the threat or attack it had experienced" (McCormack, 1991:38). The proportionality requirement entails two main conditions. First, the degree of force exercised would have to be proportional in terms of intensity and magnitude. Second, the duration of the preemptive attack would have to be strictly limited to the removal of the threat. The incident that provided the basis of the most commonly accepted formulation of proportionality is the *Caroline* incident: "It will be for [the British Government] to show, also, that the local authorities of Canada, even supposing the necessity of the moment . . . did nothing unreasonable or excessive; since the act, justified by the necessity of self-defense, must be limited by that necessity, and kept clearly within it" (Webster, cited in Jennings, 1938). This raises two important questions: How much is proportional, and who decides that enough is done?

4.5.2.1 How Much is Proportional?

Beck and Arend identify (1994:206) three approaches to the principle of proportionality in response to terrorism. The first approach may be called "eye for an eye" or "tit for tat" proportionality. This means that a victim state must respond proportionately to some prior act of terrorism. The claim of self-defense must be rejected if "the nature and amount of force used is disproportionate to the character of the initiating coercion" (Intoccia, 1987:206).

The second approach may be called "cumulative proportionality." The proponents of this approach contend that the victim state's forcible measures should be proportionate to an aggregation of past illegal acts. For instance, Roberts (1987:281–82) says that the equivalence in number of deaths and extent of property damage is the sine qua non of proportionality. He asserts that proportionality must be calculated on the basis of prior events. An accumulation of small events can justify a single, larger retaliatory response in certain cases.

The third approach may be called "deterrent proportionality." This approach argues that the victim state's use of force must be proportionate to the overall terrorist threat faced by the state. O'Brian (1990:472) believes that counterterror measures should be proportionate to the purposes of counter terror deterrence and defense and the referent of proportionality should be the "overall pattern of past and projected acts." Schachter (1989) contends that "tit for tat" is not the only test for proportionality. There are two others: the response in relation to a continuing pattern of attack rather than the last one and proportionality judged in terms of the ends sought, that is, the cessation of attacks and the means used. Similarly, Baker

(1987–88) states that self-defensive measures should be weighed against all attacks prior to the response and the probability and size of future attacks.

The first two approaches make more sense as it will be easy to measure the damage done in the case of one or more attacks. The third approach seems to be risky in that the size and probable damage cannot be measured in the case of probable future attacks. No one knows the exact size of damage in any probable attack. For instance, in the case of September 11, 2001 attacks, one plane did not hit its target and fell into the fields of Pennsylvania. It raises two issues: the probable attack may be aborted and does not occur at all and the planned attack might not happen in the manner it is planned. Hence this approach, or at least the part dealing with "probable and size of future attack," is problematic, and it would be very hard to decide what is proportional. Greater risk of abuse is involved in this approach.

4.5.2.2 Who Decides the Question of "Enough"?

The right of self-defense is a self-judging principle, but the international community must judge its propriety (Waldock, 1952). If the victim state claims that it has the exclusive authority to determine the lawfulness of the use of force in self-defense, then "the law has reached a vanishing point" (see Schachter, 1987). The International Tribunal also rejected this argument when the Nazi leaders argued that Germany had acted in self-defense and in any given case, it is to the state to decide whether it has such a right (Schachter, 1987). The right of self-defense can be initiated at the discretion of the state, that is, when a state believes that it has been attacked or such an attack is imminent. However, the final assessment of its lawfulness lies with the larger community. Sir Hersch Lauterpacht (1933:179–80) said:

> The right of self-defense is a general principle of law. . . . It is recognized to the extent . . . that recourse to it is not itself illegal. It is regulated to the extent that it is the business of the courts to determine whether, how far and for how long there was a necessity to have recourse to it. There is not the slightest relation between the content of the right of self-defense and the claim that it is above the law and not amenable to evaluation by the law. Such a claim is self-contradictory inasmuch as it purports to be based on legal right and as, at the same time, it dissociates itself from regulation and evaluation by the law.

A state has an initial power to qualify its actions as being in self-defense, and this classification continues to operate unless the international community determines otherwise. The same is true with regard to the termination of the right to act in self-defense. If, despite a call for a cease-fire by the Security Council, hostilities continue, it is for the community to decide upon the consequences that flow from the failure to abide by the Security Council's decision (Greig, 1991:392). Waldock (1952) asserts that it is for the Security Council to determine whether the right to self-defense has ended. "If the Council is paralysed and fails to take any measure necessary to maintain international peace and security, the legal position is equally obvious: a Member State exercising the right of self-defense may persist in the use of force" (Dinstein, 1988:196).

The right to self-defense is the natural and independent right of a state. It can be initiated and may continue as long as is necessary, in the opinion of the victim state, until either the objective for using force is achieved or the Security Council has taken effective measures. However, to decide on its lawfulness and propriety is for the international community at large and organizations, such as the United Nations, regional organizations, and interested individuals.

4.6 Conclusion

Terrorism is a serious threat to peace, security, and human lives. It must be dealt with rigorously. However, the struggle against terrorism must be within the limits of law. States that take responsibility to implement international law or the resolutions of the Security Council must uphold the rule of law. Illegal terrorist acts must be defeated by the strength of law. The argument that the current norms of international law are inadequate to deal with the threat of terrorism is not convincing. The current international legal order provides for self-defense, anticipatory self-defense in credible cases, and for any other situation threatening peace and security to be reported to the Security Council for determination and necessary action. What is needed is to make the Security Council a reliable and effective body, which requires the political will of the international community to meet the challenge. The doctrine of preemption cannot fit into the current international legal system, and it does not present compelling arguments for it to be accepted as new norm of international law.

References

Baker, M. (1987–88) Terrorism and the inherent right of self-defence (a call to amend Article 51 of the United Nations Charter). *Houston Journal of International Law*, 10, pp.25–49.

Beck, R. and Arend, C. (1994) Don't tread on us: International law and forcible state responses to terrorism. *Wisconsin International Law Journal*, 12, pp.153–219.

Bothe, M. (2003) Terrorism and the legality of pre-emptive force. *European Journal of International Law*, 14 (227).

Bowett, D. (1972) Reprisals involving recourse to armed force. *American Journal of International Law*, 66, pp.1–36.

———. (1958) *Self-defence in international law*. Manchester: Manchester University Press.

Brownlie, I. (1963) *International law and the use of force by states*. Oxford: Clarendon Press.

———. (1961) The use of force in self-defence. *British Yearbook of International Law*, Vol. 37, pp.183–268.

———. (1955–56) Collective self-defence under the Charter of the United Nations. *British Yearbook of International Law*, 32, pp.130–61.

Byers, M. (2002) Iraq and the "Bush Doctrine" of pre-emptive self-defence. *Crimes of war project*. Available at: http://www.crimesofwar.org/expert/bush-byers.html.

Cassese, A. (2001) Terrorism is also disrupting some crucial categories of international law. *European Journal of International Law*, 21(5), pp.993–1001.

———. (1989) The international community's "Legal" response to terrorism. *International and Comparative Law Quarterly*, 38, pp.589–608.

Chambers Compact Dictionary, 2001.

Charney, J. (2001) The use of force against terrorism and international law. *American Journal of International Law*, 95, pp.835–39.

Chayes, A. (1991) The use of force in the Persian Gulf. *In* Damrosch, L. and Scheffer, D. (eds.). *Law and force in the New International Order*. Boulder, CO: Westview Press.

Coll, A. (1987) The legal and moral adequacy of military responses to terrorism. *American Society of International Law Proceedings*, 81, pp.297–306.

Crawford, J. (2003) *The international law commission's articles on state responsibility: Introduction, text and commentaries*. Cambridge: Cambridge University Press.

Damrosch, L. (2000) Sanctions against perpetrators of terrorism. *Houston Journal of International Law*, 22, pp.63–76.

Dickson, B. (2005) Law versus Terrorism: Can Law Win? *European Human Rights Law Review*, 1, pp.11–28.

Dinstein, Y. (2003) Self-defence in an age of terrorism. *American Society of International Law Proceedings*, 97, pp.147–49.

———. (1988) *War, aggression and self-defence*. Cambridge: Cambridge University Press.

Farer, T. (2002) Beyond the Charter Frame: Unilateralism or Communism? *American Journal of International Law*, 96, pp.359–64.

Frank, T. (2002) Iraq and the "Bush Doctrine" of pre-emptive self-defence. *Crimes of War Project*. Available at: shttp://www.crimesofwar.org/expert/bush-franck.html.

———. (2001) When, if ever, may states deploy military force without prior Security Council authorisation. *Washington University Journal of Law and Policy*, 5, pp.51–68.

Frank, T. and Patel, F. (1991) Police action in lieu of war: The old order changeth. *American Journal of International Law*, 85, pp.63–74.

Frowein, F. (1988) The present state of research carried out by the English-speaking section of the Centre for Studies and Research. In *Legal Aspects of International Terrorism* pp.55–96.

General Assembly (1974) Resolution 3314. April 12.

General Treaty for the Renunciation of War (Kellog-Briand) 1928.

Glennon, M. (2002) The fog of law: Self-defence, inherence, and incoherence in Article 51 of the United Nations Charter. *Harvard Journal of Law and Public Policy*, 25, pp.539–58.

———. (2003) Why the Security Council failed? *Foreign Affairs*, 82, pp. 16–35.

Goldsmith, Lord. (2003) Iraq: Resolution 1441 (Secret Memo to the Prime Minster). March 7. Available at: http://image.guardian.co.uk/sys-files/Guardian/documents/2005/04/28/legal.pdf.

Greenwood, C. (2002) The legality of using force against Iraq. Memorandum to the UK Government on October 12, 2002. Available at: http://www.publications.parliament.uk/pa/cm200203/cmselect/cmfaff/196/2102406.htm.

Greig, D. (1991) Self-defence and the Security Council: What does Article 51 require? *International and Comparative Law Quarterly*, 40, pp.366–402.

Gross, E. (2001) Thwarting terrorist acts by attacking the perpetrator or their commanders as an act of self-defence: Human rights versus the state's duty to protect its citizens. *Temple International and Comparative Law Journal*, 15, pp.195–245.

Grotius, H. (1913) *De jure belli ac pacis libire tres* (*Three books on the law of war and peace*) (Kelsen, trans) (Original work published 1625).

Halberstam, M. (1996) The right to self-defence once the security council takes action. *Michigan Journal of International Law*, 17, pp.229–48.

Henkin, L. (1979) *How nations behave*. New York: Columbia University Press.

Higgins, R. (1994) *Problems and process: International law and how we use it*. Oxford: Oxford University Press.

Hole, L. (2004) Anticipatory self-defence under international law. *American University International Law Review*, 19, pp.69–106.

I.C.J. (2005) *Democratic Republic of Congo v. Uganda*. December 19.

———. (2004) *Legal consequences of the construction of a wall in the occupied Palestinian territory*. July 9.

———. (1986) *Nicaragua v. United States of America*. June 27.

———. (1949) *Albania v. United Kingdom* (The Corfu Channel Case). April 9.

I.C.T.Y. (1997) *Prosecutor v. Tadic*. July 14. Available at: http://www.un.org/icty/tadic/appeal/decision-e/51002.htm.

Inter-American Reciprocal Assistance and Solidarity (Act of Chapultepec), 1945.

Intoccia, G. (1987) American bombing of Libya: An international legal analysis. *Case W. Res. Journal of International Law*, 19, pp.177–213.

Jinks, D. (2003) Self-defence in an age of terrorism. *American Society of International Law Proceedings*, 97, pp.144–46.

Jennings, R.(1938) The Caroline and McLeod Cases. *American Journal of International Law*, 32, pp.82–99.

Kelsen, H. (1948) Collective security and collective self-defence under the Charter of the United Nations. *American Journal of International Law*, 42, pp.783–96.

Knauft, S. (1996) Proposed guidelines for measuring the propriety of armed state responses to terrorist attacks. *Hastings International and Comparative Law Review*, 19, pp.763–88.

Kunz, J. (1947) Individual and collective self-defence in Article of 51 of the Charter of the United Nations. *American Journal of International Law*, 41, pp.872.

Lauterpacht, H. (1933) *The function of law in international community*. Oxford: Claredon Press.

League of Nations (1919) Covenant of the League of Nations.

Lobel, J. (1999) The use of force to respond to terrorists attack: The bombing of Sudan and Afghanistan. *Yale Journal of International Law*, 24, pp.537–57.

McCormack, T. (1991) Anticipatory self-defence in the legislative history of the United Nations history. *Israel Law Review*, 25(1), pp.1–41.

McDougal, M. (1963) The Soviet-Cuban quarantine and self-defense. *American Journal of International Law*, 57, pp.597–604.

McDougal, M. and Feliciano, F. (1961) *Law and minimum world public order: The legal regulation of international coercion*. New Haven: Yale University Press.

Murphy, S. (2002) Terrorism and the concept of "armed attack" in Article 51 of the U.N. Charter, *Harvard International Law Journal*, 43, pp.41–51.

O'Boyle, F. (1987) Military responses to terrorism. *American Society of International Law Proceedings*, 81, pp.287–96.

O'Brien, W. (1990) Reprisals, deterrence and self-defence in counterterror operations. *Virginia Journal of International Law*, 30, pp.421–79.

O'Connell, M. (2002) The myth of preemptive self-defence. ASIL Task Force on Terrorism. pp.1–22. Available at: http://www.asil.org/taskforce/oconnell.pdf.

Paust, J. (2004) Post-9/11 overreaction and fallacies regarding war and defence, Guantanamo, the status of persons, treatment, judicial review of detention, and due process in military commissions. *Notre Dame Law Review*, 79, pp.1335–64.

———. (2002) Use of armed force against terrorists in Afghanistan, Iraq and beyond. *Cornell International Law Journal*, 35, pp.533–57.

Reisman, M. (2003) Self-defence in an age of terrorism. *American Society of International Law Proceedings*, 97, pp.141–52.

———. (1991) Allocating competences to use coercion in the post-cold world order: Practices, conditions, and prospects. *In* Damrosch, F. and Scheffer, D. (eds.) *Law and Force in the New International Order*. Boulder, San Francisco, Oxford: Westview Press.

———. (1985) Criteria for the lawful use of force in international law. *Yale Journal of International Law*, 10, pp.279–85.

Roberts, G. (1987) Self-help in combating state-sponsored terrorism: self-defense and peacetime reprisal. *Case W. Res. Journal of International Law*, 19, pp.243–94.

Rogers, A. P. V. (2001) Terrorism and the law of war: September 11 and its aftermath. *Crimes of War Project*. Available at: http://www.crimesofwar.org/expert/attack-apv.html.

Rostow, E. (1991) Until what? Enforcement action or collective self-defence. *American Journal of International Law*, 85, pp.506–16.

Rowles, J. (1987) Military responses to terrorism. *American Society of International Law Proceedings*, 81, pp.307–17.

Sapiro, M. (2003) Iraq: The shifting sands of pre-emptive self-defence. *American Journal of International Law*, 97, pp.599–607.

Schachter, O. (1991) Authorised uses of force by the United Nations and regional organisations. I*n* Damrosch, F. and Scheffer, D. (eds.) *Law and force in the New International Order*. Boulder, San Francisco, Oxford Westview Press.

———. (1989) The extra territorial use of force against terrorists. *Houston Journal of International Law*. 11, pp.309–16.

———. (1987) Self-judging self-defence. *Case Western Reserve Journal of International Law*, 19, pp.121–27.

———. (1986) "In Defence of International Use of Force" *University of Chicago Law Review*. 53 pp.113–46.

———. (1984) The right of states to use armed force. *Michigan Law Review*, 82, pp.1620–46.

Security Council (2001) Resolution 1373. September 28.

——— (2001) Resolution 1368. September 12.

Sofaer, A. (2003) On the necessity of pre-emption. *European Journal of International Law* 4(2):209–26.

———. (1989) "Terrorism, the law and the national defence. *Military Law Review*, 95, pp.89–123.

Taft and Buchwald (2003) Pre-emption, Iraq and international law. *American Journal of International Law*, 97, pp.557–63.

Townsend, G. (1997) State responsibility for acts of de facto agents. *Arizona Journal of International and Comparative Law*, 14, pp.635–78.

Travalio, G. (2000) Terrorism, international law, and the use of military force. *Wisconsin International Law Journal*, 18, pp.145–91.

United Nations (1945) The Charter of the United Nations.

United States (2006) The national security strategy of the United States of America. Available at: http://www.whitehouse.gov/nsc/nss/2006/nss2006.pdf.

——— (2002) The national security strategy of the United States of America. Available at: http://www.whitehouse.gov/nsc/nss.html.

Waldock, C. (1952) The regulation of the use of force by individual states in international law. *Recueil Des Cours*, Vol. II, pp.451–515.

Webster, D. (1840–41) Letters from U.S. secretary of State Daniel Webster to *British Minister Mr. Fox, 29 British and Foreign Papers*, pp.1129, 1137–38.

Wedgwood, R. (2003) The fall of Saddam Hussein: Security Council mandates and pre-emptive self-defense. *American Journal of International Law*, 97, pp.576–85.

———. (1999) Responding to terrorism: The strikes against Bin Laden. *Yale Journal of International Law*, 24, pp.559–79.

Yoo, J. (2004) Using force. *The University of Chicago Law Review*, 71(3), pp.729–97.

CHAPTER 5

Legality of Iraq Invasion

The 2003 invasion of Iraq had divided world opinion from the very beginning. The war has strong supporters as well as serious and articulate critics. A considerable scholarship is in the making on the different aspects of invasion of Iraq. Philosophers tend to analyze it from the Judo-Christian theory of "just war" perspective, whereas political scientists look at its political and strategic fallout. Economists focus on the economic costs of the war, while human rights breaches have outraged the prophets of human rights. Some Muslims believe or are made to believe that it is a crusade against Islam, that is, an Anglo-American led neo-imperialism. Hence, their estimation is steeped in religious colors. On the legal aspect of the Iraq invasion, international lawyers remain divided. Views range from strong support to strong opposition. However, it seems from the survey of available literature that those who support the invasion of Iraq are either on the payroll of Anglo-American administrations or politically aligned with them. The great majority of independent international lawyers view, as the rest of this chapter shows, the invasion as illegal.

This chapter examines two aspects of the 2003 invasion of Iraq. First, the evaluation of evidence regarding Iraq's weapons of mass destruction (WMD). The focus, however, is on the prewar intelligence—before March 19, 2003—in order to find out whether there was clear and convincing evidence to justify the use of force against Iraq. What happened after the fact is not within the remit of this chapter. Second, the aim is to evaluate the validity of Anglo-American "revival theory": The power to use force against Iraq was revived because the reports of UN weapons inspectors suggest that Iraq is not cooperating. The chapter also argues that whatever the technical legal ground for invasion was, the overall argument was and is self-defense, as Iraq was considered a serious threat to the security of Anglo-Americans and their allies.

5.1 Background to Invasion

On August 2, 1990, the Iraqi forces stormed into Kuwait and captured it quickly. The Security Council in resolution 660 (1990) condemned the invasion and demanded that "Iraq withdraw immediately and unconditionally all its forces to the positions in which they were located on 1 August 1990." The exiled government of Kuwait in Saudi Arabia asked the international community to assist in repelling Iraqi troops (Taft and Buchwald, 2003). The United States claimed that forces have been deployed in the region at the requests of the governments in the region (UN Doc. S/21492, 1990). In November 1990, the Security Council (resolution 678) provided one "final opportunity" to Iraq to withdraw forces from Kuwait on or before January 15, 1991. The Security Council also authorized:

> Member States [to] cooperate . . . with the Government of Kuwait . . . to use all necessary means to uphold and implement resolution 660 (1990) and all subsequent relevant resolutions and to restore international peace and security in the area.

Iraq ignored the Security Council's deadline and the coalition forces launched attacks on Iraqi troops on January 16, 1991. Soon after Kuwait was liberated, hostilities were suspended by resolution 686 (1991), and resolution 687 (1991) finally effected a cease-fire among Iraq, Kuwait, and member states cooperating with Kuwait. The main terms of that ceasefire were that Iraq must: destroy its chemical and biological weapons and ballistic missiles and agree to on-site inspections; not use, develop, construct, or acquire WMD and their delivery systems; not acquire or develop nuclear weapons or nuclear-weapons-usable material or components; and accept on-site inspection and destroy nuclear-related weapons or materials (resolution 687, paragraph 8). Resolution 687 (paragraph 34) confirms that the Security Council "remain seized of the matter and to take such further steps as may be required for the implementation of the present resolution and to secure peace and security in the area." Inspections were carried out until 1998 but then suspended because of Iraq's lack of cooperation and the dissipation of the interest of the international community (see Warbrick, 1991). Iraq became the focus of attention once again after September 11, 2001. President George W. Bush (January 29, 2002) branded Iraq as a part of the "axis of evil." In November 2002, the Security Council adopted resolution 1441, which found Iraq in "material breach" of its international obligations under a number of previous resolutions. The Security Council demanded immediate cooperation with the newly established enhanced inspection regime under resolution 1441. Otherwise, "serious consequences" would have to follow. It is against this backdrop that we need to address issues of WMD and the legality of invasion 2003.

5.2 Evidence of WMD

The United States and the United Kingdom made strong claims that Iraq possessed and was developing WMD in violation of cease-fire terms agreed in the Security Council resolution 687. Before we examine evidence regarding Iraq's WMD program as presented by the Anglo-Americans, it is important to outline what standard of appraisal of evidence might apply.

5.2.1 Clear and Convincing Evidence

There are two main standards of evidential appraisal. In civil law, the case is decided on the basis of "balance of probabilities" standard. In criminal law, a case is decided on the basis of "beyond reasonable doubt" standard. Despite over one hundred years of international adjudication and sixty years of Security Council fact-finding, we cannot point to any well-established set of rules governing evidence in international law in general or in the case of self-defense in particular (O'Connell, 2002:2). Questions involving the standards and mechanisms for assessing complicated factual inquiries are generally not accorded the same treatment given by the legal academy to the more abstract issues involved in defining relevant international law standards. Unfortunately, international incidents generally involve disputed issues of fact, and, in the absence of an international judicial or other centralised fact-finding mechanism, the *ad hoc* manner in which nations evaluate factual claims is often decisive (Lobel, 1999:538). Apart from the two standards previously outlined, the greater weight of authority favors a "clear and convincing" standard in cases of armed force to justify the use of force in self-defense: The party making the claim must show "clear and convincing" evidence that the circumstances warrant the use of force (O'Connell, 2002:3). The international authority for this standard consists of several decisions of international courts and tribunals, including the implicit standard found in the International Court of Justice's decision on the use of force in the *Nicaragua* case (1986) and in the opinion of international lawyers (O'Connell, 2002:3; see also *Democratic Republic of Congo* case, 2005).

In the case of *Nicaragua* (1986), paragraph 110), the International Court of Justice did not enunciate a standard but referred to "sufficient proof." "By implication this means a standard of convincing evidence. The judgement certainly does not reveal that the International Court of Justice required proof beyond a reasonable doubt. On the other hand, in rejecting some of Nicaragua's claims, the Court appeared to require more than a mere preponderance of the evidence"(O'Connell, 2002:4). In an arbitration between the United States and Canada (cited in O'Connell, 2002) where the United States claimed that Canada was responsible for environmental damage, it was found that "no State has the right to use or permit the use of its territory in a manner as to cause injury . . . to the territory of another, when the case is of serious consequence and the injury is established by clear and convincing evidence." Greenwood (1987:935) argues for a "sufficiently convincing" evidence standard.

> Given the potential for abuse of the right of national self-defense, international law must require that a nation meet a clear and stringent evidentiary standard designed to assure the world community that an ongoing terrorist attack is in fact occurring before the attacked nation responds with force. Such a principle is the clear import of the International Court of Justice's decision in Nicaragua v. United States. (Lobel, 1999:547)

The decisions of different adjudicating bodies and views of international lawyers reflect that to use force against a sovereign nation (including non-state actors), the "clear and convincing" evidence standard must be used. The principles of justice and reason demand that the use of force, which invariably results in violence and loss of life and property, must be based on verifiable, clear, and convincing evidence. The use of force in self-defense (article 51) is an exception to the Charter's proscription on the use of force (article 2[4]), and to rely on this exception, one must provide evidence, which is verifiable, clear, and seems convincing to the international community, international organizations, and individuals.

5.2.2 United States' Evidence on WMD

Before the invasion of Iraq in 2003, Anglo-Americans made strong claims that intelligence suggested that Iraq possessed and was developing nuclear weapons and WMD and supporting terrorist organizations, such as Al-Qaeda. President Bush (March 17, 2003) said to his nation:

> Intelligence gathered by this and other governments leaves no doubt that the Iraq regime continues to possess and conceal some of the most lethal weapons

> ever devised. This regime has already used weapons of mass destruction against Iraq's neighbors and against Iraq's people. . . . And it has aided, trained and harbored terrorists, including operatives of al Qaeda. The danger is clear: using chemical, biological or, one day, nuclear weapons, obtained with the help of Iraq, the terrorists could fulfil their stated ambitions and kill thousands or hundreds of thousands of innocent people in our country, or any other. . . . We are now acting because the risks of inaction would be far greater. In one year, or five years, the power of Iraq to inflict harm on all free nations would be multiplied many times over. With these capabilities, Saddam Hussein and his terrorist allies could choose the moment of deadly conflict when they are strongest. We choose to meet that threat now, where it arises, before it can appear suddenly in our skies and cities.

Vice president Dick Cheney (September 8, 2002) said that "we know, with absolute certainty, that [Saddam] is using his procurement system to acquire the equipment he needs in order to enrich uranium to build nuclear weapon." Former Secretary of State Colin Powell said (September 8, 2002): "There is no doubt that he has chemical weapons stocks"). Powell (February 5, 2003) made similar claims in the Security Council and shared U.S. evidence with other members. He told the Security Council that "leaving Saddam Hussein in possession of weapons of mass destruction for a few more months or years is not an option, not in a post-September 11th world."

The statements of the president, vice president, and secretary of state reflect clearly that Iraq had nuclear weapons and WMD. They are the ones who had complete access to intelligence, or it might be more appropriate to say that the intelligence community worked at their behest. They had first-hand knowledge of the evidence and, according to them, the prewar evidence against Iraq was *absolute* and without *doubt*.

5.2.3 United Kingdom's Evidence on WMD

The United Kingdom also made a strong claim that Iraq possesses and is developing WMD. In his foreword to the *Iraq's Weapons of Mass Destruction: The Assessment of the British Government* September 2002 dossier, former Prime Minister Tony Blair wrote:

> In recent months, I have been increasingly alarmed by the evidence from inside Iraq that . . . Hussein is continuing to develop WMD, and with them the ability to inflict real damage upon the region, and the stability of the world . . . I and other Ministers have been briefed in detail on the intelligence and are satisfied as to its authority. . . . What I believe the assessed intelligence has

> established beyond doubt is that Saddam has continued to produce chemical and biological weapons, that he continues in his efforts to develop nuclear weapons, and that he has been able to extend the range of his ballistic missile programme. . . . I am in no doubt that the threat is serious and current, that he has made progress on WMD, and that he has to be stopped. . . . And the document discloses that his military planning allows for some of the WMD to be ready within 45 minutes of an order to use them. . . . The threat posed to international peace and security, when WMD are in the hands of a brutal and aggressive regime like Saddam's, is real.

On March 18, 2003, former Prime Minster Blair said to the House of Commons "[Saddam's] weapons of mass destruction programme is active, detailed and growing. . . . The intelligence picture that they paint is one accumulated over the last four years. It is extensive, detailed, and authoritative." Former Prime Minister Blair told Parliament and his nation that there is no doubt that Iraq is developing nuclear weapons and WMD. The intelligence is detailed and his Cabinet is satisfied of its probity, he claimed. "Iraq continues to deny it has any WMD, though no serious intelligence service anywhere in the world believes them" (Blair, March 18, 2003). The same claim was echoed by Former British Foreign Secretary, Jack Straw, in the Security Council on February 5, 2003.

5.2.4 Negation of the United States' Evidence

After invading Iraq and the ensuing frustration in finding WMD, demands for reassessing the prewar intelligence on Iraq's WMD resonated from different quarters. This demand was made very strongly in the United States and the United Kingdom. In June 2003, the United States' Senate Select Committee on Intelligence (hereinafter, Committee on Intelligence) began a formal review of the United States' intelligence into the existence of Iraq's weapons of mass destruction, Iraq's ties with terrorist groups, and so on. In the process of the review, the Committee on Intelligence requested that the White House provide Presidential Daily Briefs relevant to Iraq's weapons of mass destruction and links to terrorist groups but the White House turned down the request. "Without examining these documents [Presidential Daily Briefs], the Committee is unable to determine fully whether Intelligence Community judgements were properly disseminated to policy makers in the executive branch" (Committee on Intelligence, 2004:3). On the basis of whatever evidence was made available to it, the Committee on Intelligence (2004) reached the following conclusions regarding prewar intelligence:

> Most of the major key judgments in the Intelligence Community's October 2002 National Intelligence Estimate (NIE), Iraq's Continuing Programs for Weapons of Mass Destruction, either overstated, or were not supported by, the underlying intelligence reporting. A series of failures, particularly in analytic trade craft, led to the mischaracterization of the intelligence. (paragraph 14)
>
> The Intelligence Community (IC) suffered from a collective presumption that Iraq had an active and growing weapons of mass destruction (WNW) program. This "group think" dynamic led Intelligence Community analysts, collectors and managers to both interpret ambiguous evidence as conclusively indicative of a WMD program as well as ignore or minimize evidence that Iraq did not have active and expanding weapons of mass destruction programs. This presumption was so strong that formalized IC mechanisms established to challenge assumptions and group think were not utilized. (paragraph 18)
>
> The Committee found significant shortcomings in almost every aspect of the Intelligence Community's human intelligence collection efforts against Iraq's weapons of mass destruction activities, in particular that the Community had no sources collecting against weapons of mass destruction in Iraq after 1998. (paragraph 24)
>
> The Central Intelligence Agency (CIA), in several significant instances, abused its unique position in the Intelligence Community, particularly in terms of information sharing, to the detriment of the Intelligence Community's prewar analysis concerning Iraq's weapons of mass destruction programs. (paragraph 27)

President Bush constituted a Commission on the Intelligence Capabilities of the United States Regarding Weapons of Mass Destruction (Silberman-Robb Commission) in February 2004. The Commission (March 31, 2005) reported the following to the president.

> On the brink of war, and in front of the whole world, the United States government asserted that Saddam Hussein had reconstituted his nuclear weapons program, had biological weapons and mobile biological weapon production facilities, and had stockpiled and was producing chemical weapons. All of this was based on the assessments of the U.S. Intelligence Community And not one bit of it could be confirmed when the war was over. . . . Much of what they [intelligence agencies] did collect was either worthless or misleading [and] . . . intelligence analysts were too wedded to their assumptions about Saddam's intentions.

In a transmittal letter, the authors of the report noted in very naked terms: "We conclude that the Intelligence Community was dead wrong in almost all of its pre-war judgments about Iraq's weapons of mass destruction."

In his comprehensive report of September 30, 2004 on the context and analysis of Iraq Survey Group findings, Charles Duelfer, Special Advisor to the Director of Central Intelligence, concluded:

> *From the evidence available through the actions and statements of a range of Iraqis, it seems clear that the guiding theme for WMD was to sustain the intellectual capacity. . . . [And] . . . as resources became available and the constraints of sanctions decayed, there was a direct expansion of activity that would have the effect of supporting future WMD reconstitution.* (emphasis in original)

The declassified National Intelligence Estimate (NIE), October 2002 contained forty distinct caveats or conditions usually dropped by officials (Carnegie Endowment for International Peace, 2004:17). Two key intelligence offices disputed the NIE nuclear assessments (see Carnegie Endowment for International Peace, 2004:22).

After examining the conclusions of different U.S. commissions and the Committee on Intelligence, the following conclusions may be drawn. First, the intelligence community either overstated or distorted the prewar intelligence on Iraq's WMD. The CIA abused its power by either suppressing or fabricating evidence. The case of uranium transaction from Niger, discussed later in this chapter, is a case in point. The White House seemed to be comfortable (if not complicit) with this role for the CIA and may be suspected of hiding something because it turned down the request of the Committee on Intelligence to provide it with the Presidential Daily Briefs on Iraq's WMD. Second, the caveats and warnings of the intelligence reports were deliberately suppressed. The disputed assessments within intelligence reports were either ignored or presented as authoritative and absolute. Third, the intelligence community turned presumption into conviction and remained wedded to the idea that Saddam had the intention to develop WMD. Before the invasion, Iraq had neither WMD nor the capacity to build WMD but only had the intention to do so when possible. The suggestion that Iraq had used chemical weapons against Kurds in the past and must have had them before the invasion in 2003 is not tenable, because Iraq's weapons program was "neutralised" by the UN inspectors in 1998 (ElBaradei, February 14, 2003). The grand edifice of Iraq's WMD was raised on the presumption of intention, not on clear and convincing evidence.

5.2.5 Negation of the United Kingdom's Evidence

Coming under pressure from the public after chaos and the killings of soldiers in Iraq, in February 2003 the British government set up an independent commission under the headship of Lord Butler to review the collection, assessment, and use of intelligence leading to the invasion of Iraq. Lord Butler's commission concluded that "there was limited intelligence suggesting Iraqi attempts to expand its missile programme, to lay the foundations of a revived nuclear programme, and to develop facilities which could be used for chemical and biological programmes" (July 14, 2004, paragraph 19). The commission also said (paraghraph 24):

> During the spring and summer of 2002 . . . further intelligence came in and the tone of JIC [Joint Intelligence Committee] judgements became firmer but successive JIC assessements warned that the intelligence remained limited. . . . In translating material to the dossier [Govt. September 2002 dossier outlining the evidence of Iraq's WMD], warnings in the JIC assessments were lost about the limited intelligence base on which some aspects of these assessments were being made. . . . It was a serious weakness that the JIC's warning on the limitations of the intelligence were not made sufficiently clear in the dossier.

The commission further concluded (parapgraph 32):

> The [government's] report that [claims that] Saddam could deploy chemical and biological weapons within 45 minutes . . . was unclear and the JIC should not have included it in this form. . . . Mobile laboratories have been found in Iraq but do not match the ones in the intelligence reports which were relied on for evidence of Iraq's production of biological agent. Moreover, we now know the one described by the source would not have been capable of producing *stocks* of such agent.

Former British Foreign Secretary, Robin Cook (Guardian, 18 June 2003) said:

> I think it would be fair to say there was a selection of evidence to support a conclusion. I fear we got into a position in which the intelligence was not being used to inform and shape policy, but to shape policy that was already settled.

The conclusions of Butler's report suggest that the intelligence agencies reported to the government that evidence on Iraq's WMD is limited, which the government ignored when making a case for war before the public. The government also dropped all warnings and caveats about the uncertainity of evidence and presented it as beyond doubt, extensive, and authoritative. The evidence was presentated in much stronger and firmer terms, claiming that WMD may be moblized within forty five miuntes. I fully agree with Lord Butler when he said that more burden was placed on evidence than it could bear. It reflects deliberate efforts on the part of the government of embellishing and screening the evidnece.

5.2.6 United Nations' Evidence on WMD

Under resolution 1441, the Security Council set up an enhanced inspection regime. The inspectors resumed inspection on November 27, 2002. The Director General of International Atomic Energy Agency (hereinafter, IAEA), ElBaradei, reported on February 14, 2003:

> The IAEA concluded, by December 1998, that it had neutralized Iraq's past nuclear programme and that, therefore, there were no unresolved disarmament issues left at that time. . . . We have to date found no evidence of ongoing prohibited nuclear or nuclear related activities in Iraq. However, as I have just indicated, a number of issues are still under investigation and we are not yet in a position to reach a conclusion about them.

On March 7, 2003, few days before invading Iraq, ElBaradei reported to the Security Council that the inspection is moving forward:

> There is no indication of resumed nuclear activities in those buildings that were identified through the use of satellite imagery as being reconstructed or newly erected since 1998, nor any indication of nuclear-related prohibited activities at any inspected sites.
>
> There is no indication that Iraq has attempted to import uranium since 1990.
>
> There is no indication that Iraq has attempted to import aluminum tubes for use in centrifuge enrichment. Moreover, even had Iraq pursued such a plan, it would have encountered practical difficulties in manufacturing centrifuges out of the aluminium tubes in question.
>
> Although we are still reviewing issues related to magnets and magnet production, there is no indication to date that Iraq imported magnets for use in a centrifuge enrichment programme.

In the same report, ElBaradei informed the Security Council:

> Based on thorough analysis, the IAEA has concluded, with the concurrence of outside experts, that these documents—which formed the basis for the reports of recent uranium transactions between Iraq and Niger—are in fact not authentic. We have therefore concluded that these specific allegations are unfounded.

The prewar evidence gathered by the IAEA points toward the same conclusion: There was no evidence of nuclear weapons and WMD until the date of report. However, it did say that some issues were under investigation and needed more time. The report indicated that there was no evidence of prohibited nuclear activities so far. The result of further investigation was uncertain as to whether Iraq had or was developing WMD. Only time could tell, which was denied to inspectors as the invasion began on March 19, 2003. Hans Blix (2004:5) says that "others [except the US and the UK] in the Security Council thought the process of inspection required more time." The sum total of the IAEA inspection is that there was no evidence of WMD before the invasion, although some issues were under investigation requiring more time. One of the former UN senior weapons inspectors, Scott Ritter, addressed the Iraqi Parliament on September 8, 2002:

> The rhetoric of fear that is disseminated by my government and others has not to date been backed up by hard facts that substantiate any allegations that Iraq is today in possession of weapons of mass destruction or has links to terror groups responsible for attacking the United States. Void of such facts, all we have is speculation.

In the final analysis on the prewar evidence of Iraq's WMD, it may be concluded that there was no clear and convincing evidence that Iraq had or was developing WMD. The claims of the United States and the United Kingdom administrations were based on deliberately distorted (suppressing caveats and warnings contained in intelligence reports), and in some cases the United States attempted to fabricate evidence. For instance, IAEA concluded that the documents provided by the United States showing uranium transactions between Iraq and Niger "are in fact not authentic" (ElBaradei, March 7, 2003). The "Bush administration passed on forged documents to U.N. weapons inspectors to support allegations that Iraq had sought uranium from the African nation of Niger" (see Senator Rockefeller, July 30, 2006). On July 7, 2004, the United States Intelligence Committee concluded that "the Central Intelligence Agency's (CIA) comments and assessments about the Iraq-Niger uranium reporting were inconsistent and, at times contradictory." President Bush "was thinking of flying U2 reconnaissance aircraft with fighter cover over Iraq, painted in UN colours. If Saddam fired on them, he would be in breach" (Gibbon, February 2, 2006). Former Prime Minister Blair made an unwarranted claim in his foreword to the 2002 dossier on Iraq's WMD that Iraq's WMD might be deployed within forty-five minutes, which Lord Butler (July 14, 2004, paragraph 32) said should not have been inserted. The intelligence agencies never advised the former Prime Minister Blair about forty-five-minute deployment time.

The politicians in the United States and the United Kingdom seem to blame the intelligence agencies for flaws or intelligence failures. That does not seem to be the case, however. On the contrary, both the United States' and the United Kingdom's intelligence agencies warned that intelligence is limited and added several caveats and warnings. Experts within the intelligence services seriously disputed some intelligence assessments. In fact, the administrations in two countries suppressed the warnings and caveats and presented the evidence as "absolute[ly] certain" and "without doubt" to their nations and the world at large. It must be frankly admitted that the intelligence reports suffered from serious flaws but the intelligence agencies in both countries never claimed that the evidence was clear and convincing. It seems that conscious efforts were made by both administrations to make a stronger case for invading Iraq. In order to do so, they went to the extent to suppress disputed aspect of evidence. In fact, they did not stop there. They fabricated evidence, such as the British forty-five minutes claim in what is known as the September dossier and Niger-Iraq uranium deal. The IAEA also never reported that there was evidence of WMD development in Iraq. On the contrary, ElBaradei reported that there was no such evidence so far and some issues were under investigation. It simply means that IAEA had not found evidence but did not rule out that there will be no such evidence had investigation been allowed to continue.

President Bush (December 14, 2005) admitted that "much of the intelligence turned out to be wrong. As President, I'm responsible for the decision to go into Iraq." Former Prime Minister Blair (July 14, 2004) also admitted that the intelligence on WMD was wrong and he took full responsibility. There are two important issues involved here. First, shifting the blame to the intelligence community in the United States and the United Kingdom might save the faces of administrations and take political pressure off them at domestic level. The tactic, however, would not stand the test of international law. Intelligence agencies are state organs and, according to international law, a state is responsible for the actions of its organs. This is an effective principle of international law (see Crawford, 2003). For the purpose of international law, it is irrelevant who got it wrong: President Bush, CIA, former Prime Minister Blair, or MI6. Second, the admissions of both President Bush and former Prime Minister Blair have confessional value for any future trial (of which there is no possibility under the current world order) for crime of aggression, violating humanitarian law, and crime against humanity. President Bush and former Prime Minister Blair may get out of the political fog over Iraq by shifting the blame to intelligence failures, but that would not save them if they ever came to face the test of international law. Another issue is the importance of Iraq's intention to develop WMD. The intelligence of the United States strongly suggests that Saddam has the intention to develop nuclear weapons and WMD. Let us accept, without further independent evidence, this was the case. The mere intention to develop WMD has no value, legally speaking. First, international law does not allow the use of force against a state if it has the intention to develop WMD (see Warbrick, October 30, 2002). Second, if Saddam was harboring the intention of acquiring WMD, Iraq had no capacity to develop WMD, as ElBaradei reported on March 7. 2003.

As indicated above, both President Bush and former Prime Minister Blair admitted, after the invasion, that there were no WMD in Iraq. The most significant question, however, is whether they had the knowledge before the invasion that Iraq did not possess WMD. The evidence, which was available to President Bush and former Prime Minister Blair before the invasion and to the public only after the invasion, suggests that both of them knew well before the invasion that Iraq did not possess WMD. The evidence also points toward the conclusion that selective evidence was used and, in some cases, overstated to achieve their policy goal: the use of military force to change the unwanted regime in Baghdad. Based on the leaked Manning's memo (2002), the *Washington Post* (May 13, 2005:A18) reported that seven months before the invasion of Iraq, the head of the British foreign intelligence (MI6, Richard Dearlove) informed former Prime Minister Blair that President Bush wanted to topple Saddam by military action and warned that, in Washington, intelligence was "being fixed around the policy." Former Prime Minister Blair privately conceded two weeks before the invasion of Iraq that Saddam did not possess any usable weapons of mass destruction. John Scarlett, Chairman of the Joint Intelligence Committee of the United Kingdom, also "assented" that Saddam had no such weapons (Cook, October 5, 2003). Former Secretary Cook (October 5, 2003) said that the government misled the House of Commons and asked members of Parliament to vote for war on a "false prospectus." The man who told the world on behalf of the United States, former Secretary Powell, admitted (September 8, 2005) that "his speech to the United Nations [Security Council on 5 February 2003] accusing Iraq of harbouring weapons of mass destruction was a 'blot' on his record."

> My speculation . . . is that the Bush administration decided in the summer of 2002 . . . it should be ready to preemptivly to strike any identified enemy, which it feared might pose a threat to the U.S. It saw Saddam Hussien as personifying evil . . . [and] having declared war on terrorism, needed to eliminate this perceived threat well before the next presidential election. (Blix, 2004:12)

President Bush and former Prime Minister Blair knew that Iraq did not possess WMD, but they posed before the international community that Iraq had WMD, had link with Al-Qaeda, and posed a serious threat the Anglo-American security. The United States planned regime change in Iraq long before the invasion in 2003. The Congress of the United States passed on January 27, 1998 the "Iraq Liberation Act 1998." The act says: "It should be the policy of the United States to support efforts to remove the regime headed by Saddam Hussein from power in Iraq and to promote the emergence of a democratic government to replace that regime."

5.3 The Revival Theory

The thrust of the "revival theory" is that resolution 678 authorized the use of force against Iraq. Resolution 687 suspended, not terminated, that authority as a cease-fire agreement reached among Iraq, Kuwait, and nations that cooperated with Kuwait. Iraq did not fulfil her obligations under resolution 687. Resolution 1441 found Iraq in "material breach" and, therefore the authority to use force against Iraq, contained in resolution 678, is revived. The Anglo-Americans argued that coalition forces are authorized to use force to disarm Iraq without further Security Council resolutions. "Under Resolutions 678 and 687—both still in effect—the United States and our allies are authorized to use force in ridding Iraq of weapons of mass destruction" (Bush, March 17, 2003). Former Prime Minister Blair (March 18, 2003) told the House of Commons: "Iraq having failed to comply and Iraq being at the time of Resolution 1441 and continuing to be in material breach, the authority to use force under Resolution 678 has revived and so continues today."

To reach a plausible interpretation, we need a careful examination of the language of resolutions 678, 686, 687, and 1441 and the attending political circumstances of those times. The four main questions that need to be answered are: (a) Did Iraq violate the cease-fire terms?; (b) Did resolution 687 suspend or terminate resolution 678?; (c) Did resolution 1441 authorize the automatic use of force?; and (d) If not, did customary law of armed conflict authorize, under those circumstances, the resumption of hostilities?

5.3.1 Did Iraq Violate the Cease-fire Agreement?

On November 8, 2002, the Security Council adopted resolution 1441 (paragraph 1) deciding that "Iraq has been and remains in material breach of its obligations under relevant resolutions, including resolution 687 (1991), in particular through Iraq's failure to cooperate with United Nations inspectors and the IAEA, and to complete the actions required under paragraphs 8 to 13 of resolution 687 (1991)." Resolution 1441 (paragraph 2) set up "an enhanced inspection regime with the aim of bringing to full and verified completion the disarmament process established by resolution 687 (1991) and subsequent resolutions." Paragraph 4 says that any "false statements or omissions . . . [or] failure by Iraq at any time to comply with, and cooperate fully in the implementation of this resolution shall constitute a 'further material breach' of Iraq's obligations and will be reported to the Council for assessment in accordance with paragraphs 11 and 12 below." Paragraph 11 directs "the Executive Chairman of UNMOVIC and the Director-General of the IAEA to report immediately to the Council any interference by Iraq with inspection activities, as well as any failure by Iraq to comply with its disarmament obligations." Paragraph 12 decides "to convene immediately upon receipt of a report in accordance with paragraphs 4 or 11 above, in order to consider the situation and the need for full compliance with all of the relevant Council resolutions in order to secure international peace and security." Resolution 1441 (paragraph 2) afforded Iraq "a final opportunity to comply with its disarmament obligations" otherwise "serious consequences as a result of its continued violations of its obligations" (paragraph 13) would follow. The Security Council decided "to remain seized of the matter" (paragraph 12).

It is clear that resolution 1441 obligated the inspectors to report Iraq's noncompliance to the Security Council, and it is the responsibility of the Security Council to make an "assessment" and "consider the situation" and how full compliance may be achieved. The United States argues that any member state can report Iraq's noncompliance to the Security Council (Negroponte, November 8, 2002). This view, however, is not persuasive when we read the text of resolution 1441. The language used in operative paragraphs 4, 11, and 12 is plain and simple: Iraq is required to cooperate unconditionally with the enhanced inspection regime and the inspectors would report any noncompliance to the Security Council for assessment. Logically speaking, the Security Council set up the inspection regime, so it is expected that the inspectors will report to the same body unless expressly provided otherwise. The previous practice of the Security Council points to the following interpretation: Inspectors, not member states, can report Iraq's noncompliance to the Security Council.

Now let us see what the inspection regime's different reports, from November 8, 2002 to March 19, 2003, suggest. The two last reports, March 7, 2003, of Dr. Hans Blix and Dr. Mohamed ElBaradei need careful examination. On February 14, 2003, ElBaradei reported that "the Agency's inspection activities had moved well beyond the 'reconnaissance phase' . . . into the 'investigative phase'." On inspections, ElBaradei (March 7, 2003) reported that "the IAEA has now conducted a total of 218 nuclear inspections at 141 sites, including 21 that had not been inspected before. In addition, IAEA experts have taken part in many joint UNMOVIC-IAEA inspections." Individuals are consenting to interviews without escorts and tape recorders. "In the last few weeks, Iraq has provided a considerable volume of documentation relevant to the issues I reported earlier as being of particular concern, including Iraq's efforts to procure aluminium tubes, its attempted procurement of magnets and magnet production capabilities, and its reported attempt to import uranium" (ElBaradei, March 7, 2003).

> In conclusion, I am able to report today that, in the area of nuclear weapons . . . inspections in Iraq are moving forward. Since the resumption of inspections . . . the IAEA has made important progress in identifying what nuclear-related capabilities remain in Iraq, and in its assessment of whether Iraq has made any efforts to revive its past nuclear programme during the intervening four years since inspections were brought to a halt. (ElBaradei, March 7, 2003)

The IAEA will continue further investigation and to scrutinise these issues, ElBaradei said.

Dr Hans Blix (March 7, 2003) reported to the Security Council that "in matters relating to process, notably prompt access to sites, we have faced relatively few difficulties and certainly much less than those that were faced by UNSCOM in the period 1991 to 1998." "Initial difficulties raised by the Iraqi side about helicopters and aerial surveillance planes operating in the no-fly zones were overcome at this juncture we are able to perform professional no-notice inspections all over Iraq and to increase aerial surveillance" (Blix, March 7, 2003).

It is obvious that, while the numerous initiatives, which are now taken by the Iraqi side with a view to resolving some long-standing open disarmament issues, can be seen as "active," or even "proactive," these initiatives 3–4 months into the new resolution cannot be said to constitute "immediate" cooperation. They are nevertheless welcome and UNMOVIC is responding to them in the hope of solving presently unresolved disarmament issues. While cooperation can and is to be immediate, disarmament and at any rate the verification of it cannot be instant. Even with a proactive Iraqi attitude it would still take some time to verify sites and items, analyze documents, interview relevant persons, and draw conclusions. It would not take years, nor weeks, but months (Blix, March 7, 2003).

The United States (Department of State, March 10, 2003) was quick to conclude from these reports that "Iraq and its leadership have pursued a consistent strategy of concealing its weapons of mass destruction and deceiving inspectors in direct violation of its international obligations." "UNMOVIC's document lays bare that Iraq's strategy today has not changed. Inspectors are faced with deception, concealment and changing stories" (Department of State, March 10, 2003). Former Prime Minister Blair (March 18, 2003) said: "Iraq has not co-operated actively, unconditionally and immediately with the weapons inspectors, and has rejected the final opportunity to comply and is in further material breach of its obligations under successive mandatory UN Security Council Resolutions."

However, careful analysis of these reports reflects cooperation rather than noncooperation. The cooperation does not seem to be immediate and unconditional but, as ElBaradei and Blix noted, there was definitely progress and the investigation was moving forward. Both reports indicate that further time was required to complete the process of disarmament. These reports end on positive notes, expecting further progress. The inspectors were tasked to report to the Security Council, but neither Blix nor ElBaradei reported that the inspection regime was not moving forward. It is admitted that some issues of concern still needed investigation and clear answers, but both Blix and ElBaradei, were convinced that further inspections would resolve those issues. Time was of the essence; Blix indicated that even if Iraq was actively cooperating, more time was required to make final conclusions on Iraq's WMD. Further investigation became crucial when the inspectors reported progress and, most significantly, when ElBaradei reported that so far no evidence of nuclear weapons had been found. These reports cast serious doubt on the United States and the United Kingdom claim of the unassailable intelligence on Iraq's WMD. This reduces the case for invasion. Hans Blix (2004:3) aptly says:

> Although the inspection organisation was now operating at full strength and Iraq seemed determined to give it prompt access everywhere, the United States appeared as determined to replace our inspection force with an invasion army.

The Security Council remained content with the progress of inspection reports and did not deem it necessary to convene a meeting to "consider the situation" under paragraph 12 of resolution 1441. On each occasion of reporting, the Security Council did not consider Iraq in further material breach. None of the inspectors, who were under obligation to report, reported Iraq's noncooperation. It suggests that the Security Council,

Anglo-Americans as the exception, was satisfied with the level of cooperation. The conclusions of reports, by Blix and ElBaradei, indicate that Iraq had no nuclear, chemical, or biological weapons. It means that Iraq had not breached cease-fire agreement terms to the extent that justified military action—there was no absolute noncooperation with the inspectors. "I felt the armed action taken was not in line with what the Security Council had decided five months earlier. The Council had not set a three-and-a-half month deadline for inspections. Had there been any denials of access? Any cat-and-mouse play? No. Had the inspections been going well? Yes. . . . Since [Iraq's] level of cooperation was much better than it had rendered inspectors in earlier years, I did not think that inspections should be curtailed and declared a failure . . . and used as a justification to go to war" (Blix, 2004:10–12).

5.3.2 Does Resolution 1441 Authorize Force?

The examination of the language of resolution 1441, its debating history, and the ensuing statements by the five permanent members of the Security Council show that resolution 1441 does not authorize automatic use of force against Iraq. The joint statement of Russia, China, and France (November 8, 2002) reads:

> Resolution 1441 (2002) adopted today by the Security Council excludes any automaticity in the use of force. . . . In case of failure by Iraq to comply with its obligations, the provisions of paragraphs 4, 11 and 12 will apply. Such failure will be reported to the Security Council by the Executive Chairman of UNMOVIC or the Director General of the IAEA. It will be then for the Council to take position on the basis of that report.

The United Kingdom's Permanent Representative to the United Nations, Greenstock (November 8, 2002) said:

> We heard loud and clear during the negotiations the concerns about "automaticity" and "hidden triggers"—the concern that on a decision so crucial we should not rush into military action; that on a decision so crucial any Iraqi violations should be discussed by the Council. Let me be equally clear in response, as a co-sponsor with the United States of the text we have adopted. There is no "automaticity" in this Resolution. If there is a further Iraqi breach of its disarmament obligations, the matter will return to the Council for discussion as required in Operational Paragraph 12. We would expect the Security Council then to meet its responsibilities.

The United States' Permanent Representative to the United Nations, Negroponte (November 8, 2002) said:

> As we have said on numerous occasions to Council members, this Resolution contains no "hidden triggers" and no "automaticity" with respect to the use of force. If there is a further Iraqi breach, reported to the Council by UNMOVIC, the IAEA, or a member state, the matter will return to the Council for discussions as required in paragraph 12. . . . If the Security Council fails to act decisively in the event of a further Iraqi violation, this resolution does not constrain any member state from acting to defend itself against the threat posed by Iraq, or to enforce relevant UN resolutions and protect world peace and security.

These statements by the permanent members of the Security Council show express consensus on the language and meanings of resolution 1441. They were clear about what they were voting on: If Iraq fails to take the final opportunity by not cooperating with the inspectors, inspectors will report the matter to the Security Council for assessment. The United States, however, had a different view: The inspectors as well as a member state may report Iraq's noncooperation to the Security Council. In addition, resolution 1441 does not constrain a member state's right to the use of force in self-defense, argued the United States. It is correct that resolution 1441 does not constrain any state to use force in self-defense nor does the Security Council have the power to restrict it, as self-defense is an inherent right recognized by the Charter. However, to argue that a member state can use force to enforce the Security Council resolutions without express authority is arrogating to itself the power of the Security Council. Mary Ellen O'Connell argues (November 21. 2002):

> "Material breach" never was a viable basis for using force against Iraq. Security Council resolutions are not like treaties or other agreements reached through negotiations aimed at achieving consensus. Rather, Security Council resolutions are mandates upon parties and must be respected with or without their consent. . . . They are enforced, modified, or terminated by the Security Council, not by states in general. Neither the explicit terms of the UN Charter nor the practice of the Security Council supports any other interpretation. . . . The Security Council's history with respect to its resolutions on Iraq makes clear that it has not relinquished to the US the right to enforce its resolutions unilaterally.

In their legal opinion to the Campaign for Nuclear Disarmament (CND), a UK based non-governmental organization, Singh and Kilroy (November

15, 2002) argue that resolution 1441 does not authorize the use of force by member states of the United Nations. They argue that the United Kingdom would be in breach of international law if it were to use force without a further Security Council Resolution.

> It may appear profoundly unsatisfactory that a State such as Iraq may, as it has been put, flout the will of the international community by continuing in breach of its obligations. But this misrepresents the situation. The will of the international community is expressed in this context by the Security Council. It is for the Council to decide, on behalf of the international community, what steps should be taken: that is not a determination which individual States may make. (Lowe, 2003:867)

Lowe (2003:865) further argues that the United Kingdom was quite right to press hard for a second resolution from the Security Council explicitly authorizing the use of force against Iraq and, having failed to secure one, the invasion lacked legal justification.

The United States even did not observe its own interpretation of resolution 1441 (2002): Both inspectors and a member state may report Iraq's noncompliance to the Security Council. The inspectors reported that inspection was moving forward. The Security Council never determined that Iraq was in material breach of its international obligations after November 2002. However, neither the United States nor the United Kingdom reported to the Security Council that Iraq was in further material breach. They interpreted these reports as constituting noncooperation. First, they fiercely lobbied for a resolution authorizing the use of force. When that became impossible, they turned to the revival theory. It seems that they wanted to go to the Security Council only if to endorse what they had already decided—the use of military force. They perhaps did not want the Security Council to play its role independently (see generally, Taft, 2006). "Even though the U.K. and the U.S. pointed to the threat of a veto from France as the reason for this debacle . . . a majority of the Council had, in fact if not in form, refused to legitimise armed action" (Blix, 2004:8).

5.3.3 Did Resolution 687 Suspend or Terminate Resolution 678?

This point is discussed under three subheads: suspension or termination, the Security Council practice on the use of force, and restoring peace and security language.

5.3.3.1 Suspension or Termination?

The U.S.-led coalition argues that resolution 687 suspended resolution 678 whereas independent commentators contend that resolution 678 has run its course and remains terminated after hostilities ended in 1991. Let us examine these two resolutions. To determine the true intention and interpretation of the Security Council resolutions, the International Court of Justice has laid down the following guidelines:

> The language of a resolution of the Security Council should be carefully analyzed . . . having regard to the terms of the resolution to be interpreted, the discussions leading to it, the Charter provisions invoked and, in general, all circumstances that might assist in determining the legal consequences of the resolution of the Security Council (Legal Consequences for States of the Continued Presence of South Africa in Namibia (South West Africa). (1971, paragraph 114)

The great majority of Security Council resolutions deal with a particular situation or dispute. In such cases, it is necessary to have as much knowledge as possible of the political background and of the whole of the Security Council's involvement, both prior to and after the adoption of the resolution under consideration (Murphy, 2004). Sir Michael Wood (1998:79) argues that when interpreting the Security Council resolutions, we need to have particular regard to the overall political background and the background of Council's related action. We also need to understand the role of the Security Council under the Charter, its working methods, and the way resolutions are drafted.

Resolution 660 (1990) determined that the invasion of Kuwait by Iraq constituted breach of peace and security. Resolution 678 (1990) authorized the use of all necessary means to liberate Kuwait as envisaged in resolution 660 (1990). Charlesworth and Byrnes (March 19, 2003) argue that resolution 678 (1990) is tied to a particular historical event and cannot be read as a standing authorization for the use of force by a United Nations member against Iraq:

> No provision of resolution 687 links Iraq's duty to destroy all weapons of mass destruction to the authorisation to use force set out in resolution 678. Indeed, the final paragraph of resolution 687 gives the Security Council the power to decide "such further steps as may be required for the implementation of the present resolution and to secure peace and security in the area," implying further Security Council consideration will be needed. (Charlesworth and Byrnes, March 19, 2003)

"Any claim that 'material breach' of cease-fire obligations by Iraq justifies the use of force by the United States is unavailing. The Gulf War was a Security Council authorized action, not a state versus state conflict; accordingly, it is for the Security Council to determine whether there has been a material breach *and* whether such breach requires renewed use of force" (Ratner and Lobel, October 2, 2002). They add: "Following the formal cease-fire recorded by Resolution 687 in 1991, there has been no Security Council resolution that has clearly and specifically authorized the use of force to enforce the terms of the cease-fire, including ending Iraq's missile and chemical, biological, and nuclear weapons programs" (Ratner and Lobel, October 2, 2002). O'Connell (November 21, 200) argues that "Resolution 1441 provides no new authorization for using force. It states in paragraph 12 that a meeting of the Security Council will be the first step upon a report by inspectors that Iraq has obstructed their activities. Consequences will follow a meeting."

Warbrick (October 30, 2002) argues that resolution 678 (1990) authorizes "states cooperating with the government of Kuwait" to take action effectively to restore the authority of the government of Kuwait (no longer an issue) and to restore international peace and security in the area. The coalition is no longer in existence and the power being sought is related to the implementation of resolutions subsequent to resolution 678. The argument that resolution 678 is a residuary right to use force fails to take into account the original reassertion of authority over the situation by the Council in resolution 687. There are no longer "states co-operating with the Government of Kuwait" to restore its authority. It might even be argued that resolution 678 is no longer a "relevant" resolution in the terms of resolution 1154 (paragraph 5), wherein the Security Council decided "in accordance with its responsibilities under the Charter, to remain actively seized of the matter, in order to ensure its implementation of this resolution, and to secure peace and security in the area" (cf Rogers, 2003:645–46). Elizabeth Wilmshurst (March 18, 2003), Deputy Legal Adviser of the British Foreign and Commonwealth Office, in her letter of resignation said: "I cannot agree that it is lawful to use force against Iraq without a second Security Council resolution to revive the authorisation given in SCR 678."

> I cannot in conscience go along with advice—within the Office or to the public or Parliament—which asserts the legitimacy of military action without . . . [second resolution], particularly since an unlawful use of force on such a scale amounts to the crime of aggression; nor can I agree with such action in circumstances which are so detrimental to the international order and the rule of law. (Wilmshurst, March 18, 2003)

It is clear from the terms of resolution 687 and from the context in which it was adopted that the formal cease-fire, once effected, terminated the authorization to use force in resolution 678, and that any step to be taken for the implementation of resolution of 687 and to restore peace and security in the region were now once more a matter for the Security Council and not for the member states, (Singh and Kilroy, January 23, 2003). Resolution 686 provides the clearest possible indication that resolution 687 was not intended to continue the authorization to use force in resolution 678. Resolution 686 was adopted in acknowledgement of the suspension of hostilities, which had occurred by that point. It required Iraq to abide by the terms of a provisional cease-fire with the ultimate aim of achieving "a definitive end to the hostilities." The resolution (paragraph 4) recognized that during the period required for Iraq to comply with the terms of the provisional cease-fire, the authorization to use force in resolution 678 would remain valid. Paragraph 4 provided this explicit recognition despite the fact that paragraph 1 had affirmed that resolution 678 continued to have full force and effect (Singh and Kilroy, January 23, 2003).

No such explicit language is used in resolution 687. On the contrary, resolution 687 (paragraph 6) clearly provides for the member states cooperating with Kuwait to bring their military presence to an end following the deployment of the United Nations observer unit, and for a formal cease-fire to be effective upon official notification by Iraq of "its acceptance" of the provisions of Resolution 687. Resolution 687 affirmed resolution 678 "except as expressly changed . . . to achieve the goals of the present [687] resolution, including a formal cease-fire." If the Security Council had sought to keep the authorization to use force contained in resolution 678 alive pending Iraq's compliance with the provisions of resolution 687, resolution 686 demonstrates that it could and would have done so (Singh and Kilroy, January 23, 2003). It is clear from the language of resolution 687 that, the coalition having achieved its main goal—the liberation of Kuwait and the restoration of international peace and security in the area at that time at least—the Security Council imposed a cease-fire and then assumed its proper responsibility for the long-term restoration of international peace and security in the area. It expressly remained seized of the matter (Singh and Kilroy, January 23, 2003).

> The Security Council has authorized a combined military operation; has terminated a combined military operation; has established the terms under which various UN agency actions will occur to supervise the cease-fire, to establish the standards with which Iraq must comply; has established the means by which it may be determined whether those standards have been met (and this

> has been done through a flock of reports by the inspection system); and has engaged in negotiations to secure compliance. After all these actions, to now state that the United Nations has not in fact occupied the field, that there remains under Article 51 or under Resolution 678, which authorized the initial use of force, which authorization was terminated in Resolution 687, a collateral total freedom on the part of any UN member to use military force against Iraq at any point that any member considers there to have been a violation of the conditions set forth in Resolution 678, is to make a complete mockery of the entire system. (Frank, 1998:139)

Lowe (2003:865) argues that:

> It is simply unacceptable that a step as serious and important as a massive military attack upon a State should be launched on the basis of a legal argument dependent upon dubious inferences drawn from the silences in Resolution 1441 and the muffled echoes of earlier resolutions, unsupported by any contemporary authorisation to use force. No domestic court or authority in the United States or the United Kingdom would tolerate governmental action based upon such flimsy arguments.

The structure of resolution 678 suggests that it is focused on Iraqi compliance with the Security Council's resolutions adopted after Iraq's invasion of Kuwait but before November 29, 1990, the date of resolution 678 itself. The phrase "all subsequent relevant resolutions" in paragraph 1 appears to be a reference back to the ten resolutions specified in the preamble. Further, the authorization in paragraph 2 only becomes effective if Iraq fails to comply with such resolutions by January 16, 1991. In other words, had Iraq complied with the obligations set forth under those ten resolutions, which related to Iraq's withdrawal from Kuwait, return of Kuwaiti nationals and property, and other matters, but which did not relate to weapons of mass destruction on or before January 15, 1991, then the authorization contained in paragraph 2 would not be effective. Given that Iraq could not possibly comply by January 16 with resolutions that did not exist as of that date, the only reasonable interpretation of the language is that "all subsequent relevant resolutions" refers to the ten resolutions existing at the time resolution 678 (1990) was adopted and not resolutions adopted thereafter (Murphy, 2004:180–81). On this interpretation, resolution 687 does not even seem to be relevant. Fifteen leading lawyers of international law wrote a letter to the former Prime Minister Blair on March 6, 2003 to preempt a claim, which they thought was unfounded:

> We are teachers of international law. On the basis of information publicly available, there is no justification under international law for the use of military

> force against Iraq. . . . Neither Security Council resolution 1441 nor any prior authorise the proposed use of force in the present circumstances. (cited in Sands, 2005:187)

Anne-Marie Slaughter, (cited in Sands, 2005:175; see Moir, 2005) argues that the "invasion was both illegal and illegitimate." Kofi Anan (*Guardian*, September 16, 2004), the United Nations Secretary General said:

> I have indicated [that the invasion of Iraq] was not in conformity with the UN charter. From our point of view and from the Charter point of view it was illegal.

5.3.3.2 The Practice of Security Council

The analysis of the practice of the Security Council sheds further light on getting to the most plausible interpretation of resolutions under consideration. The followers of "revival theory" such as Yoo (2003:567) argue that the Security Council has not readily authorized the use of force in the past nor has it rescinded those decisions lightly. When the Security Council has taken the serious step of ending its authorization to use force, it has only done so in one of two ways: either by expressly terminating the prior authorization or by setting an up-front time limit on the authorization. With regard to Bosnia, for example, the Security Council by resolution 1031 (December 15, 1995) ended the legal authority for the use of force by expressly terminating the previous authorization in a separate resolution, while in Somalia, the Security Council by resolution 954 (November 4, 1994) explicitly established a sunset date when it extended the authorization. In fact, when the Security Council has wanted to reserve for itself whether the conditions for termination of its authorization have been met rather than leave the matter to the member states, it has explicitly done so. In the case of Haiti, the Security Council by resolution 940 (July 31, 1994) decided that "the multinational force will terminate its mission . . . when a secure and stable environment has been established . . . [as determined] by the Security Council, taking into account recommendations from the Member States of the multinational force."

Challenging Yoo's argument, Murphy (2004:187) argues that this position is doubtful. Resolution 678 was the third authorization by the Security Council allowing states to use military force since the inception of the Charter. In neither of the earlier situations (Korea and Southern Rhodesia) did the initial authorization contain a sunset clause nor was the authorization subsequently expressly terminated, yet neither authorization was regarded as remaining available after the passage of time and the immediate crisis at hand. Rather, the original authorizations to use force for Korea (resolution 83, 1950) and for Southern Rhodesia (resolution 221, 1966) were ultimately regarded as having dissipated in light of further developments. So, when resolution 678 was adopted in 1990, there was no consistent and certainly no substantial practice suggesting that the authorization to use force should be temporally conditioned *ab initio* nor that the failure to do so would result in an authorization of indefinite duration. The fact that the Security Council regularly sets time limits on peacekeeping operations, such as UNOSOM II in Somalia, is not relevant to the issue of authorizations for member states to use force acting in their national capacity, because such limitations in peacekeeping practice historically have been driven by the need to obtain consent of the host states and to manage the fiscal concerns of the United Nations. Gray (2004:139–40) argues that: "Resolution 686 preserved the authorization to use force in Resolution 678 for the purposes set forth in that resolution, but might not have extended such authorization to compliance with paragraphs two and three of Resolution 686" (see also White and Cryer, 1999:272).

Blokker (2000:541) argues that both the Charter system and principles of delegation reject carte blanche delegations and favor authorizations that respect the authority and responsibility of the Security Council in the United Nations collective security system. Examining the views of member states, Blokker finds the model of authorization resolutions as generally acceptable, although some states have expressed a concern for greater United Nations control. Keeping in view the experience of Iraq and interpretation of related resolutions, China and Russia were wary of the language used in the Security Council's resolution 1695 (July 15, 2006) against North Korea. China threatened to veto it if reference to chapter VII was not removed. Therefore, resolution 1695 was adopted unanimously without a reference to chapter VII. "China and Russia wanted no mention of Chapter VII for fear that it could be used to justify military strikes on North Korea. Opposition by both countries to the Chapter VII rubric has grown since the war in Iraq and what Beijing and Moscow see as the Bush administration's resort to military means to remove governments it opposes" (*New York Times*, July 16, 2006).

It is a misreading of resolution 687 to argue that failure to comply with its terms and conditions would result in the automatic use of force against Iraq by a member state. When resolution 687 was drafted, there was concern that Iraq might not comply with the provisions for the destruction, removal, or rendering harmless its weapons of mass destruction. To address that concern, the Security Council could have repeated, but did not repeat, in resolution 687 the same type of provision that appeared in resolution 686 regarding the continuing validity of resolution 678 pending Iraqi compliance with the disarmament provisions. Rather, the Security Council expressly provided for an alternative means of coercing compliance with resolution 687 in paragraph 22. The resolution provides that the economic sanctions imposed on Iraq during the 1990–91 crises would remain in place until a Security Council agreement was reached indicating that Iraq had complied with its disarmament obligations. Moreover, the Security Council would review the sanctions every sixty days for the purpose of determining whether they should be reduced or lifted in light of Iraqi compliance.

The former British Attorney General, Lord Goldsmith, has given a detail opinion to the former Prime Minister Blair on the legality of the use of force against Iraq. After reading it, one may draw two important inferences: To obtain a second resolution was the safest way and that the British view of "revival" differs from that of the United States. Relevant paragraphs of his opinion are reproduced below:

> 26. To sum up, the language of resolution 1441 leaves the position unclear and the statements made on adoption of the resolution suggest that there were differences of view within the Council as to the legal effect of the resolution. Arguments can be made on both sides. A key question is whether there is in truth a need for an assessment of whether Iraq's conduct constitutes a failure to take the final opportunity or has constituted a failure fully to cooperate within the meaning of OP4 such that the basis of the ceasefire is destroyed. If an assessment is needed of that situation, it would be for the Council to make it. A narrow textual reading of the resolution suggests that sort of assessment is not needed, because the Council has predetermined the issue. Public statements, on the other hand, say otherwise.
>
> 27. In these circumstances, I remain of the opinion that the safest legal course would be to secure the adoption of a further resolution to authorise the use of force.[. . .]The key point is that it should establish that the Council has concluded that Iraq has failed to take the final opportunity offered by resolution 1441, as in the draft which has already been tabled.
>
> 28 Nevertheless, having regard to the information on the negotiating history which I have been given and to the arguments of the US Administration which I heard in Washington, I accept that a reasonable case can be made that resolution 1441 is capable in principle of reviving the authorisation in 678 without a further resolution.
>
> 29. However, the argument that resolution 1441 alone has revived the authorisation to use force in resolution 678 will only be sustainable if there are strong factual grounds for concluding that Iraq has failed to take the final opportunity. In other words, we would need to be able to demonstrate hard evidence of non-compliance and non-cooperation. Given the structure of the

> resolution as a whole, the views of UNMOVIC and the IAEA will be highly significant in this respect. In the light of the latest reporting by UNMOVIC, you will need to consider very carefully whether the evidence of non-cooperation and non-compliance by Iraq is sufficiently compelling to justify the conclusion that Iraq has failed to take its final opportunity.
>
> 30. In reaching my conclusion, I have taken account of the fact that on a number of previous occasions, including in relation to Operation Desert Fox in December 1998 and Kosovo in 1999, UK forces have participated in military action on the basis of advice from my predecessors that the legality of the action under international law was no more than reasonably arguable. But a "reasonable case" does not mean that if the matter ever came before a court I would be confident that the court would agree with the view. I judge that, having regard to the arguments on both sides, and considering the resolution as a whole in the light of the statements made on adoption and subsequently, a court might well conclude that OPs 4 and 12 do require a further Council decision in order to revive the authorisation in resolution 678. But equally I consider that the counter view can be reasonably maintained.

I agree with the opinion of the former Attorney General to the extent that we need "strong factual grounds" to convince ourselves that Iraq is in further material breach of resolution 1441, which can be gathered from the examination of inspectors reports (as previously shown). If any assessment of material breach by Iraq is required, it will be for the Security Council to do so. Again, in principle, a case may be made in favor of "revival theory," but that is not persuasive and that is why the then British Attorney General rightly said that he is not confident about winning if the case comes before a court of law. When this opinion is juxtaposed with the U.S. view (Taft and Buchwald, 2003), one sees the difference between the views of two allies: The U.S. view is strong and certain whereas the British view carefully recognizes weakness of the "revival theory" and considers a second resolution to be the safest legal way. The British position favors greater control by the Security Council in contrast to American unilateralism.

The general political climate is always helpful in aiding to determine the true intention of the Security Council resolutions. As previously indicated, the immediate statements of the five permanent members had a consensus that Iraq's noncooperation would be reported to the Security Council, and it would be up to the Security Council to make an assessment on whether Iraq was in material breach of its obligations and to consider the need for compliance. This consensus remained intact until the last few days before the invasion of Iraq. The United States and the United Kingdom made fierce efforts to garner support for a second resolution stating that Iraq was in further material breach of resolution 1441, but France threatened to veto it (Blair, March 18, 2003). They quickly declared the French veto as "unreasonable." As previously stated, President Bush was determined to topple Saddam's regime and former Prime Minster Blair was supportive of the U.S. plan (Sands, 2005:182). Their lawyers wove the "revival" theory out of twelve-year-old resolutions as a last option to afford the invasion a legal cover. There was concern that the UN inspection team, led by Blix, had unearthed insufficient evidence. Other options were considered (Sands, 2005), such as the revival theory. At the same time, statements playing down the importance of second resolution were made claiming that it was meant to show the resolve of the international community rather than to provide the legal basis for military action.

> For its part, the United States made clear that it would have preferred the Council to adopt a second resolution. Its view was that such a resolution would have operated as an important demonstration of resolve by the international community to increase the pressure on Iraq and, ultimately, to reduce the likelihood that resort to force would be necessary. While the Council's inability to come together for such a resolution may have misled Iraq into believing it could wait out the process in New York, the absence of Council action in no way diminished the effect of what the Council had previously authorized. (Taft and Buchwald, 2003:note 23)

On the contrary, former British Foreign Secretary Cook (March 17, 2003) said that "now that those attempts have failed, we cannot pretend that getting a second resolution was of no importance." The "revival theory" seems to be a last legal resort, which pushed the region into violent conflict "by a US Administration with an agenda of its own" (Secretary Cook, March 17, 2003).

The then British Attorney General advised former Prime Minister Blair that French veto could not be considered unreasonable if the world opinion was opposed to military action, and an unreasonable veto would not entitle the coalition to proceed on the basis of presumed authorization:

> The analysis set out above applies whether a second resolution fails to be adopted because of a lack of votes or because it is vetoed. As I have said before, I do not believe that there is any basis in law for arguing that there is an implied condition of reasonableness which can be read into the power of veto conferred on the permanent members of the Security Council by the UN Charter. So there are no grounds for arguing that an "unreasonable veto" would entitle us to proceed on the basis of a presumed Security Council authorisation. In any event, if the majority of world opinion remains opposed to military action, it is likely to be difficult on the facts to categorise the French veto as "unreasonable." The legal analysis may, however, be affected by the course of events over

> the next week or so, eg the discussions on the draft second resolution. If we fail to achieve the adoption of a second resolution we would need to consider urgently at that stage the strength of our legal case in the light of circumstances at the time. (Goldsmith, March 7, 2003, paragraph 31)

Lowe (2003:867) argues:

> Any suggestion that "unreasonable" uses of the veto or unreasonably withheld authorisations of the use of force could be ignored cannot be accepted, if the Security Council is to survive. The discounting of votes cast or withheld in "bad faith" is incompatible with the Charter, and with the very idea of representative bodies upon whom legal powers are conferred, whether they exercise executive, legislative or judicial functions.

I completely agree with the views of Goldsmith and Lowe that any use of veto cannot be characterized as unreasonable in the first place, and in the second place, any veto used in good or bad faith does not per se allow member states to resort to the use of force. The following citation from Lowe (2003:866–67) illustrates the entire picture on the use of force under the Charter and the status of veto locked Security Council:

> It is tempting to regard a malfunctioning Council as a simple failure of one international mechanism among many, entitling the members of the international community to resort to some other means for securing, in such instances, international peace and security. The problem with this approach is that the UN Charter is a binding treaty. Indeed, the priority given to Charter obligations over other obligations by article 103 of the Charter signals that it has a particularly clear and strong binding quality. States cannot simply ignore it. The prohibition on the threat or use of force against other states in article 2(4) of the Charter cannot be disregarded, if (as is the assumption [in the case of French veto]) action involving the threat or use of force is in question. Nor is it easy to see how any of the doctrines that are recognized in the Vienna Convention on the Law of Treaties as permitting the suspension of treaty obligations-material breach, rebus sic stantibus, and so on could be applied to release states from their Charter obligations in such situations.

5.3.3.3 Resolution 678: Restoring Peace and Security

Paragraph 2, of course, speaks of using force not just to uphold subsequent Security Council resolutions but also "to restore international peace and security" in the area. The United States legal theory relies on this language to say that since Iraq failed to comply with the relevant resolutions prior to January 16, the use of force was authorized both to uphold those resolutions and to do more to go beyond them so as to restore peace and security in the region. Thus, if resolution 687 is viewed as setting the terms for what was necessary to restore peace and security in the region, then the use of force authorization carried forward to the upholding of resolution 687, including compliance with the WMD regime. This approach is a more tenable interpretation of resolution 678, since some content must be given to the "restore" language and that content must be something different than upholding Security Council resolutions existing as of November 1990 (Murphy, 2004:181–82).

There is, however, a far more plausible interpretation, which is that the "restore" language was intended to provide the coalition in early 1991 with considerable leeway in carrying out "Operation Desert Storm"—including not just those operations designed to compel Iraq to withdraw from Kuwait but also those aimed at the broader threat Iraq was posing to her neighbors in the region. Thus, when expelling Iraqi military forces from Kuwait and securing Kuwait's border, the 1990–91 coalition found it necessary to cross into and occupy a swath of territory in Southern Iraq as a buffer zone. Had the "restore" language not existed, then the crossing of military forces into Iraq would have been outside the scope of resolution 678, since none of the ten preceding resolutions ordered Iraq to allow such a buffer zone. Moreover, and with particular relevance to the invasion of Iraq in 2003, the "restore" language could properly be interpreted as allowing "Operation Desert Storm" to include operations in 1991 to destroy Iraq's WMD infrastructure on grounds that the WMD threatened Iraq's neighbors. Yet, once "Operation Desert Storm" ended and a new regime was developed in resolution 687 to address the "restoration of peace and security in the region," the "restore" language of resolution 678 is best seen as having run its course (Murphy, 2004:182–83).

To accept the United States' interpretation in respect to the "restore" language would lead to more extreme outcomes. If resolution 678 authorizes the use of military force indefinitely to restore any "international peace and security in the area," where does the authorization end? If current efforts to set up a post-Hussein Iraqi government fail in ten years, leading to a civil war, is resolution 678 still capable of supporting the use of force by outside states? Could Iran invoke such authority to intervene in Iraq because of civil war? The United States' interpretation need not even be confined to Iraq. If the United States were to decide that "international peace and security in the region" required intervention in Syria and Iran because, according to President Bush (July 16, 2006) and former Prime Minister Blair (July 16, 2006), they support a terrorist organization, Hizbullah, then resolution 678 may be stretched to authorize such invasions. In the summer 2006 war between Israel, Hezbollah, and Lebanon, Israel did not invoke such authority but rather relied on the self-defense argument. I do not believe that such a broad interpretation of resolution 678 was envisaged in November 1990, and it cannot be sustained (see Murphy, 2004:184). The entirety of resolution 678 points toward the goal of restoring the Kuwaiti sovereignty and independence, and the authorization to restore peace and security must be seen in congruence with that goal (Schaller, cited in Murphy, 2004:184).

To sum up, the revival theory is not persuasive. The basic understanding of resolution 1441 was that inspectors would report Iraq's noncooperation to the Security Council for further assessment, which would consider the need for compliance. When the French veto stood in the way to obtain a second resolution authorizing the use of force against Iraq, the United States and the United Kingdom turned to the revival theory. The weight of scholarly opinion suggests that resolution 686 suspended resolution 678 as a measure of temporary cease-fire and resolution 687 effected definitive cease-fire terminating the authority to use force in resolution 678.

5.3.4 Resumption of Hostilities: Law of Armed Conflict

Yoo (2003:568) argues that, under article 60(2) of the Vienna Convention on the Law of Treaties, 1969, a material breach of a treaty by one of the parties entitles a party "specially affected" by the breach to suspend the operation of the treaty in whole or in part vis-à-vis the defaulting state. Even if a state party were not "specially affected" however, a material breach that "radically changes" the position of the parties also permits complete or partial suspension. Greenwood (October 24, 2002), does not agree with this interpretation of armistice law:

> The suggestion that, because Iraq has violated the terms of the ceasefire embodied in Resolution 687 (1991), any of the coalition States which were engaged in the hostilities of 1990–91 would be justified in resuming hostilities seems to me to be based on a pre-1945 view of international law which cannot prevail against the clear language of the UN Charter. Violation of a ceasefire does not in itself justify reversion to military action today unless the original legal basis for the use of force remains in place. . . . [The United Kingdom] does not have an automatic right to resume belligerency simply because it was a party to the 1990–91 hostilities and Iraq has violated the ceasefire.

Tony Rogers (2006) argues that, according to article 40 of the Hague Convention IV (1907) "any serious violation of the armistice by one of the parties gives the other party the right of denouncing it, and even, in cases of urgency, of recommencing hostilities immediately." I agree with Rogers and Yoo on the point of law that hostilities may be resumed if one party to the cease-fire breaches its terms and it is urgent to take action. However, I disagree with Yoo on the point of fact that Iraq did not breach cease-fire terms to the extent to justify the use of military force.

5.4 Is the Invasion Self-defense?

The grounds given for invading Iraq in 2003 are diverse. In some instances, the United States expressed concern for national security, sometimes relating to the threat of terrorism. In other instances, the United States asserted a need to protect Iraq's neighbors or the international community at large, including the need to uphold resolutions of the United Nations Security Council ordering Iraqi disarmament of WMD. At times, attention was called to the welfare of the Iraqi people and the need to help them throw off a despotic and abusive ruler (Murphy, 2004:173). In general, two main arguments may be identified: the Security Council argument (i.e., Iraq is in breach of the Security Council resolution) and the self-defense argument (i.e., Iraq posses a threat to the Anglo-American security and their allies) (see Warbrick, 2002). As previously indicated, the Anglo-Americans claimed that resolution 1441 had found Iraq in "material breach" of its international obligations contained in resolution 687, and the reports of weapons inspectors show that Iraq is in further breach of the terms of resolution 1441. Therefore, the authority to use force under resolution 678 was revived to disarm Iraq. It may be called the Security Council argument.

However, the language used before and after invading Iraq suggests that self-defense was the main ground for invading Iraq. In the run up to the invasion of Iraq, the United States claimed that it had the right of "pre-emptive self-defense" under international law (National Security Strategy, 2002). President Bush (March 17, 2003) said: "The United States of America has the sovereign authority to use force in assuring it national security." "The United States and the international community had a firm basis for using preemptive force in the face of the past actions by Iraq and the threat that it posed." Taft and Buchwald (2003:563) assert that "Preemption of Iraq's possession and use of weapons of mass destruction was a principal objective of the coalition forces." The Congress of the United States (October 2, 2002), in a joint resolution, alleged that Iraq continues "to possess and develop a significant chemical and biological weapons capability, actively seeking a nuclear weapons capability, and supporting and harboring terrorist organizations" (preambular paragraph 6). It further noted that "the risk that the current Iraqi regime will either employ those weapons to launch a surprise attack against the United States or its Armed Forces or provide them to international terrorists who would do so, and the extreme magnitude of harm that would result to the United States and its citizens from such an attack, combine to justify action by the United States to defend itself" (preambular paragraph 13). The Congress (section 3) authorized the president of the United States to "defend the national security of the United States against the continuing threat posed by Iraq." The United Kingdom also articulated national security as the main ground for invading Iraq. In his national speech, the former British Prime Minster (March 18, 2003) said: "My judgement, as Prime Minister, is that this threat is real, growing and of an entirely different nature to any conventional threat to our security that Britain has faced before." He further said (July 6, 2006): "Ever since September 11th, the US has embarked on a policy of intervention in order to protect its and our future security. Hence Afghanistan. Hence Iraq." As previously stated, the actual invasion was based on the revival theory, but self-defense remained the main overall unstated ground before and after the invasion (see Murphy, 2004). Even if the revival theory is accepted, for the sake of argument, the Secuirty Council authorized necessary steps to liberate Kuwait: The authorization was in collective self-defense. If the power to use force is revived, force could be used only for self-defense or collective self-defense as that was the original ground for the authorization of force. The only other course open for intervention is on humanitarian grounds, which was neither the ground for the first Gulf war nor for the 2003 invasion of Iraq.

Let us deal with the allegation that Iraq poses a serious threat to the United States and the United Kingdom. First, Iraq had no useable WMD nor the capacity to develop WMD at the time of invasion. Second, if Iraq were in possession of WMD, she had no delivery system as ElBaradei and Blix confrimed in the above reports. There was not a remote possiblity that Iraq would attack the United States or the United Kingdom. Even countries in the region such as Kuwait neither reported to the Security Council nor asked the United States for assistance because Iraq was posing immediate threat to their security. The use of force is allowed only when there is an armed attack against a state or such attack is imminent. Iraq posed no such threat either to the United States or the United Kingdom. Iraq was also not an immediate threat to neighboring countries in the region. The prewar intelligence suggests that the allegation that Iraq was suporting terrorists such as Al-Qaeda was basless. "The JIC found no evidence of co-operation between the Iraqi regime and Al-Qaida" (Butler's Report, July 14, 2004, paragraph 32). There is no arguable case that the United States or the United Kingdom were acting in self-defense in invading Iraq (see Lowe, 2003), because Iraq posed no threat to their security.

5.5 Conclusion

The United States and the United Kingdom together with their allies invaded Iraq on March 19, 2003 on the basis of seriously flawed intelligence and without clear and convincing evidence. The revival theory is not persuasive. The legal case for the invasion is very thin. Iraq did flout Security Council resolutions for years, but that does not per se allow member states to use force or regime change. It is very hard to accept the United States' and the United Kingdom's case for war based on such evidence, more specifically when there was a risk of loss of thousands of human lives and enormous damage to property and infrastructure. I agree with former Secretary Cook (March 17, 2003) who did give a timely warning:

> The threshold for war should always be high. None of us can predict the death toll of civilians from the forthcoming bombardment of Iraq, but the US warning of a bombing campaign that will shock and awe makes it likely that casualties will be numbered at least in the thousands.

References

Annan, K. (2004) Iraq War was illegal and breached UN Charter. Available at: http://www.guardian.co.uk/Iraq/Story/0,2763,1305709,00.html.

Associated Press. (2002) Joint statement by China, France and Russia interpreting UN Security Council Resolution 1441. November 8. Available at: www.accessatlanta.com/ajc/news/1102/09interpretation.html.

Blair, T. (2006) Speech in Loss Angeles USA. July 6. Available at: http://www.pm.gov.uk/output/Page9948.asp.

———. (2004) Statement on Butler Report. July 14. Available at http://www.number10.gov.uk/output/Page6109.asp.

———. (2003) The debate in the House of Commons "Iraq." March 18. Available at: http://www.publications.parliament.uk/pa/cm200203/cmhansrd/v030318/debtext/30318-06.htm.

Blix, H. (2004) *Disarming Iraq: The search for weapons of mass destruction*. London: Bloomsbury Publishing.

———. (2003) Oral introduction of the twelfth quarterly report of UNMOVIC. March 7. Available at: http://www.un.org/Depts/unmovic/SC7asdelivered.htm.

Blokker, N. (2000) Is the authorisation authorised? *European Journal of International Law*, 11, pp.541.

Bush, G. (2006) Bush blames Hezbollah, Syria for mildest violence. Available at: http://www.foxnews.com/story/0,2933,203756,00.html.

———. (2005) President discusses Iraqi elections, victory in the war on terror. December 14. Available at: http://www.whitehouse.gov/news/releases/2005/12/20051214l.html.

———. (2003) President Bush Addresses the Nation. March 17. Available at: http://www.whitehouse.gov/news/releases/2003/03/20030319-17.html.

———. (2002) State of the Union Address. January 29. Available at: http://www.whitehouse.gov/news/releases/2002/01/20020129-11.html.

Butler, Lord (2004) Review of intelligence on weapons of mass destruction. July 14. Available at: http://www.butlerreview.org.uk/.

Carnegie Endowment for International Peace (2004) WMD in Iraq: Evidence and implications. Available at: http://www.carnegieendowment.org/npp/iraqintell/home.cfm.

Charlesworth, H and Byrnes, A (2003) No, this war is illegal. March 19. Available at: http://www.theage.com.au/articles/2003/03/18/1047749770379.html.

Cheney, D. (2002) *Meet the Press* NBC with Tim Russert. September 8. Available at: http://www.whitehouse.gov/vicepresident/news-speeches/speeches/print/vp20020324.html.

Cook, R. (2003) Blair "Knew Iraq Had No WMD interview with David Cracknell. October 5. Available at: http://www.commondreams.org/headlines03/1005-01.htm.

———. (2003) Personal Statement. March 17. Available at: http://www.publications.parliament.uk/pa/cm200203/cmhansrd/vo030317/debtext/30317-33.htm.

Crawford, J. (2003) *The international law commission's articles on state responsibility: Introduction, text and commentaries.* Cambridge: Cambridge University Press.

Dinstein, Y. (2005) *War, aggression and self-defence.* Cambridge: Cambridge University Press.

ElBaradei, M. (2003) The status of nuclear inspections in Iraq: An update. March 7. Available at: http://www.iaea.org/NewsCenter/Statements/2003/ebsp2003n006.html.

———. (2003) The status of inspections in Iraq. February 14, 2003 update. Available at: http://www.iaea.org/NewsCenter/Statements/2003/ebsp2003n005.shtml.

Gibbon, G. (2006) The Whitehouse memo. February 2. Available at: http://www.channel4.com/news/special-reports/special-reports storypage.jsp?id=1661.

Goldsmith, L. (2003) Iraq: Resolution 1441 (Secret Memo to the Prime Minster). March 7. http://image.guardian.co.uk/sys-files/Guardian/documents/2005/04/28/legal.pdf.

Gray, C. (2004) *International law and the use of force.* Oxford: Oxford University Press.

Greenwood, C. (2002) The legality of using force against Iraq. Memorandum to the UK parliamentary Committee on Foreign Affairs on October 12, 2002. http://www.publications.parliament.uk/pa/cm200203/cmselect/cmfaff/196/2102406.htm.

———. (1987) International law and the United States' air operation against Libya. *W. Va. L Rev.*, 89, pp.933.

Greenstock, (2002) Statement by Ambassador Greenstock to the Security Council. 8 November. Available at: http://www.ukun.org/xq/asp/SarticleType.17/Article_ID.516/qx/articles_show.htm.

Hague Convention IV (1907). Available at: http://www.icrc.org/ihl.nsf/FULL/195.

Hoge, W. (2006) U.N. Council, in weakened resolution, demands end to North Korean missile program. *The New York Times*. July 16. Available at: http://www.nytimes.com/2006/07/16/world/asia/16nations.html?ex=1310702400&en=6a3db996ff85c4bf&ei=5088&partner=rssnyt&emc=rss.

I.C.J. (1986) *Nicaragua v. United States of America*. June 27. Available at: http://www.icj-cij.org/icjwww/icases/inus/inusframe.htm.

———. (1971) Legal consequences for states of the continued presence of South Africa in Namibia and the West Africa notwithstanding the Security Council Resolution 276 (1970). June 21. Available at: http://www.icj-cij.org/icjwww/idecisions/isummaries/inamsummary710621.htm.

I.C.T.Y. (1997) *Prosecutor v. Tadic*. May 17. Available at: http://www.un.org/icty/tadic/appeal/decision-e/51002.htm.

Lobel, J. (1999) The use of force to respond to terrorist attacks: The bombing of Sudan and Afghanistan. *Yale Journal of International Law*, 25, pp.537–57.

Lowe, V. (2003) The Iraq crisis: What now? *International and Comparative Law Quarterly*, 52, pp.859.

Manning, D. (2002) Secret Downing Street Memo. July 23. Available at: http://www.timesonline.co.uk/article/0,,2087-1593607,00.html.

Moir, L. (2005) Reappraising the resort to force? Jus ad bellum and the war on terror. *New Zealand Yearbook of Jurisprudence*, 8.1, pp.1–31.

Murphy, S. (2004) Assessing the legality of invading Iraq. *Georgetown Law Journal*, 92, pp.173–258.

Negroponte, J. (2002) USUN Press Release # 187 (02) (Revised). November 8. Available at: http://www.un.int/usa/02_187.htm.

O'Connell, M. (2002) Evidence of terror. *Journal of Conflict and Security Law*, 7, pp.19.

———. (2002) UN Resolution 1441: Compelling Iraq, restraining Bush. *Jurist*. November 12. Available at: http://jurist.law.pitt.edu/forum/forumnew73.php.

Powell, C. (2005) Powell calls UN speech painful *Associated Press*. September 8. Available at: http://www.cbsnews.com/stories/2005/09/08/politics/main829085.shtml.

———. (2003) Remarks to the United Nations Security Council. January 5. Available at: http://www.state.gov/secretary/former/powell/remarks/2003/17300.htm.

———. (2002) Interview Fox News Sunday by Tony Snow and Brit Hume. September 8. Available at: http://www.state.gov/secretary/former/powell/remarks/2002/13324.htm.

Ratner and Lobel, (2002) The United Nations Charter and the use of force against Iraq. October 2. Available at: http://www.lawyersagainstthewar.org/legalarticles/ratner.htm.

Ritter, Scott (2002) Address to Iraqi Parliament. September 8. Available at: http://news.bbc.co.uk/1/hi/not_in_website/syndication/monitoring/media_reports/2244614.stm.

Rockefeller, Senator. (2006) Report on pre-war intelligence lagging. Interview by Dafna Linzer. *Washington Post*. July 30. Available at: http://www.washingtonpost.com/wp-dyn/content/article/2006/07/29/AR2006072900608.html.

Rogers, APV (2006) Personal Communication at Lauterpacht Centre for International Law. August.

——— (2003) Comments on Resolution 1441 (2002). *Yearbook of International Humanitarian Law*, 3.

Sands, P. (2005) *Lawless world: America and the making and breaking of global rules.* London: Allen Lane.

Security Council (2006) Resolution 1695. July 15.

——— (2002) Resolution 1441. November 8.

——— (1998) Resolution 1154. March 2.

——— (1995) Resolution 1031. December 15.

——— (1994) Resolution 954. November 4.

——— (1994) Resolution 940. July 31.

——— (1991) Resolution 687. April 3.

——— (1991) Resolution 686. November 2.

——— (1990) Resolution 661. August 6.

——— (1990) Resolution 660. August 2.

——— (1990) Resolution 678. November 29.

——— (1966) Resolution 221. April 9.

——— (1950) Resolution 83. June 27.

Singh and Kilroy (2003) Opinion given to the Campaign for Nuclear Disarmament (CND). January 23. Available at: http://www.inlap.freeuk.com/caw_chapter_10.pdf.

——— (2002) Opinion given to the Campaign for Nuclear Disarmament (CND). November 15. Available at: http://www.inlap.freeuk.com/caw_chapter_04.pdf.

Taft, W. (2006) A view from the top: American perspectives on international law after the cold war. *Yale Journal of International Law*, 31, pp.503–12.

Taft and Buchwald (2003) Pre-emption, Iraq and international law. *American Journal of International Law*, 97, pp.557–63.

United Kingdom, (2002) Iraq's weapons of mass destruction: The assessment of the British government. September 24. Available at: http://www.number10.gov.uk/output/Page271.asp.

United Nations (1945) The Charter of the United Nations.

United States (2006) The National Security Strategy of the United States of America. Available at: http://www.whitehouse.gov/nsc/nss/2006/nss2006.pdf.

———, (2005) Commission on the intelligence capabilities of the United States regarding weapons of mass destruction's report. March 31. Available at: http://www.whitehouse.gov/wmd/.

——— (2004) Comprehensive report of the special advisor to the Director Centre Intelligence on Iraq's WMD. September 30. Available at: https://www.cia.gov/cia/reports/iraq_wmd_2004/.

——— (2002) The National Security Strategy of the United States of America. Available at: http://www.whitehouse.gov/nsc/nss.html.

United States, Congress (2002) Joint resolution to authorize the use of United States armed forces against Iraq. October 2. Available at: http://www.whitehouse.gov/news/releases/2002/10/20021002-2.html.

——— (1998) Iraq Liberation Act, 1998.

United States, Department of State, (2003) Historic Review of UNMOVIC's Report on Unresolved Disarmament Issues. March 10. Available at: http://www.state.gov/r/pa/prs/ps/2003/18513.htm.

United States, Senate Select Committee on intelligence (2004) Report on the U.S. Intelligence Community's Pre-war Intelligence Assessment on Iraq. Available at: http://intelligence.senate.gov/108301.pdf.

Vienna Convention on the Law of Treaties, 1969.

Warbrick, C. (2002) Adjudication of Professor Colin Warbrick. October 30. Available at: http://www.inlap.freeuk.com/caw_chapter_03.pdf.

———. (1991) The invasion of Kuwait by Iraq. *International and Comparative Law Quarterly*, 40, pp.482–92.

Washington Post, Pincus, W. (2005) British intelligence warned of Iraq War. May 13. Available at: http://www.washingtonpost.com/wp-dyn/content/article/2005/05/12/AR2005051201857.html.

White and Cryer (1999) Unilateral enforcement of Resolution 687: A threat too far. *California Western International Law Journal*, 29, pp.243–82.

Wilmshurst, E. (2003) Wilmshurst resignation letter. Available at: http://news.bbc.co.uk/1/hi/uk_politics/4377605.stm.

Wood, M. (1998) The interpretation of the Security Council resolutions. *Max Planck Yearbook of U.N. Law*, 2, pp.73–95.

Yoo, J. (2003) International law and the war in Iraq. *American Journal of International Law*, 97, pp.563–76.

PART III

CHAPTER 6

Self-defense in Islamic and International Law

Part I of this book is focused on the right of self-defense in Islamic law and on testing Al-Qaeda's declaration of Jihad against that criterion. Part II is devoted to the right of self-defense in international law questioning the legality of Anglo-American led invasion of Iraq in 2003. The purpose of Part III is to compare the rules of self-defense in Islamic and international law in order to find whether both are compatible. A final conclusion to the issues of terrorism and the "war on terror" is also presented in this part.

The view has been expressed that Islamic law is in conflict with international law. David Westbrook (1993) contends that Islamic law is an expression of world order that is different from international legal order. Abdullahi An-Na'im's (1988) line of argument on the use of force in self-defense (Jihad) shows Islamic law as incompatible with international law. Neither An-Na'im's nor Westbrook's views are new. Both views are heavily indebted to Majid Khadduri's (1955) position. Islamic law, by its very nature, is considered supreme by its followers who struggle incessantly to ensure that Islamic law shall prevail over all other legal systems. Khadduri's view suggests that there is a built-in force in the Islamic legal system constantly struggling to trump all other legal systems in the world. It is argued in this chapter, contrary to Khadduri's view, that Islamic and international rules on the use of force, discussed in Chapters 2 and 4 respectively, are compatible.[1] Compatibility refers to the spirit and broader frameworks of both legal systems. Certainly, there was no document, such as the Charter of the United Nations, in the seventh-century Arab tribal social set up; but there was definitely a code in theory, although not followed in the majority of cases, regulating the relations between various tribes. By demonstrating the compatibility of both legal systems, it does not mean that one should replace the other. The aim rather is to show that both systems are complementary and can coexist. In addition, both systems can borrow elements from each other. Islamic law might influence the development of international law because it is practiced in many member states of the United Nations, and it can influence international law as international law recognizes state practice and decisions by its highest courts as a source of international law.[2] In the same way, in the past, Islamic law had accepted foreign influences (Shah, 2006), and there is no reason why Islamic law should not get guidance from international law on matters on which Islamic law is silent.

6.1 Prohibition of Aggression

Before the emergence of Islam, the rules on the use of force in Arab tribal society were based on the might and economic and political interests of powerful tribes (Smith, 1903). For instance, if the economic interests of a particular tribe were in jeopardy, but it was powerful enough to protect these by force, there was no real mechanism to prevent the use of force by the powerful tribe. However, it does not mean that in theory, as previously indicated, there were no rules to regulate the relations between different tribes. After the birth of Islam in the seventh century, the Koran laid down a complete prohibition on the use of force, allowing it only as an exception, that is, in self-defense. The 1945 Charter of the United Nations prohibits the use or the threat of using force in international relations save in self-defense or as an enforcement measure authorized by the Security Council of the United Nations. Islamic and international law, on the point of prohibiting aggression, are compatible.

6.2 Use of Force in Self-defense

As previously indicated, Islamic and international law allows the use of force in self-defense as an exception. The Koran allows necessary and proportionate use of force when a Muslim land is attacked or when a group of Muslims are persecuted for their belief in Islam. In Islamic law, self-defense can be individual (using force when a Muslim state is attacked) or collective (defending Muslims who are persecuted for believing in Islam but are unable to defend themselves). International law also recognizes the use of force in self-defense when there is an armed attack against a state or such an attack is imminent. Self-defense may be individual or collective. For instance, Israel habitually cites the right to self-defense when using force against either neighboring Arab states or Palestinians groups. A recent case of collective self-defense is that of Kuwait when it asked the international community in 1990 to assist in pushing out Iraqi forces from Kuwait. In both legal systems, the use of force is recognized as an exception. The grounds for the use of force are also the same: When there is an armed attack or such an attack is imminent, force may be used.

Intervention on humanitarian grounds is the emerging principle of international law. For instance, in 1990 NATO intervened, which was later endorsed by the United Nations, to prevent further killing of Bosnians. In contrast, Islamic law centuries ago recognized the use of force in defense of those Muslims who are persecuted for being Muslim but are unable to defend themselves. However, it is a narrow principle in the sense that its application is limited to Muslims whereas international law is applicable to all nations. Having said that, it does not mean that Islamic law cannot be expanded to cover the protection of non-Muslims. The Koran does not prevent a Muslim state from intervening on humanitarian grounds to protect non-Muslims. The Koran leaves it open.

6.2.1 Anticipatory Self-defense

Islamic law not only recognizes the use of force when a Muslim land is attacked but also allows the use of force when such an attack is imminent. If the other party breaks the terms of an existing treaty by proceeding to attack Muslim land, the Koran states to repudiate the treaty before they launch an attack in order to be on equal terms with them. If there is no treaty but the threat of attack is real and imminent, the same rule shall apply as the Koran allows the use of force in anticipation. In international law, there are two views regarding anticipatory self-defense. On the restrictive interpretation of article 51 of the Charter, force cannot be used unless there is an armed attack against a state. On the expanded interpretation of article 51, imminent attack is included in the meanings of phrase "armed attack," and force may be used if an armed attack is imminent. The followers of this argument hold that self-defense is an inherent right of a state, which article 51 recognizes, including the customary right of anticipatory self-defense within the limits of the *Caroline* doctrine. A slightly different argument for supporting anticipatory self-defense is that due to the advancement in weaponry and its delivery systems, it will be suicidal for a state to wait for the first strike. The wise thing to do is to prevent the attack by using force in anticipation. The expanded interpretation of article 51 is gaining credence, which makes it compatible with Islamic rules on anticipatory self-defense. If the expanded interpretation is not considered an accepted interpretation, then at least the Islamic standard is compatible with the restrictive interpretation of international law. As I argue for the expanded interpretation of article 51, in my opinion Islamic and international standards are compatible on the point of anticipatory self-defense.

6.2.2 When Self-defense Ends?

Islamic law does not allow the use of force in self-defense indefinitely. It stipulates two conditions for ending self-defense: when the oppression of Muslims and tumult ends or when the opposite party ceases fighting Muslims. If any of these conditions is met, Islamic law requires Muslims to end the use of force in self-defense. However, fighting would continue with those elements who do not cease fighting. In international law, by one interpretation, the right to self-defense continues until the matter is reported to the Security Council of the United Nations and after it had taken adequate and effective measures against the attacker. If, in the opinion of the victim, these measures are not adequate and effective, its right of self-defense continues until the objectives are achieved. These objectives, in general, could be repelling an ongoing attack or thwart an imminent attack and stop its recurrence. According to another interpretation, the Security Council may take necessary measures even if the victim state does not report the matter to it.

The Islamic legal system does not include the system of collective security but the first interpretation of article 51—ending self-defense after achieving objectives—is compatible with Islamic law. There is also no reason why collective security system cannot be developed within the Islamic legal system. Islamic law allows for diplomacy, which might be used individually or together with other states. For instance, the Organisation of Islamic Conference and the League of Arab States could be strong candidates to be invested with powers of collective security system for the regions they represent.

6.2.3 Offensive Jihad and Preemptive Self-defense

Muslims consider Islam a religion meant for humankind. Therefore, its message should be spread to the rest of the world. The majority of scholars agree with this view, but they do not share the view of some conservative scholars as to how to propagate Islam. The conservatives argue that Islam should be propagated peacefully, however, if obstructions are placed in the way, then force should be used. This is known as the offensive theory of Jihad. I submit that the Koran allows the use of force in self-defense, ruling out the use of force for propagating Islam as the Koran advocates freedom of religion. The conservative view is considered militant. There is a risk that it might be used for political motives, such as removing those governments that pursue different Islamic interpretation or oppose the conservative view.

International law makes a clear distinction between preemption and anticipatory self-defense. International law does not recognize preemption as a rule. There is greater risk that preemptive force may be used with unfounded fears of security threats or armed attacks. In addition, it is also probable that it may be resorted to for political or strategic motives, thereby eliminating opposing governments. Iran could be cited as a good case of regime opposed by the Anglo-Americans. The theory of offensive Jihad and the doctrine of preemption have some similarities despite their apparent difference of purposes: The former seems to fulfil a divine command of spreading Islam, whereas the latter seems to be focused on self-protection from a perceived external threat. The conservatives in Islamic circles believe in the offensive theory of Jihad, whereas the Anglo-American right wing (and Israel) argue for the preemptive use of force in the face of a perceived security threat posed by what they call terrorists. As previously indicated, the apparent aims of both these theories look different, but both are vulnerable to misinterpretation and might be misused.

6.2.4 Limitations on the Use of Force

Islamic law imposes three limitations on the use of force in self-defense: necessity, proportionality, and requiring Muslims to accept an offer of peace from the opposite party. Force should be used only when it becomes necessary, that is, in case of an armed attack or when such an attack is imminent. The use of force shall not exceed the extent of damage done or prevent imminent damage. When there is an offer of peace from the opposite party, it shall not be rejected and Muslims shall engage in the peace process.

International law also imposes two limitations on the use of force in self-defense: necessity and proportionality. There should be an armed attack or such an attack must be imminent to trigger the use of force in self-defense. In addition, any state claiming self-defense has to show to the international community that the force used was proportionate to the actual damage suffered or to eliminate the threat of such an attack. Both systems seem to have similar limitations except that there is no written international legal rule requiring belligerents to accept an offer of peace from the other party. On the contrary, Islamic law seems more specific. It might, however, be that by custom modern nation-states tend to engage in diplomacy first, whereas in seventh-century pre-Islamic tribal society that was not a common practice.

6.3 Use of Force by Non-state Actors

In the Islamic political system, the head of a Muslim state shall take all decisions related to public safety after consultation with the *Shura* (Council/Parliament). Once such a decision is taken, the citizens have to observe it. The declaration of Jihad (war) is an important national issue and the head of a state has to make such a declaration after due consultation. Islamic law does not leave any room for non-state actors such as Al-Qaeda to declare Jihad unless the ruler is working against the interests of a Muslim state and mainstream Muslims leaders, by consensus, declare Jihad. International law is very clear on the point: It recognizes states as sovereign bodies and only they have the authority to declare war in self-defense under article 51 of the Charter of the United Nations. The defense of self-defense is not available to non-state actors. Islamic as well as international law treat non-state actors in the same way with one exception, that is, a declaration of Jihad by consensus of Muslim leadership when the Muslim ruler is on the side of the invaders and cannot protect Muslims.

6.4 Use of Force against Non-State Actors

If non-state actors such as a tribe or group of individuals from a neighboring country damages the interests of a Muslim state by looting, plundering, or attacking a section of the Muslim population, Islamic law treats such individuals as criminals. Islamic legal practice was to contact the head of that particular tribe or state and ask for the surrender of these criminals. If the matter was not resolved in this manner and the tribe or the state tried to protect these criminals or had no control over such criminals, Islamic law allowed the use of force against the criminals as well as the protecting state (Smith, 1903). According to international law, the victim state may ask for the extradition of a non-state attacker, and if the host state refuses to do so and is protecting the attacker, then force may be used subject two conditions: The scale and effect of the attack must amount to that of a regular armed attack and the host state has effective or over all control over the non-state attacker. The positions of Islamic and international law are compatible except that Islamic law is silent on the nature of attack and size of damage. It means that the standard is open and each case will be decided according to a given set of circumstances. Islamic law may get guidance from international law on this point.

6.5 Different Interpretation of Law

All laws, municipal and international, are susceptible to various interpretations. Islamic law is not an exception to this rule. In the Islamic legal system, Jihad has two interpretations. By contextual interpretation (the approach of this author), the Koran allows the use of force in self-defense only. On the contrary, conservative scholars argue that the use of force is also allowed if propagation of Islam is obstructed. My argument is that when the incumbent Muslim government is either on the side of a foreign power or corrupt and incapable of protecting Muslims, then mainstream Muslim leaders, by consensus, may declare Jihad in defense of a Muslim land. The majority of militant organizations are currently relying on this interpretation. For instance, Al-Qaeda argues that the Saudi regime is corrupt and is the agent of the United States.

Similarly, there are two main interpretation of the use of force in self-defense under article 51—the restrictive and the expanded, which were previously discussed. Moreover, we now have a new interpretation of the rules of self-defense—which may be called Bush doctrine of preemption—contained in the National Security Strategy of the United States, 2002 (revised in 2006). According to this doctrine, force or tactical strikes may be used against targets wherefrom future possible threats of terrorism might emerge. As stated in Chapter 4 in this book, international law does not recognize the Bush doctrine of preemption. It can be justifiably called an extreme interpretation of international law. Those who rely on such an interpretation might be rightly called aggressors or extremists. It is not only Islamic law, which may be interpreted in a manner and might look like an Islamic extremism. We may not be accustomed to describing international law using such terms, but that does not make it fair. We cannot choose to describe only one legal system in a way that brings negative connotation.

6.6 Misapplication of Law

As any law may be interpreted differently, in the same way any law may be misapplied. It will be wrong to say that international law or British law cannot be misapplied. One can find, without any difficulty, plenty of instances of misapplication of different laws. For instance, Al-Qaeda is subverting a sound rule of Islamic law: the use of force in self-defense by arrogating to itself the authority of the head of a Muslim state to declare Jihad. Similarly, the weight of scholarly authority shows that the invasion of Iraq by an Anglo-American led coalition in 2003 is illegal. The Anglo-Americans arrogated to themselves the power to implement the resolutions of the Security Council without its express approval. The irony is that the misapplication of Islamic law is called Islamic extremism. In contrast to this, no one is calling the misapplication of international law as international legal or Anglo-American extremism. In my opinion, both are cases of misapplication of the same legal principles from two different legal regimes and should be treated as such.

6.7 Violence in Islamic and International Law

There is a belief that Islamic law espouse violence against non-believers during war. To substantiate this view, its supporters cite examples of violence committed by Muslim militant organizations, such as the killing of civilians by Al-Qaeda. I have two objections to this argument. The first one is the known and obvious one: Mainstream Muslims do not share the view of militant Muslim organisations. Muslims around the world condemned the tragic incidents of September 11, 2001, in the United States. The second and the most important is that it is a common practice that militant organizations take Koranic verses out of their context leading to a distorted (extremist) view regarding the use of force. As stated in Chapter 2, the Koranic verses fall in more than one category. The real meanings of these verses emerge when interpreted in these categories. For instance, some verses state the grounds when force shall be used in self-defense, while other verses exhort Muslims to be strong and firm in the battlefield once the Koranic criterion for declaring Jihad is met. Again, many verses deal with the conduct of war, negotiation of peace, and resumption of hostilities. The critics of Islamic law, like militant organizations, fall in the same trap, citing verses out of their proper context. For example, they would cite verses related to the conduct rather than justification of war. The classic example is verse 9:5, which commands Muslims to kill unbelievers whenever you meet them. The order contained in verse 9:5 is limited to the conduct of war together with other limitations, such as fight only those who fight you.

In contrast, a lot of violence took place in World Wars I and II where no Muslims were directly involved. Thousands of Muslims were killed in Bosnia in the 1990s. The International Court of Justice (2007) held that there was a failure to prevent the genocide of Muslims. All this either happened in the

Christendom or Christians were involved in these conflicts. However, there is no argument that the Bible or Christians support violence. I am sympathetic to the argument that many states in the West are not following Biblical precepts. They are rather secular. Again, no one is blaming the secular law to be intrinsically violent. Another illustration is international humanitarian law (see generally Rogers, 2004). It does not prohibit the killing or maiming of combatants. It is legal to kill or maim those who are fighting. Why is international humanitarian law not regarded as a regime supporting violence? The position of Islamic and international law is the same: Do not kill or maim non-combatants. Similarly, violations of international law do not constitute precedents.

A slightly different but closely related point is that, in many conflicts, Muslim militant organizations do not follow the rules of Islamic humanitarian law. For instance, Al-Qaeda's targeting and killing of civilians. If members of Al-Qaeda are tried in an Islamic court, they will receive a severe punishment (see Vogel, 2002). The point is that the professed followers of Islamic law may be guilty of violating Islamic law in the same manner as the subjects of international law. Islamic legal system punishes breaches of Islamic law. They do not constitute Islamic legal precedents. The international community must treat the actions of militant organizations as violations of Islamic law rather than its true application.

6.8 Conclusion

Islamic and international rules of self-defense are compatible. There may be minor differences in details, but the notions of both systems on the subject of self-defense are similar. For instances, the grounds and limitations on the use of force are the same, but the element of collective security system is missing in Islamic law. However, Islamic law provides for diplomacy to secure peace, which may be used individually or collectively. It also means that Muslim states can work within the current international collective security system under the United Nations. Any law, municipal or international, may be susceptible to multiple interpretations and can be misapplied. Any particular interpretation or misapplication of particular law should be treated as such instead of regarding it as the reflection of the very system.

References

An-Na'im, A. (1988) Islamic ambivalence to political violence: Islamic law and international terrorism. *German Yearbook of International Law*, 31, pp.307–36.

International Court of Justice (2007) *Bosnia and Herzegovina v. Serbia and Montenegro.*

Khadduri, M. (1955) *War and peace in the law of Islam*. Baltimore: John Hopkins University Press.

Rogers, APV. (2004) *Law in the battlefield*. Manchester: Manchester University Press.

Smith, W. R. (1903) *Kinship and marriage in early Arabia*. Cook (ed.) London: Adam and Charles Black.

Vogel, F. (2002) The trial of terrorists under classical Islamic law. *Harvard International Law Journal*, 43, p.53.

Westbrook, D. (1992–93) Islamic international law and public international law: Separate expression of world order. *Virginia Journal of International Law*, 33, pp.819–97.

CHAPTER 7

Conclusion

The conclusions of different chapters are not restated here at great length. They are thoroughly discussed individually in each chapter. It is clear that Islamic and international law on self-defense are compatible with each other. It is also clear that, like any other legal rule, Islamic legal rules may be either misinterpreted or misapplied. The message regarding the changing nature of conflicts in Iraq and Afghanistan is clear: The loss of Muslim lives and damage to their property is enormous, and the Anglo-Americans and the pro-Western governments are unable to prevent the catastrophe. These conflicts are deteriorating so fast that soon they might become contenders for the declaration of Koranic (legitimate) Jihad. Al-Qaeda's declaration of Jihad in 1996 and 1998 cannot be justified, that is, it is un-Islamic. However, it is attracting greater sympathy from peaceful Muslims, because of the changing nature of conflicts and the hypocrisy of the Anglo-Americans and their Western allies. This is multiplying the level of threat to peace and security of the world. To avoid that, here are some points for consideration.

7.1 Fair International Legal Order

It is very difficult to look at the formulation and implementation of international law without keeping in sight international relations and politics. To expect compliance with international law, just international legal and political orders are essential. To command greater moral authority, countries that are considered the seats of powers should be at the forefront of setting up the best precedents of compliance with international law. If an international legal order is the result of a formulative process where all members of the international community played an equal role and all states have a fair say in the running of international institutions, then there will hardly be an opportunity to use force for compliance. Absent these, expecting greater compliance seems unrealistic. This is what is exactly missing in the current international legal regime and the composition of the international institutions.

7.1.1 International Nuclear Legal Regime

Let us take the example of the international legal regime dealing with nuclear weapons. It is extremely significant to have a nuclear weapons free world. However, the current international legal regime is choreographed to keep nuclear weapons in the hands of those who have them but does not allow others to develop or receive expertise of nuclear capability. The objectives of the Non-Proliferation Nuclear Weapons Treaty (1968) are "to prevent the spread of nuclear weapons and weapons technology." The treaty imposes an obligation on nuclear states not to transfer, and on non-nuclear states not to receive any, nuclear weapons or related technology. It is highly important to prevent the spread of nuclear weapons. However, why does the international law allow some countries to have nuclear weapons while others are not allowed to acquire them? To make the world a safer place, the international community needs a Nuclear Weapons Elimination Treaty together with a Non-Proliferation Treaty. The best example can be set by the nuclear weapons states to start the process of denuclearization. If they do so, they will be standing on high moral ground to ask others to follow suit. For example, South Africa has greater moral authority, as it has abandoned its nuclear program, than the United States, which not only possesses nuclear weapons but has also used them, to ask Iran to give up its nuclear ambition. Nuclear states such as the United Kingdom and the United States not only possess nuclear capability but are also further developing their nuclear weapons system. It is not surprising that Iran does not pay heed to their calls for halting its uranium enrichment. To get a greater impact, the call, perhaps, should come from non-nuclear weapon states, such as Germany.

The current international nuclear legal regime is not only unjust but also not followed consistently. India and Pakistan tested nuclear devices in 1998 followed by little reaction or sanctions from the international community. Israel is considered an undeclared nuclear state. Its nuclear program does not concern the United States or European Union the way Iran's nuclear program does. North Korea tested a nuclear device in 2006 without a military action taken against it. Iran, a Muslim country, is under tremendous pressure and, most of the time, is threatened with military action to give up its nuclear ambitions by those who possess nuclear weapons.

7.1.2 Composition of International Institutions

International institutions are also dominated by powerful states, such as the United States and the United Kingdom. The current composition of the Security Council is a good example. The big fives—the veto powers—have monopolized power in their hands. In fact, the Security Council seems to be designed so that power remains in their hands. The Security Council seems to be based on the idea that these states are in charge of world security. In addition, they will never break international law. Let us turn to three real cases, Iraq, Lebanon, and Iran-UK sailors' crisis.

The Anglo-Americans made strong allegations that Iraq is in possession of and developing weapons of mass destruction. After the invasion in March 2003, the allegation turned out to be false. Thousands and thousands of people have been killed since the invasion. The security situation in the region requires the immediate attention of the Security Council, but it has taken no action so far. In addition, there is no hope that the Security Council will take any effective measure to restore peace and security, preventing further killing of people.

In the summer of 2006, Israel attacked south of Lebanon to free its three abducted soldiers. The Israeli bombardment killed hundreds and rendered thousands of people homeless. The United States and the United Kingdom argued that they would not convene the session of the Security Council until the job is done, that is, until the soldiers are freed and Hezbollah (who allegedly abducted Israeli soldiers) is either destabilized or eliminated. After the failure of Israel to achieve these objectives, it accepted the ceasefire terms of the Security Council resolution 1701 in 2006.

In March 2007, Iran captured fifteen British sailors claiming that they illegally entered Iran's waters. The British Ministry of Defense claimed that they were in Iraqi waters, which they patrol under the mandate of the United Nations. The reaction of the Security Council and European Union to the incident is noteworthy. On March 29, 2007, "Members of the Security Council expressed grave concern at the capture by the Revolutionary Guard [of Iran], and the continuing detention by the Government of Iran, of 15 United Kingdom naval personnel." The Security Council did not ask Iran to present evidence but took for granted the British version of the incident. European Union (March 31, 2007) issued a statement demanding that Iran release, immediately and unconditionally, the British sailors and warned of undefined "appropriate measures" if Tehran did not comply. The European Union also did not invite Iran to present its version of the incident. What can the Muslims in the region expect from these institutions? Muslims may ask why they should trust these institutions. The Security Council met and passed several resolutions when the Anglo-Americans alleged that their security is threatened by Iraq. However, when thousands of Iraqis are killed, the Security Council does not even convene. In this situation, the call of Bin Laden might sound more convincing to many Muslims: the United Nations is the tool of the Western powers. For any fair international legal order, we should begin with Sellers' work: *Republican Theory of International Law: The Fundamental: Requirements of Just World Order* (Palgrave Macmillan, 2006).

7.2 Democracy and the Muslim World

The United States and the United Kingdom justify their continued presence in Muslim countries because they want to promote democracy and freedom in the Muslim world. It will be very good to have democracy in the Muslim world, which unfortunately had remained under colonial, dynastic, and military rulers for too long. In many cases, it was (and is) with the covert and overt Western support, such as Saudi Arabia and Pakistan. However, three important aspects of Anglo-American's claim need examination: their level of commitment; whose democracy is it; and the way they introduce democracy in the Muslim world.

7.2.1 Level of Commitment

Let us start with the level of commitment to the introduction of democracy and freedom in the Muslim world, by the Anglo-Americans in specific and the West in general. The history of their actions reflects very low levels of commitment and, in fact, is hypocritical. For instance, they support the Saudi regime, which is dynastic and unelected. The regime has a very poor record of human rights and is considered a corrupt country. In the case of Pakistan, they supported General Zia ul-Haq in the 1980s and now support General Musharaf who is running the country. There are many other dynastic rulers in the Middle East who they support. On the contrary, Iran, although it has a very poor human rights record, has far better democratic institutions compared to other dynastic regimes in the Middle East. The United Kingdom and the United States, however, are against Iran.

7.2.2 Whose Democracy?

The second question is what kind of democracy the Anglo-Americans want to promote in the Muslim world. Is it Islamic or Anglo-American? The Anglo-Americans believe that their brand of democracy is the best. They seem committed to introduce liberal secular democracy in the Muslim world. The majority of Muslims suspect it to be a cultural invasion and suspect that their efforts will change Islamic values system. This is why there is greater resistance, which makes it very hard for Anglo-Americans to succeed. The case of Hamas in Palestine is good example. Hamas is a militant organization but it chose to be the part of democratic process. Hamas defeated the secular Fatah party by winning the general election in 2006. Instead of accepting the result of election in a democratic spirit, the United States, the European Union, and Israel froze all aid to Palestine, as if they wanted to punish the voters for electing Hamas. For many Muslims it means that they are not committed to promote democracy in the Muslim world. They, in fact, promote a particular kind of democracy—that is, secular and liberal democracy represented by parties, such as Fatah. Their attitude toward the Muslim world is the proof of what Bin Laden said in his declarations of 1996 and 1998: They are against the Islamic value system.

Anglo-Americans, in general, tend to claim, that there is no democracy in Islam, which is ignorance of Islam. It is true that there is no model of Islamic democracy in the current Muslim world, but that does not mean that Islam does not have the concept of democracy. It is argued that there is a genuine scope for developing an Islamic democratic system based on the Koran, which, as a system of government, will be compatible with basic democratic values. How this could be accomplished shall be a subject for another book. The key, however, for peace and stability in the Muslim world is to promote the development of Islamic democracy, a system acceptable to Muslims and compatible with tenets of democracy. Muslims have never accepted the imposition of Western democracy. The chances are very slim that they will accept it now.

7.2.3 Method of Democratisation

The third important question is how the Anglo-Americans introduce democracy in the Muslim world. The evidence shows that they follow either the secretive approach or the short-cut. There is no evidence that they ever followed an honest (consistent) democratic approach to introduce democracy in the Muslim world. The secretive approach is in that they provide covert support to opposition and insurgent groups in a particular country in order to topple regimes they oppose. For instance, they promoted opposition to Saddam Hussein abroad. Some insurgent groups, such as the Kurdish movement, were funded and armed inside Iraq. The Northern Alliance was armed and funded against the Taliban in Afghanistan. Iran claimed that the Anglo-Americans are promoting insurgency in areas bordering Pakistan. The short-cut approach is to go into a country for one reason or another, overthrow the government they oppose, conduct elections under their supervision, and bring in power government that are pro-victors. Afghanistan and Iraq are classic cases. The West in general and Anglo-Americans in particular never followed a democratic approach when introducing democracy in the Muslim world, that is, to educate people, make them economically capable over longer period, and give them the choice to determine how to govern themselves. For any successful attempt to introduce democracy in the Muslim world, two further points must be kept in view. First, democracy must be introduced by democratic means, which means let the people choose their leaders and type of democracy. Second, international institutions such as the United Nations must be based on democratic principles dispensing justice to everyone.

7.3 Islamic Extremism and Anglo-American Hubris

The two major issues of concern today are the rise of Islamic extremism and Anglo-American hubris. In fancy terms of international relations, Anglo-American hubris is described as "unilateralism." Islamic extremism is often times called terrorism. These two issues are closely related. Anglo-Americans helped and are helping Islamic extremism in two ways. First, the Anglo-Americans fund and support Islamic militant organizations. They helped in founding and funding Al-Qaeda and the Taliban. Israel and the United States created and support Hamas in order to destabilize pro-Russian Fatah of Yasser Arafat. They also support those countries that follow the extreme interpretation of Islam, such as Saudi Arabia. They not only support them politically but also arm them by selling them billions of dollars worth of weapons. Second, they are using military means to take out Islamic extremism. Their military operations cost innocent Muslim lives and damage their properties. The pro-Western Muslim regimes, in many instances, are unable to protect Muslims. In return, this causes anger and anxiety among Muslims who start sympathizing with militant groups. To cause change, the Anglo-Americans and the West in general, have to change their policies toward the Muslim world by introducing democracy by democratic means in the Muslim world and developing respect for international law. Once the major grievances of the Muslims are addressed, there will be a major decline in hostility toward the West. It will become evident that the majority of Muslims are not against the West per se, but they oppose what they think are unjust policies of the West. The people of Western countries can play a major role by compelling their political leadership to change polices vis-à-vis the Muslim world.

Notes

Chapter 1

1. This approach refers to when the victors hold elections soon after victory under their supervision and install, in general, a government loyal to the victors. Mr Maliki's government in Iraq and Mr Karzai's government in Afghanistan are good examples.
2. World Islamic Front is an organization comprising Al-Qaeda, Jihad Group in Egypt, Egyptian Islamic Group, Jamiat-ul-Ulema-e-Pakistan, and Jihad Movement in Bangladesh.

Chapter 2

1. This chapter is published in a different form in the *Yearbook of Islamic and Middle Eastern Law*, 2005–6. vol. 12.
2. It seems different volumes of the Koranic commentary were produced over long periods so it is difficult to find an exact date for the online version that I use in this book.
3. In general, Maududi's interpretation of the Koran and his historical accounts of different events are considered authoritative. However, I respectfully disagree with some of his views, such as the offensive theory of Jihad.
4. The sayings (*hadiths*) of the Prophet Muhammad constitute an important portion of the second source of Islamic law. However, many *hadiths* are considered controversial.

Chapter 3

1. Most of the elegance is lost in translation.
2. The United Kingdom's "Countering International Terrorism" (2006:8) argues that the Muslim world's list of grievances is a one-sided story. It explains how much money the United Kingdom is spending on development and other programs, such as brining scholars to the United Kingdom from the Muslim world. Any fair commentator would give some credit to the "Engaging with Islamic World" program of the United Kingdom. However, its positive impact is underminded by

the self-defeating British policies in the Muslim world. The Senlis Council, an independent think-tank, submitted a Memorandum (March 15, 2007) to the United Kingdom Parliamentary Defense Committee: "By seeking to defeat the Taliban militarily and at the same time destroying people's livelihoods through misguided policies, the stabilisation mission in southern Afghanistan is at great risk." The Council recommended: "Counter-insurgency strategy in Afghanistan must be a complete package of diverse development-based interventions along with a military response. A comprehensive development policy that tackles the real causes of the rise in grassroots insurgency and addresses the real needs of the Afghan people must be in place." Christian Aid, another NGO, also submitted a Memorandum to the same committee: "While public attention has been drawn to the military dimensions of Britain's engagement, Christian Aid believes that a renewed focus by the UK on the conflict's underlying causes would bring benefits for Afghans in 2007."

3. The argument that Iraqis, not Anglo-Americans, kill Iraqis is not convincing. Iraqis were not killing Iraqis when Anglo-Americans were not in Iraq. The Anglo-Americans are like a farmer who prepares the field, sows the seed, and then watches the plant growing while he is unable to prevent its growth. They share responsibility for the killing of Iraqis along with those who are individually responsible for these killings.
4. The *New York Times* (May 6, 2007) reported that senior officers viewed the killings as a potential public relations problem that could fuel insurgent propaganda against the American military; the officers' immediate response had been intentionally misleading. Tim McGirk's report (Times, March 19, 2006) exposed the incident of the Haditha killings. The Annual Report on Human Rights by the British Foreign and Commonwealth Office (April 18, 2007:31) also indicated American's involvement in the cover-up of the Haditha incident.
5. Col. John Nicholson, the U.S. commander, said: "I stand before you today, deeply, deeply ashamed and terribly sorry that Americans have killed and wounded innocent Afghan people" (*New York Times*, May 9, 2007).
6. "Scores of civilian deaths over the past months from heavy American and allied reliance on air strikes to battle Taliban insurgents are threatening popular support for the Afghan government and creating severe strains within the NATO alliance" (*New York Times*, May 13, 2007).
7. Continuing probes into arm deals with Tanzania, the Czech Republic, South Africa, Chile, Qatar, and Romania were also halted (*The Observer*, May 13, 2007).
8. President Bush (May 2, 2007) vetoed a Congressional Bill, which set the date for withdrawal from Iraq. No withdrawal strategy is in sight. In contrast, the United States is thinking of having a long-term military presence in Iraq on the style of Korea, called the Korean Model (*New York Times*, June 3, 2007). This confirms what Bin Laden has been saying since 1996.
9. The DSB is a body that advises Pentagon on strategic communication.
10. More and more people in Pakistan are supporting the Taliban and the government is losing grip in areas bordering Afghanistan. The document, prepared by the

Interior Ministry of Pakistan says that "Taliban fighters were rapidly spreading beyond the country's lawless tribal areas and that without 'swift and decisive action,' the growing militancy could engulf the rest of the country" (*New York Times*, June 28, 2007). A strong belief exists that Pakistan's all-powerful Inter Intelligence Service (ISI) is covertly supporting Taliban (*New York Times*, January 21, 2007).

11. Rambo III, the movie, is dedicated "to the gallant people of Afghanistan."
12. In "Fascist America, in 10 Easy Steps," Naomi Wolf (*New York Times*, April 30, 2007) succinctly describes ten steps—from Hitler to Pinochet—which any would-be dictator must take to destroy constitutional freedoms. Wolf argues that the administration of President Bush seems to be taking them all. These steps are: *invoke* a terrifying internal and external enemy; create a gulag; develop a thug caste; step up an internal surveillance system; harass citizens' group; conduct arbitrary detention and release; target key individuals; control the press; dissent equal reason; and suspend the rule of law.
13. The argument that Kashmiri should quit militancy and join in the democratic process is misleading. The purpose of Kashmir militancy is not to elect members of State Assembly or Central Parliament (i.e., Indian Congress). Rather the point is to hold a referendum under the United Nations resolutions and let Kashmiris decide their fate, that is, whether to be with Pakistan or India. There is also a debate on a third option: an independent Kashmir.

Chapter 4

1. This chapter is published in a different form, in *The Journal of Conflict and Security Law*. 2007, Vol. 12(1).
2. Mr. Taft was the Legal Adviser of the United States Department of State. Mr Buchwald is the Assistant Legal Adviser for Political-Military Affairs of the United States Department of State.

Chapter 6

1. I have discussed in another place (Shah, 2006) how greater compatibility between Islamic and international human rights standards might be achieved.
2. I am grateful to Melissa Perry, QC, (New South Wales, Australia) for raising this point during my presentation in January 2006 at the Lauterpacht Research Centre for International Law, Cambridge University.

Selected Bibliography

AbuKhalil, A. (2002) *Bin Laden, Islam and America's new "war on terrorism."* New York: A Seven Stories Press & Open Media Book.

Ali, Y. (1989) *The meaning of the holy Qur'an*. Maryland: Amana Corporation.

An-Na'im, A. (1988) Islamic ambivalence to political violence: Islamic law and international terrorism. *German Yearbook of International Law*, 31, pp.307–36.

Ali, S. S. and Rehman, J. (2005) The concept of Jihad in Islamic international law. *Journal of Conflict and Security Law*, 10, pp.321–45.

An-Na'im, A. (1987) Islamic law, international relations, and human rights challenge: Challenge and response. *Cornell International Law Journal*, 20, pp.317–36.

Asad, M. (1997) *The message of the Koran*. Gibraltar: Dar Al-Andalus.

Azzam, A. (1985) Defence of Muslim lands: The first obligation after Iman [Faith]. Available at: http://www.religioscope.com/info/doc/jihad/azzam_defence_1_table.htm.

Baker, M. (1987–88) Terrorism and the inherent right of self-defence (a call to amend Article 51 of the United Nations Charter). *Houston Journal of International Law*, 10, pp.25–49.

Beck, R. and Arend, C. (1994) "Don't tread on us": International law and forcible state responses to terrorism. *Wisconsin International Law Journal*, 12, pp.153–219.

Blix, H. (2004) *Disarming Iraq: The search for weapons of mass destruction*. London: Bloomsbury Publishing.

Blokker, N. (2000) Is the authorisation authorised? *European Journal of International Law*, 11, pp.541.

Bloom, M. (2005) *Dying to kill: The allure of suicide terror*. New York: Columbia University Press.

Bothe, M. (2003) "Terrorism and the legality of pre-emptive force. *European Journal of International Law* 14 (227)

Bowett, D. (1972) Reprisals involving recourse to armed force *American Journal of International Law*, 66, pp.1–36.

———. (1958) *Self-defence in international law*. Manchester: Manchester University Press.

———. (1955–56) Collective self-defence under the charter of the United Nations *British Yearbook of International Law*, 32, pp.130–61.

Brownlie, I. (1963) *International law and the use of force by states*. Oxford: Clarendon Press.

———. (1961) The use of force in self-defence. *British Yearbook of International Law*, Vol. 37, pp.183–268.

Cassese, A. (2001) Terrorism is also disrupting some crucial categories of international law. *European Journal of International Law*, 21(5), pp.993–1001.

———. (1989) The international community's "legal" response to terrorism. *International and Comparative Law Quarterly*, 38, pp.589–608.

Charlesworth, H. and Byrnes, A. (2003) No, this war is illegal. March 19. Available at http://www.theage.com.au/articles/2003/03/18/1047749770379.html.

Charney, J. (2001) The use of force against terrorism and international law. *American Journal of International Law*, 95, pp.835–39.

Chayes, A. (1991) The use of force in the Persian Gulf. In Damrosch, L. and Scheffer, D. (eds.) *Law and force in the new international order*. Boulder, CO: Westview Press.

Claridge, D. (2000) Exploding the Myths of Superterrorism. In Taylor, M. and Horgan, J. (eds.) *The future of terrorism*, London: Frank Cass. pp.69–78.

Coll, A. (1987) The legal and moral adequacy of military responses to terrorism. *American Society of International Law Proceedings*, 81, pp.297–306.

Coll, S. (2005) *Ghost Wars: The secret history of the CIA, Afghanistan and Bin Laden*. London: Penguin Books Ltd.

Crawford, J. (2003) *The international law commission's articles on state responsibility: Introduction, text and commentaries*. Cambridge: Cambridge University Press.

Council of Europe (2007) Dick Marty's report "Alleged secrete detentions flights in the council of Europe member states." June 8. Available at: http://assembly.coe.int/Main.asp?link=/CommitteeDocs/2006/20060124_Jdoc032006_E.htm.

Dale, S. F. (1988) Religious suicide in Islamic Asia: Anticolonial terrorism in India, Indonesia, and the Philippines. *The Journal of Conflict Resolution*, March, pp.37–59.

Damrosch, L. (2000) Sanctions against perpetrators of terrorism. *Houston Journal of International Law*, 22, pp.63–76.

Daryabadi, A.M. (2001) *The glorious Quran: Text, translation & commentary*. Leicester: The Islamic Foundation.

Dickson, B. (2005) Law versus terrorism: Can law win? *European Human Rights Law Review*, 1, pp.11–28.

Dinstein, Y. (2003) Self-defence in an age of terrorism. *American Society of International Law Proceedings*, 97, pp.147–49.

———. (1988) *War, aggression and self-defence*. Cambridge: Cambridge University Press.

Donner, F. (1991) The sources of Islamic conception of Jihad. In Kelsey, J. and Johnson, J. (eds.) *War and Jihad: Historical and theoretical perspectives on war and peace in Western and Islamic traditions*. New York: Greenwood Press.

Esposito, J. and DeLong-Bas, N. J. (2001) *Women in Muslim family law*. 2nd ed., Syracuse: Syracuse University Press.

Fanon, F. (2005) *The wretched of the earth*. New York: Grove Press.

Farer, T. (2002) Beyond the charter frame: Unilateralism or communism? *American Journal of International Law*, 96, pp.359–64.

Frank, T. (2001) When, if ever, may states deploy military force without prior security council authorisation. *Washington University Journal of Law and Policy*, 5, pp.51–68.

Frank and Patel (1991) Police action in lieu of war: The old order changeth. *American Journal of International Law*, 85, pp.63–74.

Frowein, F. (1988) The present state of research carried out by the English-speaking section of the Centre for Studies and Research. In *Legal aspects of international terrorism*, pp.55–96.

Glennon, M. (2003) Why the security council failed? *Foreign Affairs*, 82, pp.16–35.

———. (2002) The fog of law: Self-defence, inherence, and incoherence in Article 51 of the United Nations Charter. *Harvard Journal of Law and Public Policy*, 25, pp.539–58.

Goldsmith, Lord. (2003) Iraq: Resolution 1441 (Secret Memo to the Prime Minster). March 7.

Gray, C. (2004) *International law and the use of force*. Oxford: Oxford University Press.

Greenwood, C. (2002) The legality of using force against Iraq. Memorandum to the UK Government on October 12, 2002.

———. (1987) International law and the United States. Air Operation against Libya" *W. Va. L Rev*. 89, pp.933.

Greig, D. (1991) Self-defence and the security council: What does Article 51 require? *International and Comparative Law Quarterly*, 40, pp.366–402.

Gross, E. (2001) Thwarting terrorist acts by attacking the perpetrator or their commanders as an act of self-defence: Human rights versus the state's duty to protect its citizens. *Temple International and Comparative Law Journal*, 15, pp.195–245.

Grotius, H. (1913) *De jure belli ac pacis libire tres* (*Three books on the law of war and peace*) (Kelsen, H. trans). (Original work published 1625).

Halberstam, M. (1996) The right to self-defence once the security council takes action. *Michigan Journal of International Law*, 17, pp.229–48.

Hallaq, W. (2005) *The origins and evolution of Islamic law*. Cambridge: Cambridge University Press.

Hamidullah, M. (1956) *The Muslim conduct of state*. Lahore, Pakistan: Ashraf Publishers.

Henkin, L. (1979) *How nations behave*? New York: Columbia University Press.

Higgins, R. (1994) *Problems and process: International law and how we use it*. Oxford: Oxford University Press.

Hitti, P. (1961) *History of the Arabs*. London: McMillan.

Hoffman, B. (2003) The logic of suicide terrorism. *The Atlantic Monthly*. June. Available at: http://www.theatlantic.com/doc/200306/hoffman.

Hole, L. (2004) Anticipatory self-defence under international law. *American University International Law Review*, 19, pp.69–106.

Honderich, T. (2002) *After the terror*. Edinburgh: Edinburgh University Press.

Intoccia, G. (1987) American bombing of Libya: An international legal analysis. *Case W. Res. Journal of International Law*, 19, pp.177–213.

Jackson, S. (2002) Jihad and the modern world. *Journal of Islamic Law and Culture*, Spring/Summer, pp.1–26.

Jinks, D. (2003) Self-defence in an age of terrorism. *American Society of International Law Proceedings*, 97, pp.144–46.

Jennings, R. (1938) The Caroline and McLeod cases. *American Journal of International Law*, 32, pp.82–99.

Kamali, M. H. (2000) Law and society, the interplay of revelation and reason in the Shariah. In Esposito, J. (eds.) *Oxford history of Islam*. Oxford University Press.

Kathir, Ibn. (2000) *Tafsir Ibn Kathir* (Al-Mubarakpuri, S. trans). Vol I & IV. Riyadh: Darussalam. (Original work published in 1301–73).

Kelsay, J. (1993) *Islam and War: A study in comparative study*. Kentucky: John Knox Press.

Kelsen, H. (1948) Collective security and collective self-defence under the charter of the United Nations. *American Journal of International Law*, 42, pp.783–96.

Khadduri, M. (1956) Islam and the modern law of nations. *American Journal of International Law*, 50, pp.358–71.

———. (1955) *War and peace in the law of Islam*. Baltimore: John Hopkins University Press.

Knauft, S. (1996) Proposed guidelines for measuring the propriety of armed state responses to terrorist attacks. *Hastings International and Comparative Law Review*, 19, pp.763–88.

Kruse, H. (1956) *The foundation of Islamic international law*. Karachi: Pakistan Historical Society.

Kunz, J. (1947) Individual and collective self-defence in Article of 51 of the charter of the United Nations. *American Journal of International Law*. 41, pp.872.

Laden, B. (1996) Declaration of war against the Americans occupying the land of the two Holy Places. Available at: http://www.pbs.org/newshour/terrorism/international/fatwa_1996.html.

Lauterpacht, H. (1933) *The function of law in international community*. Oxford: Claredon Press.

Lawrence, B. (2005) *Messages to the world: The statements of Bin Laden*. (Howarth, J. trans) London: Verso.

League of Nations (1919) Covenant of the League of Nations.

Lewis, B. (2004) *The crises in Islam: Holy war and unholy terror*. London: Phoenix.

———. (1998) License to kill. *Foreign Affairs*. November–December.

Lobel, J. (1999) The use of force to respond to terrorists attack: The bombing of Sudan and Afghanistan. *Yale Journal of International Law*, 24, pp.537–57.

Lowe, V. (2003) The Iraq crisis: What now?. *International and Comparative Law Quarterly*, 52, pp.859.

Mann, M. (2003) *Incoherent empire*. London: Verso.

Maududi, S. A. (1996) *Al-Jihad Fil-Islam* (Urdu). Lahore, Pakistan.

———. (1990) *Towards understanding the Quran*. (Ansari, trans) Vol. III. Delhi: Markazi Maktaba Islami. (Original work published 1942–73).

McCormack, T. (1991) Anticipatory self-defence in the legislative history of the United Nations history. *Israel Law Review*, 25(1), pp.1–41.

McDougal, M. (1963) The Soviet-Cuban quarantine and self-defense. *American Journal of International Law*, 57, pp.597–604.

McDougal, M. and Feliciano, M. (1961) *Law and minimum world public order: The legal regulation of international coercion*. New Haven: Yale University Press.

Mohammad, N. (1985) The doctrine of Jihad: An introduction. *Journal of Law and Religion*, 3, pp.381–98.

Moir, L. (2005) Reappraising the resort to force? Jus ad bellum and the war on terror. *New Zealand Yearbook of Jurisprudence*, 8(1), pp.1–31.

Murphy, S. (2004) Assessing the legality of invading Iraq. *Georgetown Law Journal*, 92, pp.173–258.

———. (2002) Terrorism and the concept of "armed attack" in Article 51 of the U.N. Charter *Harvard International Law Journal*, 43, pp.41–51.

Mushkat, R. (1986–87) Is war ever justifiable? A comparative survey. *Loyola of Los Angles International and Comparative Law Journal*, 9(2), pp.227–318.

Mutahhari, M. (1986) Jihad in the Qur'an: First lecture. In Abedi, Mehdi and Legenhausen, Gary (eds.) *Jihad and Shahadat: Struggle and martyrdom in Islam: Essays and addresses by Ayatollah Mahmud Taleqani, Ayatullah Murtada Muttahari and Dr. Ali Shari'ati*. Houston: Institute for Research and Islamic Studies.

O'Boyle, F. (1987) Military responses to terrorism. *American Society of International Law Proceedings*, 81, pp.287–96.

O'Brien, W. (1990) Reprisals, deterrence and self-defence in counterterror operations. *Virginia Journal of International Law*, 30, pp.421–79.

O'Connell, M. (2002) Evidence of terror. *Journal of Conflict and Security Law*, 7, pp.19.

———. (2002) The myth of Preemptive Self-defence. ASIL Task Force on Terrorism. pp.1–22. Available at: at:http://www.asil.org/taskforce/oconnell.pdf.

Pape, R. (2005) *Dying to win: The strategic logic of suicide terrorism*. New York: The Random House Publishing Group.

Paust, J. (2004) Post-9/11 overreaction and fallacies regarding war and defence, Guantanamo, the status of persons, treatment, judicial review of detention, and due process in military commissions. *Notre Dame Law Review*, 79, pp.1335–64.

———. (2002) Use of armed force against terrorists in Afghanistan, Iraq and beyond. *Cornell International Law Journal*, 35, pp.533–57.

Prasad, I. (1959) *A short history of Muslim rule in India*. The Indian Press Ltd. Allabad.

Qureshi, I. (1962) *The Muslim community in the Indo-Pakistan sub-continent*. Gravenage.

Qutb, S. (2003) *In the shade of the Quran*. Vol. 8 & 9 (Salahi, M. A. trans). Leicester: The Islamic Foundation. (Original work published 1950–60s).

Rahim, A. (1911) *Muhammadan jurisprudence*. Lahore: PLD Publishers.

Rapoport, D. C. (1984) Fear and trembling: Terrorism in three religious traditions. *American Political Science Review*, 78(3), pp.668–72.

Rashid, A. (2002) *Taliban: Militant Islam, oil and fundamentalism in Central Asia*. New Haven: Yale University Press.

Reisman, M. (2003) Self-defence in an age of terrorism. *American Society of International Law Proceedings*, 97, pp.141–52.
———. (1991) Allocating competences to use coercion in the post cold world order: Practices, conditions, and prospects. In Damrosch, L. and Scheffer, D. (eds.) *Law and Force in the New International Order*, Boulder, CO: Westview Press.
———. (1985) Criteria for the lawful use of force in international law. *Yale Journal of International Law*, 10, pp.279–85.
Reuter, C. (2004) *My life is weapon: A modern history of suicide bombing*. New Jersey: Princeton University Press.
Roberts, G. (1987) Self-help in combating state-sponsored terrorism: Self-defense and peacetime reprisal. *Case W. Res. Journal of International Law*, 19, pp.243–94.
Rogers, APV. (2004) *Law in the battlefield*. Manchester: Manchester University Press.
———. (2003) Comments on Resolution 1441 (2002). *Yearbook of International Humanitarian Law*. Vol. 3, pp.
Rostow, E. (1991) Until what? Enforcement action or collective self-defence. *American Journal of International Law*, 85, pp.506–16.
Rowles, J. (1987) Military responses to terrorism. *American Society of International Law Proceedings*, 81, pp.307–17.
Sands, P. (2005) *Lawless world: America and the making and breaking of global rules*. London: Allen Lane (an imprint of Penguin Books).
Schachter, O. (1991) Authorised uses of force by the United Nations and regional organisations. In Damrosch, L. and Scheffer, D. (eds.) *Law and force in the new international order*. Boulder, CO: Westview Press.
———. (1989) The extra territorial use of force against terrorists. *Houston Journal of International Law*, 11, pp.309–16.
———. (1987) Self-judging self-defence. *Case Western Reserve Journal of International Law*, 19, pp.121–27.
———. (1986) In defence of international use of force. *University of Chicago Law Review*, 53, pp.113–46.
———. (1984) The right of states to use armed force. *Michigan Law Review*, 82, pp.1620–46.
Scheuer, M. (2004) *Imperial hubris: Why the West is losing war on terror*. Potomac Books.
Seller, M. (2006) *Republican theory of international law: The fundamental requirements of just world order*. London: Palgrave Macmillan.
Shakespeare, W. (2007) *King Lear*. London: Penguin Classics.
———. (1981) *The merchant of Venice*. London: Penguin Classics.
Shah, N. A. (2006) *Women, the Koran and international human rights law: The experience of Pakistan*. Lieden: Martinus Nijhoff.
Silverman, A. (2002) Just war, Jihad, and Terrorism: A comparison of Western and Islamic norms for the use of political violence. *Journal of Church and State*, 44, pp.73–92.
Smith, W. (1903) *Kinship and marriage in early Arabia*. Cook (eds.) Adam And Charles Black London.

Sofaer, A. (2003) On the necessity of pre-emption. *European Journal of International Law*, 4(2), pp.209–26.

———. (1989) Terrorism, the law and the national defence. *Military Law Review*, 95, pp.89–123.

Stern, J. (2004) *Terror in the name of God: Why religious militants kill.* New York: Happer Colins.

Steyn, Lord. (2006) Democracy, the rule of law and the role of judges. *European Human Rights Law Review*, 3, pp.243–53.

Stone, R. (2006) *Civil liberties and human rights.* Oxford: Oxford University Press.

Streusand, D. (1997) What does Jihad mean? *Middle East Quarterly.* September.

Tabatabai, A. (1892–1981) *Al-Mizan* (Koranic commentary online version).

Taft, W. (2006) A view from the top: American perspectives on international law after the cold war. *Yale Journal of International Law*, 31, pp.503–12.

Taft, W. and Buchwald, T. (2003) Pre-emption, Iraq and international law. *American Journal of International Law*, 97, pp.557–63.

Taymiyyah, Ibn (2005) *Risala Usul Tafseer* (Ansari Urdu, trans). Lahore, Pakistan: Al-Faisal Nashran. (Original work published 712).

Tibi, B. (1996) War and peace in Islam. In Nardin, T. (ed.) *The ethics of war and peace: Religious and secular perspectives.* New Jersey: Princeton University Press, pp.128–45.

Townsend, G. (1997) State responsibility for acts of de facto agents. *Arizona Journal of International and Comparative Law*, 14, pp.635–78.

Travalio, G. (2000) Terrorism, international law, and the use of military force. *Wisconsin International Law Journal*, 18, pp.145–91.

United Kingdom (2006) Countering international terrorism: the United Kingdom's strategy, 2006.

United Nations (1945) The charter of the United Nations.

United States (2002) The national security strategy of the United States of America.

Usmani, S.A. (1993) *Al-Koran: Translation and commentary* (Urdu). Madina, Saudi Arabia: Shah Fahad Koran Complex.

Vienna Convention on the Law of Treaties, 1969.

Vogel, F. (2002) The trial of terrorists under classical Islamic law. *Harvard International Law Journal*, 43, pp.53.

Waldock, C. (1952) The regulation of the use of force by individual states in international law. *Recueil Des Cours*, 2, pp.451–515.

Wali, Ullah. S. (2005) *Al-Fozul Al-Kabir* (Abdullah Urdu, trans). Lahore, Pakistan: Al-Faisal Nashran.

Warbrick, C. (1991) The invasion of Kuwait by Iraq. *International and Comparative Law Quarterly*, 40, pp 482 92.

Watt, W. M. (1969) *Muhammad at Medina.* Karachi: Oxford University Press.

Westbrook, D. (1992–93) Islamic international law and public international law: Separate expression of world order. *Virginia Journal of International Law*, 33, pp.819–97.

Webster, D. (1840–41) Letters from U.S. secretary of state Daniel Webster to *British Minister Mr. Fox, 29 British and Foreign Papers*, pp.1129, 1137–38.

Wedgwood, R. (2003) The fall of Saddam Hussein: Security council mandates and pre-emptive self-defense. *American Journal of International Law*, 97, pp.576–85.

———. (1999) Responding to terrorism: The strikes against Bin Laden. *Yale Journal of International Law*, 24, pp.559–79.

White and Cryer (1999) Unilateral enforcement of Resolution 687: A threat too far. *California Western International Law Journal*, 29, pp.243–82.

Wood, M. (1998) The interpretation of the Security Council resolutions. *Max Planck Yearbook of U.N. Law*, 2, pp.73–95.

Woodward, B. (2006) *State of denial: Bush at war, Part III*. UK: Cambridge: Simon & Schuster Ltd.

World Islamic Front, (1998) Jihad against Jews and Crusaders.

Yoo, J. (2004) Using force. *The University of Chicago Law Review*, 71(3), pp.729–97.

———. (2003) International law and the war in Iraq. *American Journal of International Law*, 97, pp.563–76.

Yusuf, S.D. (1991) *Koran, translation and commentary*. Junaghari (Urdu, Trans.). Madina, Saudi Arabia: Shah Fahad Koran Complex.

Index